The
30-Minute
Light Gourmet

Also by Lulu P. Grace:

Leaving Home

The
30-Minute
Light Gourmet

Lulu P. Grace

Taylor Publishing Company
Dallas, Texas

Designed by Deborah Jackson-Jones

Published by Taylor Publishing Company
              1550 West Mockingbird Lane
              Dallas, Texas 75235

Library of Congress Cataloging-in-Publication Data

Grace, Louise P.
     The 30-minute light gourmet / Lulu Grace.
        p.   cm.
     ISBN 0-87833-617-6 : $18.95
     1. Low-fat diet—Recipes.   2. Salt-free diet—Recipes.   3. Low-calorie
diet—Recipes.   I. Title.   II. Title: The thirty minute light gourmet.
RM237.7.G725   1990
641.5′635—dc20   89-71365
                                                                       CIP

Printed in the United States of America
10 9 8 7 6 5 4 3

To my dear friend and daughter Virginia Joy.

And in memory of some very special friends I said goodbye to this year . . .

Jennifer Leigh Jennings
Judith Anne Latson
James Perry Patterson
James Douglas Simril
Pandora Wilson

CONTENTS

ACKNOWLEDGMENTS

As the saying goes, two heads are better than one. Therefore, my special thanks go to my good friend and supercook, Kay Brooks Cross, who helped me create and test many of my recipes—and we're still friends today! Special thanks also go to my friend and microwave genius, Vicki Shelton White, for helping to make me microwave-literate and for sharing some of her great recipes with me. And finally, a very special "thank you" to Christopher Gerard Hibbs for his help and expertise in computer programming. Without his help and patience this cookbook would not be!

EATING HEALTHY:
THE ESSENTIAL INGREDIENTS

How I Got Started

My mother, Joy Skipwith Peal, would probably disagree, but I feel as though I were born under a stove. As a teenager I would plan and execute challenging menus on weekends. I found it fun and creative. In college, when I was trying to find my niche in life, I took an introductory course in nutrition and loved it. My future was set: I promptly changed my major and went on to earn a Bachelor of Science degree in nutrition.

Still wet behind the ears, I was accepted as a trainee by the late Helen L. Corbitt, renowned director of The Zodiac Room restaurant in Neiman-Marcus' flagship store in Dallas and other Neiman-Marcus restaurants. I managed The Mariposa Room in the Houston Galleria for Helen. She was a tough but marvelous teacher, as was my next boss, Gerald G. Ramsey, director of Food Service for Southern Methodist University. Both were recipients of the Gold Plate Award, the highest award for excellence in food service. At Southern Methodist University I coordinated food production and purchasing for the student center as well as catering for the university.

In 1973 I successfully completed my dietary internship at Presbyterian Medical Center in Dallas under Food Service Director Doris J. Wilson, an outstanding dietitian and friend. I then passed my National Boards and became a Registered Dietitian.

Since then, I have been a consultant, food service director for Highland Park Independent School District, and cookbook author, publishing *Leaving Home* in 1985.

A Light Gourmet Lifestyle

I have written *The 30-Minute Light Gourmet* to promote a healthful style of eating based on foods that are also appealing and easy to prepare. *The 30-Minute Light Gourmet* is not a diet book; it is a health-style guide. The recipes have reduced calorie contents and are lower in

1

saturated fats, sodium, and cholesterol than are most traditional recipes. Who says nutritious foods have to be bland? I hope to dispel that notion: my recipes are mouthwateringly delicious.

A healthful diet is preventive medicine—so eat right, but enjoy it!

Nutrition Data

Each of my recipes is followed by nutrition information based upon USDA findings. This will tell you the calories per serving in each recipe as well as the grams of protein, carbohydrates, fat, and fiber. I have also included information on the milligrams of cholesterol and the percentage of calories from fat in each serving. Note: where there is a range of servings (e.g., "Serves 4 to 6"), the highest serving number was the basis for the nutrition analysis.

Keep in mind that whereas protein and carbohydrates have 4 calories per gram, fat has 9 calories per gram (and alcohol has 7). For example, a serving with 75 calories and 5 grams of fat gets 60% of its calories from fat. This means that vegetables sautéed in a pat of reduced-calorie butter substitute may show a high percentage of calories from fat since the vegetables themselves contain so few calories. I use reduced-calorie butter substitutes in my sauté recipes mainly because, when you use sautéing alternatives, you sacrifice the taste that butter gives the dish. However, there are some good-tasting alternatives to butter and butter substitute sautéing: dry white wine, chicken broth, and non-stick cooking sprays. (There are even olive-oil-flavored sprays these days.) And don't forget that fresh herbs add wonderful flavors to your dishes without adding fat. However, all my recipes are lower in saturated fats than are conventional recipes. Balance is the key: ideally, only 30% of your total daily calories should come from fat.

Time Savers

The recipes in The 30-Minute Light Gourmet are broken down into simple-to-follow steps that will streamline your cooking. Here are some ways to get you out of the kitchen faster.

☐ Over the weekends I chop vegetables and put ½-cup or ¼-cup amounts in the freezer so that I can pop them out as needed. Most supermarkets now have deli counters that stock pre-cut vegetables in their salad bars.

☐ I have found rice in single-serving boiling bags to be a great time saver.

☐ Ready-cooked, frozen, packaged chicken and seafood are also available in 2-cup servings at your supermarket. It's great to add to sautéed vegetables.

☐ It's really worth it to invest in some quality kitchen equipment; it makes food preparation easier as well as quicker. Some tools that I use throughout the book are a food processor, a Mouli Julienne Machine, an electric hand blender, a mini food chopper, a garlic press, wire whisks, a metal meat thermometer, a metal meat tenderizer, a juicer, a black pepper grinder, and a set of microwave-safe bowls.

☐ Don't avoid recipes that call for marinades. Marinate overnight or during the day while you're at work—then all you have to do is fire up the grill and your meal is ready in 15 minutes.

☐ A microwave, of course, is a revolutionary time saver. I've included a variety of recipes in my "Microwave Magic" chapter to show its great versatility.

Ten Commandments for a Healthy Lifestyle

1. Don't eat because it is "meal time"; eat when your body tells you it needs fuel.

2. Eat slowly. Chew your food well. Chewing aids digestion and gives your stomach time to "tell" your brain that you're full. Before you reach for that second or third helping, wait 10 minutes: you might find that you're already satisfied.

3. Small portions, please! Portion size is the key to weight control and maintenance. There is a balance between food calories consumed (eaten) and food calories burned by internal (metabolic rate) and external activities. To maintain your weight, they must equal each other.

4. Avoid consuming "empty" calories from sugar-laden snacks such as soft drinks and candy. These provide no nutritional value.

5. Start using products such as reduced-calorie margarine; butter

substitute; egg substitute; reduced-sugar jams; 2%, 1%, or skim milk; light soy sauce; light cream cheese; light sour cream; non-fat yogurt; and reduced-calorie breads. Be alert to any new reduced-calorie products that appear on your grocer's shelves.

Caution: Read labels carefully. According to law, labels cannot legally contain false and misleading product information, yet they can be misleading. Product labels list ingredients in order of their quantity. The ingredient listed first is present in the greatest quantity by weight. For example, if the first listed ingredient is water, that product contains more water than any other listed ingredient. Each listed ingredient that follows is present in decreasing amounts.

6. Increase your intake of complex carbohydrates by eating foods such as peas, beans, potatoes, rice, pasta, and whole-grain breads such as rye, whole wheat, and oatmeal. Why? Complex carbohydrates are good sources of energy and fiber. They take a while to digest, so you'll feel full longer than you would after eating a candy bar with the same number of calories.

7. Use fresh foods when possible, and frozen foods rather than canned foods. Again, read those labels carefully. You might be in for some eye-opening surprises in the form of hidden sugars, saturated fats, and sodium.

8. No more than one-third of your daily calories should come from fat. Most Americans get 40% or more of their daily caloric intake from fat. Heart disease prevention, cancer prevention, and weight control are benefits of lowering your daily caloric intake from fat. There are three basic types of fat:

   ☐ **Saturated fats:** These fats are most common in meats and animal by-products. Saturated fats are solid at room temperature. Lard, butter and butter fat in dairy products (such as ice cream, whole milk, and cheeses), solid white shortening, tropical oils (coconut, palm, and palm kernel oils), and hydrogenated oils are a few of the most commonly used saturated fats. These fats are believed to cause elevated blood cholesterol levels. Avoid saturated fats and when cooking replace them with the ones below. Use olive oil instead of a tropical oil, for example.

☐ **Monounsaturated fats:** These fats include olive oil and peanut oil. Olives, nuts, and avocados are foods rich in monounsaturated fats. Monounsaturated fats are neutral fats that neither raise nor lower blood cholesterol levels—although some research indicates olive oil may lower blood cholesterol levels.

☐ **Polyunsaturated fats:** These are primarily of vegetable origin and include safflower, corn, canola, soybean, and cottonseed oils. They are believed to help reduce blood cholesterol levels, but should still be used in moderation.

Try to eat these types of fats in proportion: 10% calories from saturated, 10% calories from monounsaturated, and 10% calories from polyunsaturated is a good goal to begin with, but keep your overall fat consumption as low as possible.

9. Eat only 6 ounces (after cooking) of meat or meat by-products daily. This is an adequate amount for a healthful diet. Other sources of protein are milk, breads, and vegetables.

10. Exercise, exercise, exercise! In our busy times, and by the nature of the society we have created, we have become more and more sedentary, decreasing our ability to burn calories. The mouth works faster than the legs! A reasonable exercise program is an essential part of a healthy lifestyle.

Take my commandments to heart and learn to eat smart. It's fun to eat and enjoy foods that give you the perfect balance of pleasure and optimal nutrition. But allow yourself a treat once in a while. As long as you balance your caloric and fat intake, satisfying an occasional craving won't harm you. My dessert chapter has some delicious ideas for special occasions.

GREAT
BEGINNINGS

Grilled Tortilla
with Roasted Chiles and Tomatoes

T hese are tasty Southwest-style appetizers whose roasted pepper filling can be prepared several days in advance. You can use several different cheeses, but I prefer Mexican Chihuahua. Monterey Jack cheese is an acceptable substitute. Serve with tortillas, diced jalapeños, avocados, and either bottled hot sauce or my Pico de Gallo. The popular green Anaheim or Californian chile is about 8 inches long and fairly mild.

Makes 20 wedges

2 fresh Anaheim chiles
1 tablespoon olive oil
1/2 cup chopped onion
1 teaspoon chopped fresh garlic
1 cup coarsely chopped fresh tomato
1/2 teaspoon Lulu's Special Seasoning
1/4 teaspoon ground cumin
1/4 teaspoon cracked black pepper
5 6-inch flour tortillas
Light sour cream
Thinly sliced Mexican Chihuahua cheese as needed
Chopped jalapeño (optional)
Diced avocado (optional)
Pico de gallo (optional)

1 Preheat broiler. Adjust oven rack to upper third of oven.

2 Wearing disposable plastic gloves or rubber gloves, slice the Anaheim peppers lengthwise in half. Skin side up, arrange peppers on baking sheet and place under the broiler for about three minutes or until the skins pop and turn brown. Remove peppers from oven and let cool. Slip off the skins. Peel the skins and coarsely chop the peppers.

3 Heat the oil in a heavy skillet set over medium-high heat. Add the onion and garlic, cooking until onion is tender. Add the tomato, roasted chopped peppers, special seasoning, cumin, and pepper. Cook, stirring occasionally until the tomato is about half-cooked but firm. Remove from heat. Wash and dry skillet.

4 Spray the skillet with non-stick cooking spray and place over high heat. Meanwhile spread one side of each tortilla with sour

cream. Place 2 tablespoons of the tomato and chili mixture on half of each tortilla, and top with 1 or 2 thin slices of Chihuahua cheese. Fold tortilla in half.

5   Grill both sides of the tortilla until lightly browned and the cheese melts. Using a pizza cutter, cut each tortilla half into 4 wedges. Serve warm, garnished with diced jalapeños, avocados, and pico de gallo.

Per wedge: *46 calories; 1.48 gm protein; 5.42 gm carbohydrates; 2.03 gm fat; 0 mg cholesterol; .13 gm fiber; 40% of calories from fat*

Herbed Brie en Croute

*T*his *recipe has to be served as a treat. It is worth it! A must for entertaining.*

Makes 8 1-ounce wedges

1   sheet **Pepperidge Farm Puff Pastry**
1   **8-ounce wheel Brie cheese**
    Lulu's Special Seasoning to taste
    Cracked black pepper to taste
    Paprika to taste
    Crushed red pepper to taste
    Summer savory to taste
    Tarragon to taste

1   Preheat oven to 450°.

2   Place puff pastry sheet on a piece of waxed paper to thaw (about 20 minutes). You must work with the pastry while it is cool. If you let it get too warm, it will stick to everything.

3   Trim the white rind off from one side of the Brie and sprinkle the top of the cheese with the herbs.

4   Place the herbed wheel on the pastry. Cover the bottom and sides of the wheel with the pastry, trimming off excess pastry with a knife. Using the lid of the Brie container as a template, cut a circle of pastry to fit on top. Then cut five 3-by-½-inch

strips of pastry. Fit these around the top edge to seal the 2 pieces of pastry. Flute the edges as you would a pie crust. Be sure the Brie is well-sealed, for if you have any openings, the Brie will ooze out as it bakes.

5   Place the Brie on a baking sheet and bake in the preheated 450° oven for 10 minutes. Reduce the heat to 350° and bake 15 minutes longer or until crust is browned.

6   Cut into wedges and serve hot with your favorite crackers and fresh fruit.

Per wedge: *104 calories; 3.64 gm protein; 4.99 gm carbohydrates; 7.7 gm fat; 14 mg cholesterol; .25 gm fiber; 67% of calories from fat*

Cheese-Stuffed Mushrooms

These bacon-topped stuffed mushrooms just melt in your mouth. I use an 8-ounce box of mushrooms which contains 14 mushrooms. If the mushrooms have a thick skin, I peel them. Otherwise, I don't. If you hand select the mushrooms, choose mushrooms with a 1½-inch diameter cap. I also microwave the bacon because I think it comes out crisp and dry.

Makes 14

1   8-ounce box fresh mushrooms
    Lemon juice
    Non-stick cooking spray
1   tablespoon finely chopped shallot
4   ounces softened light cream cheese
2   ounces blue cheese
2   tablespoons reduced-calorie butter or margarine
¼   cup sauterne
    Chopped parsley or cilantro (optional)

1   Wipe mushrooms using a paper towel dipped in fresh lemon juice. This makes a difference. Set mushrooms aside.

2 Spray a small skillet with non-stick cooking spray. Sauté shallot until tender.

3 In a small bowl blend the cream cheese, blue cheese, and sautéed shallot. Stuff each mushroom with cheese mixture.

4 Place butter or margarine and sauterne in a skillet large enough to accommodate the mushrooms. Add the mushrooms, and over medium heat, sauté 5 to 8 minutes basting several times with the pan juices. Be sure not to turn over the mushrooms.

5 Sprinkle with chopped parsley or cilantro and serve hot.

Per mushroom: *54 calories; 2.2 gm protein; 2.03 gm carbohydrates; 3.86 gm fat; 10 mg cholesterol; .16 gm fiber; 64% of calories from fat*

Mushroom Squares

The mushroom mixture for this delightful appetizer can be prepared a day ahead. Serve with Artichoke Chicken Salad as an accompaniment to hot or chilled soups.

Makes 20 squares

4 ounces cleaned and sliced fresh mushrooms
3 slices lean bacon, cooked and crumbled
1/4 cup low-sodium grated Swiss cheese
2 tablespoons light mayonnaise
2 tablespoons chopped fresh parsley
1 green onion, sliced
1/4 teaspoon garlic pepper
1/4 teaspoon Parsley Plus
5 slices 40-calorie wheat bread
2 tablespoons reduced-calorie butter or margarine

1 Preheat oven to 400°.

2 Blend mushrooms, bacon, cheese, mayonnaise, parsley, onion, garlic pepper, and parsley plus in a small bowl.

3   Trim crusts from bread. Cut each slice into 4 squares and spread one side with butter or margarine. Place bread buttered side down on baking sheet and top each square with mushroom mixture.

4   Bake in the preheated 400° oven for 7 minutes. Serve at once.

Per serving: *32 calories; 1.03 gm protein; 3.32 gm carbohydrates; 1.6 gm fat; 1.65 mg cholesterol; .07 gm fiber; 45% of calories from fat*

Red Bell Pepper Butter

This colorful flavored butter is especially beautiful at holiday time. To serve, mold in a 1-cup or in individual molds. Select a smooth, skinned, crease-free red pepper because it is much easier to peel.

Makes 1 cup

Non-stick cooking spray
1 medium (5- to 6-ounce) red bell pepper, peeled and finely chopped
1 cup reduced-calorie butter
1/4 teaspoon fresh lemon juice
1/8 teaspoon paprika
1/8 teaspoon light salt (optional)

1   Spray a skillet with non-stick cooking spray, and sauté the chopped red peppers in 2 tablespoons of butter. Place in a paper towel and gently press out any excess liquid. Pat peppers dry. Add remaining ingredients and mix until well blended. Mold and chill until ready to use.

2   To unmold, briefly dip mold into hot water. Serve immediately.

Per teaspoon: *17 calories; .03 gm protein; .1 gm carbohydrates; 1.84 gm fat; 0 mg cholesterol; .02 gm fiber; 97% of calories from fat*

Blue Cheese Crisps

T hese flaky pastry sandwiches with a nippy blue cheese filling are an easy-to-prepare appetizer.

Makes 24 squares

3 ounces blue cheese
3 ounces light cream cheese
2 teaspoons reduced-calorie margarine
2 teaspoons finely chopped onion
1 puff pastry sheet (I prefer Pepperidge Farm)
Grated cheddar cheese (optional)
Paprika

1 Preheat oven to 425°.

2 In a small bowl, blend the blue cheese, cream cheese, margarine, and onion until light and fluffy. Cover and refrigerate.

3 Meanwhile, thaw the pastry sheet for 20 minutes. Then, on a lightly floured surface, roll out the pastry, smoothing out the creases.

4 Spread the chilled cheese mixture evenly over ½ the puff pastry. Fold the pastry in half, covering the filling. Pinch the edges, and using a sharp knife, cut pastry into 24 squares. Sprinkle the tops lightly with cheddar cheese and paprika.

5 Bake on an ungreased baking sheet in the preheated 425° oven for 12 to 15 minutes or until lightly browned and puffy. Serve at once.

Per square: 35 calories; 1.09 gm protein; .85 gm carbohydrates; 3 gm fat; 6.71 mg cholesterol; 0 gm fiber; 77% of calories from fat

Italian-Style Stuffed Artichokes

These are beautiful arranged on a pretty platter. Low in calories but nutritious for you.

4 large artichokes
2 slices reduced-calorie whole wheat bread, crumbed
1/2 cup Parmesan cheese
1/4 cup fresh chopped parsley
2 teaspoons chopped fresh garlic
1 egg or the equivalent in egg substitute
1/2 cup olive oil or salad oil

Makes 4 stuffed artichokes

1 Preheat oven to 400°.

2 Cut the stem of each artichoke so that it will sit up. With a sharp knife, cut 1 inch from the tops of the leaves. This will remove the thorny leaf-ends. Wash artichokes and drain well.

3 In a small bowl, blend the bread crumbs, Parmesan cheese, parsley, garlic, and egg or egg substitute. This is your stuffing.

4 Place artichokes in a large baking dish.

5 Bend back each leaf, pushing the stuffing down into the opening.

6 Evenly pour the oil over the artichokes. Cover the bottom of the dish with 1 inch of very hot water.

7 Cover tightly with the pan's lid or aluminum foil. Bake for 1 hour or until you can easily remove a leaf from the artichoke. Serve hot or at room temperature.

Per serving: *466 calories; 11 gm protein; 33 gm carbohydrates; 33 gm fat; 78 mg cholesterol; 1.33 gm fiber; 64% of calories from fat*

Great Ball of Fire

I refer to this appetizer as the "great ball of fire" because I coat this ham-and-chicken-flavored cream cheese ball with hot curry powder. I think the curry sets all the flavors off.

1   8-ounce package light cream cheese
1   6 3/4-ounce can drained, boned chicken
1   4 1/2-ounce can deviled ham
1   tablespoon finely chopped shallots
1   tablespoon dry vermouth
     Hot curry powder

Makes about 2 cups

1   Place all the ingredients listed in your food processor or blender and purée.

2   Chill this mixture until it is firm enough to mold or form into a ball. Sprinkle with hot curry powder. Serve with bagel chips.

Per tablespoon: *44 calories; 2.63 gm protein; .36 gm carbohydrates; 3.34 gm fat; 12 mg cholesterol; .01 gm fiber; 69% of calories from fat*

Pepper Cheese Stacks

Even though I present this as a cold appetizer, these savory cheese-stuffed peppers double nicely as a salad course. For a pretty presentation, arrange red, yellow, and green bell peppers, alternating the colors.

1   red, yellow, or green bell pepper
1   4-ounce container whipped light cream cheese with chives
2   ounces blue cheese
     Garlic pepper to taste
1   large ripe tomato
     Red leaf lettuce leaves
     Paprika

Makes 4 slices

1   Cut top and bottom from pepper and discard. Remove and discard ribs and seeds. Wash, drain, and pat dry.

2 In a small mixing bowl, blend cheeses and garlic pepper.

3 Place pepper on a small plate, and stuff pepper with the cheese mixture. Cover and chill several hours or overnight. Cheese mixture should be firm.

4 To serve, slice tomato so that you have 4 perfect center-cut slices. Slice bell pepper into 4 equal rounds. Then place a stuffed pepper slice atop a tomato slice and serve on a bed of red-leaf lettuce. Garnish with paprika.

Per serving: *161 calories; 5.5 gm protein; 3.75 gm carbohydrates; 14 gm fat; 42 mg cholesterol; .37 gm fiber; 78% of calories from fat*

Stuffed Roma Tomatoes

I prefer Roma (Italian plum) tomatoes to cherry tomatoes because their texture and sweet flavor is more consistent throughout the year. The color of the tomato is no indication of maturity. These lovely stuffed tomato halves can double as a salad (see step 4).

4 Roma tomatoes (about ¹/₂ pound), cut in half
¹/₃ to ¹/₂ cup diced ripe avocado
1 tablespoon light mayonnaise
1 teaspoon finely chopped onion
1 teaspoon prepared horseradish French endive
Fresh parsley sprigs (optional)

Makes 8

1 Using a melon ball scoop, remove the tomato seeds. Remove pulp and place on a clean cutting board. Add the diced avocados, mayonnaise, onion, and horseradish. Mash the mixture until it is almost smooth leaving some avocado chunks.

2 Evenly mound the tomato mixture back into the tomato halves. Chill at least 30 minutes or up to 1 hour.

3   Place each tomato half in a French endive leaf and serve garnished with a parsley sprig.

4   To serve as a salad, arrange 3 tomato halves, stem end pointed in and touching to form a 3-petaled flower, on a bed of red-leaf lettuce or radicchio.

Per serving: 133 calories; 2.02 gm protein; 7.68 gm carbohydrates; 12 gm fat; .5 mg cholesterol; 1.69 gm fiber; 81% of calories from fat

Cheese and Onion Canapés

Gay and festive, these hot, open-sandwich-style canapés contain Italian-style cheeses, onion, and tomato. They are easy to make and can be easily assembled at the last minute.

Makes 40

1 long loaf French bread
1/2 cup light mayonnaise
2 tablespoons horseradish
1/2 teaspoon garlic powder
4 to 5 thinly sliced Roma (Italian plum) tomatoes
1 thinly sliced red Italian onion
   Cracked black pepper to taste
1/3 pound grated fresh Parmesan cheese
1/3 pound grated fresh Romano cheese
1/4 teaspoon paprika

1   Preheat broiler.

2   Blend mayonnaise, horseradish, and garlic powder in a small bowl or jar. Cover. Chill to let the flavors blend. In a separate bowl, blend pepper, Parmesan, Romano, and paprika.

3   Cut the bread into 40 1/3-inch-wide slices and coat each cut side lightly with the mayonnaise mixture. Top one side of bread with sliced tomato and onion, and sprinkle to taste with reserved cheese mixture. Broil quickly and serve warm.

Per serving: 81 calories; 4.83 gm protein; 7.39 gm carbohydrates; 3.71 gm fat; 8.64 mg cholesterol; .290 gm fiber; 41% of calories from fat

Five-Cheese Eggplant Sticks

I offer this as an appetizer, but it doubles as a side dish with any grilled meat of your choice, especially Grilled Lamb Loin Chops with Fresh Rosemary. I suggest 5 cheeses, mainly because I generally have them on hand. But use your imagination and change them about. I don't mind! I prefer small Japanese eggplants because they are easy to handle. If they aren't available, the regular will do.

Serves 4

8 Japanese eggplants or 1 small regular eggplant (pick a small one)
2 tablespoons reduced-calorie butter or margarine
2 tablespoons coarsely grated onion
2 pressed garlic cloves
  Garlic pepper to taste
2 cups (total) of a combination of these grated cheeses: Monterey Jack, mozzarella, Mexican-style Chihuahua cheese, cheddar, or any Swiss cheese
  Grated Parmesan and Romano cheeses

1 Preheat broiler.

2 Peel and cut the eggplants into ½-inch sticks. Place on ungreased baking sheet, touching but not overlapping.

3 In your microwave, melt the butter with the onion and garlic in it. Brush the sticks with the melted butter mixture.

4 Broil the sticks for 5 minutes; turn and baste with the butter mixture. Broil 5 minutes longer.

5 Sprinkle the sticks with the garlic pepper and grated 5-cheese blend, then sprinkle with Parmesan and Romano cheeses, broiling until the cheeses melt.

Per serving: 236 calories; 15 gm protein; 2.97 gm carbohydrates; 18 gm fat; 36 mg cholesterol; .25 gm fiber; 69% of calories from fat

Marinated Vegetables

E xcept for the oil, all the goodies in this recipe are low-calorie. Great for entertaining served in combination with a cold salad plate.

Serves 4

2 pounds small whole mushrooms, cleaned

2 14-ounce cans drained, quartered artichoke hearts, drained and cut into smaller wedges

2 cups halved cherry tomatoes, or 2 medium Roma tomatoes cut into wedges

1 green bell pepper, cut into thin rings

1/2 red onion, cut into thin rings

1/2 cucumber, cut into thin circles

1 cup water

1 cup cider vinegar

1/3 cup safflower, canola, or peanut oil

1/4 cup chopped fresh parsley

1 crumbled bay leaf

1 teaspoon light salt

1 teaspoon chopped fresh garlic

1/2 teaspoon whole black peppercorns

1/2 teaspoon dried chervil

1/2 teaspoon dried oregano

1/2 teaspoon dried thyme

1/2 teaspoon dried summer savory

1 Place all vegetables in a large glass or metal bowl.

2 In a large jar, combine water, vinegar, oil, parsley, bayleaf, salt, garlic, peppercorns, chervil, oregano, thyme, and savory. Blend well. Pour marinade over vegetables. Cover and refrigerate for several hours. To serve, drain.

Per serving: *203 calories; 6.85 gm protein; 28 gm carbohydrates; 9.05 gm fat; 0 mg cholesterol; 3.21 gm fiber; 40% of calories from fat*

Shrimp Dip

This is great as a spread, as a dip, or for stuffing cherry tomatoes, mushroom caps, or leaves of Belgian endive. Or, just pile it high on cucumber circles or on a chilled avocado half. To "level," cut a lengthwise slice from the bottom of the avocado.

Makes 1 1/2 cups

8 ounces softened light cream cheese
1/2 cup finely chopped green onion (white and green part)
1 cup finely chopped fresh shrimp meat
1 tablespoon chili sauce or ketchup
1 1/2 teaspoons Tabasco sauce
1/2 teaspoon light salt
1/4 teaspoon white pepper
1/8 teaspoon paprika

Blend all listed ingredients in a medium bowl. Cover bowl and chill several hours or overnight.

Per tablespoon: *39 calories; 2.97 gm protein; .87 gm carbohydrates; 2.51 gm fat; 23 mg cholesterol; .03 gm fiber; 58% of calories from fat*

Shrimp Butter

This tasty appetizer makes a nice gift for friends, or serve with an assortment of thinly sliced bread rounds.

Makes 1 1/2 cups

1/2 pound peeled, deveined, finely chopped fresh shrimp
8 ounces light cream cheese
1/4 cup reduced-calorie butter
1/4 cup lemon juice
2 tablespoons minced green onion (tops only)
1 to 2 tablespoons salmon roe
1/4 teaspoon dill weed
1/4 teaspoon light salt
2 to 4 drops Tabasco sauce

In a mixing bowl, mix all the ingredients listed. Spoon into a decorative crock or your favorite mold sprayed with non-stick cooking spray. Refrigerate 24 hours. To unmold, quickly dip mold in hot water.

Per teaspoon: *16 calories; 1.08 gm protein; .24 gm carbohydrates; 1.15 gm fat; 8.98 mg cholesterol; 0 gm fiber; 65% of calories from fat*

Shrimp Boats

hese shrimp boats not only taste good, but are pretty and fun for entertaining. Both the preparation and assembling can be done ahead of time. Purchase fresh snow peas that are at least 3 inches long and have larger seeds, otherwise they cannot be split open.

Makes 12

12	shrimp (31 to 35 count)
12	large, fresh snow peas
4	ounces softened light cream cheese
1	tablespoon finely chopped green onion
2	tablespoons ketchup
1	teaspoon 2% milk
1/2	teaspoon Lulu's Special Seasoning
1/4	to 1/2 teaspoon Tabasco sauce
	Freshly ground black pepper to taste
	Mint leaves

1 Cook, peel, and devein shrimp.

2 Clean and split snow peas lengthwise on the seeded side of the snow pea.

3 In a small mixing bowl, blend the cream cheese, onion, ketchup, milk, special seasoning, Tabasco, and pepper.

4 Carefully fill each pea with approximately 1 tablespoon seasoned cream cheese. Top each with a shrimp, inserting the ends of the shrimp into the cream cheese to resemble a horseshoe, creating a sail effect. Insert a mint leaf in each.

Per serving: *104 calories; 15 gm protein; 2 gm carbohydrates; 4.01 gm fat; 96 mg cholesterol; 0 gm fiber; 35% of calories from fat*

Ceviche of Sole and Scallops

This delightful and popular South American hors d'oeuvre is made by marinating white-fleshed fish in lime juice. The action of the lime juice "cooks" the fish, turning it opaque. Of the fish and seafood combinations I have tried, sole and scallops are my favorite. This is a very easy recipe.

Makes 4 cups

$1/2$ pound fillet of sole, cut into bite-size pieces

$1/2$ pound sea scallops, cut in half if needed (if you use bay scallops, leave them whole)

$3/4$ cup sauterne or other dry white wine

$2/3$ cup fresh or bottled lime juice (4 to 6 limes)

$1/2$ cup coarsely chopped onion

$1/4$ cup diced red bell pepper

$1/4$ cup chopped fresh cilantro

$1/4$ cup chopped fresh parsley

2 ounces whole green chiles (from a 4-ounce can)

$1/4$ cup olive oil

$1/2$ tablespoon chopped fresh garlic

$3/4$ teaspoon chopped fresh oregano

$3/4$ teaspoon cracked black pepper

$3/4$ teaspoon light salt

$1/8$ teaspoon cayenne pepper or to taste

1 cup seeded, coarsely diced Roma tomatoes (about 4 medium)

1 sliced avocado (optional)

1 head French endive, individual leaves separated and crisped in cold water (optional)

1 Place sole and scallops in a medium-size glass bowl. Bring wine to boiling and pour over fish. Let cool completely. Pour off wine.

2 Add lime juice, onion, bell pepper, cilantro, parsley, chiles, oil, garlic, oregano, black pepper, salt, and cayenne. Stir, cover lightly, refrigerate and marinate overnight.

3 Several hours before serving, stir in the tomatoes. Transfer the seviche to a decorative glass serving bowl. In the center of the ceviche I create a flower using the endive leaves and the sliced

avocado (dipped in lemon juice to prevent it from darkening). I place one tablespoon of the ceviche into the center of the flower.

Per serving: 173 calories; 21 gm protein; 13 gm carbohydrates; .82 gm fat; 59 mg cholesterol; .84 gm fiber; 4% of calories from fat

Artichoke Bottoms Filled with a Trio of Seafood

Served with some interesting crackers this doubles as a dip. Or, you can cut a sheet of prepared puff pastry into 12 triangles, bake them, and top with the dip. Run this appetizer under the broiler, and voilà, you have a delicious hot hors d'oeuvre. It's great either way. In a pinch, you can use a 6-ounce can of white crabmeat, but it lacks the sweetness of fresh.

Makes 12 artichoke bottoms or 3/4 cup dip

1/2 cup fresh crabmeat
1/4 cup light cream cheese
1/4 cup diced cooked lobster
2 tablespoons diced cooked shrimp
6 to 8 strands saffron, soaked in water until soft, then chopped
1 tablespoon light mayonnaise
1 teaspoon lemon juice
1 teaspoon minced green onion
1/8 teaspoon Lulu's Special Seasoning
1/8 teaspoon light salt
1/8 teaspoon paprika
2 shakes cayenne pepper
2 13.75-ounce cans artichoke bottoms

1 In a bowl blend all the ingredients listed, except the artichoke bottoms. Chill.

2 Mound seafood mixture on each artichoke bottom.

Per serving: 66 calories; 3.16 gm protein; 7.94 gm carbohydrates; 2.5 gm fat; 14 mg cholesterol; .35 gm fiber; 34% of calories from fat

Stuffed Clam Appetizers

F or this elegant, low-calorie appetizer I use fresh cherrystone clams and steam them for about 5 minutes. When the shells open, the clams are cooked. If fresh clams are not available, canned clams can be used.

Makes 10

10 cherrystone clams
   Non-stick cooking spray
1/4 cup finely chopped onion
2 tablespoons finely chopped red bell pepper
1 teaspoon finely chopped fresh garlic
1 slice 40-calorie wheat bread, processed into crumbs
1 tablespoon fresh cream
2 teaspoons fresh lemon juice
1 teaspoon chopped fresh oregano or 1/2 teaspoon dried
1 teaspoon chopped fresh basil or 1/2 teaspoon dried
1/8 teaspoon black pepper
1 tablespoon each of freshly grated Parmesan and Romano cheese
2 tablespoons chopped fresh parsley

1 Preheat oven to 400°.

2 Wash clams thoroughly and place in a vegetable steamer or heavy skillet. Add about ½ inch water. Cover and steam for 5 minutes. Pry shell open. Loosen and remove meat. Drain and save the bottom shell so it can be filled with the clam mixture. Mince clams and set aside.

3 Spray a skillet with non-stick cooking spray. Add onions, red pepper, and garlic. Over medium heat, cook until vegetables are tender. Remove from heat and stir in all the remaining ingredients. Add the minced clams and mix well.

4 Spoon equal amounts of clam mixture into the reserved shells. Arrange in a baking pan, and bake in the preheated 400° oven for 8 minutes or until hot.

Per clam: *38 calories; 2.59 gm protein; 4.59 gm carbohydrates; 1.07 gm fat; 5.95 mg cholesterol; .25 gm fiber; 25% of calories from fat*

Chicken Pâté

When entertaining, you can never go wrong by serving a smooth, palate-pleasing homemade pâté. It can be molded and garnished with many things. Use your imagination!

Makes 2 cups

1 1/2 cups finely chopped cooked chicken breast, poached in low-sodium chicken broth
4 ounces softened light cream cheese
3 tablespoons chopped onion
2 tablespoons sauterne
2 tablespoons light mayonnaise
2 teaspoons fresh lemon juice
1/4 teaspoon Tabasco sauce
1/4 teaspoon Lulu's Special Seasoning
1/4 teaspoon garlic pepper
1/8 teaspoon cayenne pepper
1/8 teaspoon ground nutmeg
Non-stick cooking spray
Paprika to taste (optional)

1 Using your blender or food processor, process all the ingredients listed (except the paprika) until smooth. Pack pâté into a 2-cup mold sprayed with non-stick cooking spray. Cover and chill 3 to 4 hours or overnight.

2 Just before serving, unmold onto serving plate, garnish, and sprinkle with paprika. Serve with crisp low-calorie and low-sodium crackers and fresh vegetables.

Per tablespoon: *30 calories; 3.77 gm protein; .4 gm carbohydrates; 1.38 gm fat; 12 mg cholesterol; .01 gm fiber; 41% of calories from fat*

Meatballs in Madeira

I prepare the meat mixture for these delicious meatballs in my food processor. If you do not have one, just mix all of the ingredients together in a bowl. For entertaining, prepare them ahead of time (sauce too) and just reheat on top of the stove or in your microwave. The meatballs may be frozen — but also remember to freeze the drippings to flavor the sauce. When served with whole wheat pasta, these meatballs make a wonderful entree.

1/4 cup raisins, plumped in enough warm water to cover for 10 minutes, drained and chopped
1 slice 40-calorie wheat or white bread
1 pound lean ground beef
1/2 pound sweet Italian sausage, casing removed
3 ounces light cream cheese
2 ounces (1/4 cup) blue cheese
1/4 cup chopped fresh parsley
1 egg
1 teaspoon Lulu's Special Seasoning
1 teaspoon chopped fresh garlic
1/2 teaspoon ground black pepper

Makes 36

1 Preheat oven to 350°.

2 Process the slice of bread into crumbs. Then add all remaining ingredients, processing until all ingredients are well blended. Do not overmix.

3 Form into 36 meatballs about the size of a ping pong ball. Place meatballs on a cookie sheet, and bake in the preheated 350° oven for 20 to 25 minutes or until cooked to desired degree of doneness. Reserve drippings.

Per meatball: *61 calories; 4.24 gm protein; 1.53 gm carbohydrates; 4.18 gm fat; 23 mg cholesterol; .04 gm fiber; 62% of calories from fat*

Madeira Sauce

**Drippings from the cooked
meatballs**
1/2 cup low-sodium beef broth
3 tablespoons Madeira
**3 tablespoons crema Mexicana,
Crème Fraîche, or whipping cream
Light salt and cracked black pepper
to taste**

Whisk all ingredients in a saucepan set over medium heat. Cook until the sauce thickens slightly. Pour sauce over cooked hot meatballs and serve immediately.

Per tablespoon sauce: *18 calories; .1 gm protein; .31 gm carbohydrates; 1.46 gm fat; 3.64 mg cholesterol; 0 gm fiber; 73% of calories from fat*

SOPHISTICATED SAUCES & SEASONINGS

Lulu's Special Seasoning

I created this blend of herbs and spices to give some zip to my dishes without having to use salt. Try it. This recipe makes ¹/₂ cup seasoning, enough to fill one standard glass spice bottle.

Makes ¹/₂ cup

¹/₄ cup light salt
2 teaspoons onion powder
2 teaspoons garlic powder
2 teaspoons paprika
1 teaspoon chili powder
¹/₂ teaspoon cayenne pepper
¹/₂ teaspoon black pepper
¹/₂ teaspoon MSG (optional)
¹/₂ teaspoon curry powder (optional)

Blend all ingredients listed in a small bowl. Pour into a glass spice bottle.

Parsley Plus

This is a light and aromatic blend of herbs and spices which I use to season meat and vegetable dishes. It's salt-free. Try it in place of Mrs. Dash or Parsley Patch. Don't over-process or it will be very strong.

Makes ¹/₂ cup

1 cup parsley flakes
2 tablespoons instant minced onion
2 tablespoons instant minced garlic
1 teaspoon paprika
1 teaspoon celery seed
1 teaspoon lemon zest
1 teaspoon crushed red pepper
¹/₂ teaspoon orange peel

Put all the ingredients in a food processor or blender and rapidly process until blended but not ground. If using a blender, hit the highest button and turn it on, then off, 5 times. If using a food processor, hit the pulse button 5 times. It should only be processed a total of 5 to 8 seconds.

Cinnamon Sugar

A handy recipe to
have, and making it
*yourself is much cheaper
than buying it at the
grocery store.*

1/3 cup granulated sugar
2 teaspoons cinnamon

Makes 1/3 cup

Blend sugar and cinnamon in a small bowl. Pour into a clean 3-ounce spice jar.

Per teaspoon: *17 calories; 0 gm protein; 4.35 gm carbohydrates; 0 gm fat; 0 mg cholesterol; .08 gm fiber; 0% of calories from fat*

Mornay Sauce

A sauce mornay is
simply a white sauce
*with cheese. It's excellent
served with fish, eggs, and
vegetables.*

3/4 cup 2% milk
1/4 cup light beer
3 tablespoons all-purpose flour
2 teaspoons reduced-calorie margarine
1/4 teaspoon light salt
1/4 teaspoon white pepper
1 cup grated cheddar cheese

Makes 1 cup

1 Microwave milk and beer on high power for 1 minute in a 1-quart glass measure.

2 Whisk in flour, margarine, salt, and pepper. Microwave on high power for 2 minutes. Whisk.

3 Microwave on high power for 1 minute longer. Whisk in grated cheese. Let sauce stand 5 minutes. Serve hot.

Per tablespoon: *48 calories; 2.3 gm protein; 1.87 gm carbohydrates; 3.19 gm fat; 8.28 mg cholesterol; .02 gm fiber; 60% of calories from fat*

Cold Horseradish Sauce

I keep a jar of this in my refrigerator at all times. It's wonderful over fresh sliced tomatoes, baked ham, boiled shrimp, grilled chicken, and red meats.

¹/₂ cup light mayonnaise
2 tablespoons prepared horseradish

Makes ¹/₂ cup

Blend mayonnaise and horseradish. Place in a container with a tight-fitting lid. Refrigerate until ready to serve.

Per tablespoon: 22 calories; .05 gm protein; 2.42 gm carbohydrates; 2 gm fat; 2 mg cholesterol; .05 gm fiber; 83% of calories from fat

Easy Cream Gravy

I t's so simple with a microwave. If you're preparing beef, add 1 package low-sodium instant beef broth; for chicken, use chicken broth. Each package contains about 2 teaspoons of broth.

1   cup 2% milk
2   tablespoons flour
2   tablespoons reduced-calorie margarine
1   package of low-sodium beef or chicken broth
    Black or white pepper to taste

Makes 1 cup

1   Put milk in a 1-quart glass measure and microwave it 1 minute on high.

2   Add all remaining ingredients and, using a wire whisk, blend the ingredients together. Put into microwave and cook on high for 2 minutes.

3 Open microwave and briskly whisk sauce. Return to the microwave and cook on high for 1 minute longer. Remove from microwave and briskly whisk sauce again.

4 Let stand for 5 minutes before serving.

Per tablespoon: *18 calories; .66 gm protein; 1.55 gm carbohydrates; 1.01 gm fat; 1.19 mg cholesterol; .01 gm fiber; 50% of calories from fat*

Grapefruit Marsala Sauce

I serve this delicious, easy, make-ahead sauce with roast duck. The sauce also complements grilled pork tenderloin, chicken breasts, or venison steaks.

Makes ¹/₂ cup

4 tablespoons reduced-calorie butter
¹/₄ cup minced shallot
²/₃ cup + 1 tablespoon Marsala
³/₄ cup fresh grapefruit juice
2 tablespoons chicken stock or water
1 tablespoon honey
1 tablespoon grapefruit zest
Light salt to taste
White pepper to taste

1 Heat 3 tablespoons reduced-calorie butter in a small, heavy saucepan over low heat. Sauté shallots about 10 minutes. Add ²/₃ cup Marsala, grapefruit juice, and chicken stock or water. Cook sauce over very low heat until you have about 1 cup sauce.

2 Whisk in the remaining 1 tablespoon butter and Marsala, honey, and grapefruit zest and cook 1 to 2 minutes longer.

3 Lightly season with salt and pepper. Strain sauce through a fine-meshed strainer (a tea strainer works well).

4 Pour sauce into a thermos until ready to serve. Sauce stays hot for several hours.

Per tablespoon: *75 calories; .33 gm protein; 7.55 gm carbohydrates; 2.53 gm fat; 0 mg cholesterol; .14 gm fiber; 30% of calories from fat*

Lemon-Lime Thyme Butter

*U*se this zippy seasoned butter as a bread spread, or melt and use to baste broiled or grilled chicken and fish.

Makes 1/2 cup

1/2 cup reduced-calorie butter or margarine, softened
1 tablespoon fresh lime juice
1 teaspoon finely chopped fresh lemon thyme
A dash of light salt

Blend all ingredients. Place in a container with a tight-fitting lid. Refrigerate.

Per tablespoon: *26 calories; .01 gm protein; .23 gm carbohydrates; 2.51 gm fat; 0 mg cholesterol; .03 gm fiber; 88% of calories from fat*

Microwave Béarnaise Sauce

*S*uperb served with grilled meats and as a condiment for freshly steamed vegetables. Let the microwave do the work for you. It comes out perfect every time.

Makes 1 cup

1 cup reduced-calorie butter
2 egg yolks
2 tablespoons tarragon vinegar
1 tablespoon finely chopped green onion
2 teaspoons fresh lemon juice
1 teaspoon each dried parsley flakes, chervil, and tarragon
1/2 teaspoon dried mustard
1/4 teaspoon cracked black pepper
1/4 teaspoon Lulu's Special Seasoning
1/4 teaspoon light salt

1   Place butter in a 1-quart glass measure and microwave on high power for 1 1/2 minutes.

2   Using a blender or an electric hand-held blender (which I adore) blend egg yolks with all remaining ingredients.

3 Slowly add the melted butter to the egg yolk mixture and blend well.

4 Pour the blended mixture back into the glass measure. Microwave on high power 1 minute longer. When ready to serve, microwave another minute on high power.

Per tablespoon: 59 calories; 4 gm protein; .21 gm carbohydrates; 5.77 gm fat; 34 mg cholesterol; .01 gm fiber; 88% of calories from fat

Basic White Sauce

In case you don't yet own a microwave oven, here is the traditional method of making a medium-thick white sauce, the basis for many sauces such as mornay sauce (a white sauce with added cheese). An unadorned white sauce is often called béchamel.

2 tablespoons reduced-calorie butter or margarine
2 tablespoons all-purpose flour
1 cup 2% milk
1/4 teaspoon light salt
Black or white pepper to taste

Makes 1 cup

1 Melt the margarine or butter in a skillet over medium heat.

2 Add the flour, and stirring constantly, cook the roux until it bubbles and becomes thick and smooth (about 5 minutes).

3 Whisk in the milk, salt, and pepper and, stirring constantly, cook sauce until it thickens (about 5 minutes). Liquids, herbs, spices, and grated cheese can be added at this point.

Per tablespoon: 17 calories; .6 gm protein; 1.49 gm carbohydrates; .95 gm fat; 1.13 mg cholesterol; .01 gm fiber; 49% of calories from fat

Quick Sour Cream Cheese Sauce

G*reat over steamed
vegetables such as
broccoli, cauliflower, and
brussels sprouts.*

Makes ¹/₂ cup

3 tablespoons light sour cream
1 tablespoon 2% milk
1 tablespoon reduced-calorie butter
¹/₄ teaspoon Lulu's Special Seasoning
¹/₈ teaspoon tarragon
¹/₈ teaspoon summer savory
¹/₈ teaspoon cracked black pepper
¹/₂ cup grated cheddar cheese

In a 1-cup glass measure, blend the sour cream, milk, butter, special seasoning, tarragon, summer savory, and pepper. Microwave on high power for 1 minute. Stir in grated cheese until melted. Microwave on high power for 30 seconds longer. Let stand several minutes before serving.

Per tablespoon: *43 calories; 2.14 gm protein; .32 gm carbohydrates; 3.48 gm fat; 7.58 mg cholesterol; 0 gm fiber; 73% of calories from fat*

Tarragon Horseradish Cream

S*erve this sauce with
hot or cold roast beef,
steak, or chicken.*

Makes 1 cup

¹/₂ cup unflavored non-fat yogurt
¹/₂ cup light mayonnaise
3 tablespoons prepared horseradish
2 teaspoons tarragon vinegar
¹/₂ teaspoon white pepper
¹/₂ teaspoon dry mustard

Blend all sauce ingredients in a small bowl, cover and chill.

Per tablespoon: *16 calories; .47 gm protein; 1.92 gm carbohydrates; 1.03 gm fat; 1.13 mg cholesterol; .04 gm fiber; 59% of calories from fat*

Brandy Sauce

T his sauce is a nice
accompaniment to
any type of poultry and
game.

2 tablespoons finely chopped
   shallot
1 tablespoon reduced-calorie butter
   or margarine
3/4 cup brandy
3/4 cup sauterne
1 1/2 cups strong homemade chicken
   stock
1/2 teaspoon minced fresh ginger
1/8 teaspoon dried rosemary
1/4 cup whipping cream
1/4 cup 2% milk
1/4 teaspoon light salt
1/8 teaspoon white pepper
1 1/2 tablespoons reduced-calorie
   butter
2 teaspoons arrowroot, dissolved in
   1/4 cup bouillon or water

Makes 1 1/4 cups

1 Heat butter or margarine in a saucepan over medium heat and
sauté the shallots until they are transparent.

2 Add brandy and sauterne, scraping any residue from the bottom
of the pan. Cook until half the liquid has evaporated.

3 Add the stock, ginger, and rosemary and reduce the sauce to 1/2
cup. Strain. Return sauce to pan, and reduce heat to low. Add
the cream, milk, salt, and pepper. Do not let sauce boil.

4 Bit by bit whisk in the remaining 1 1/2 tablespoons butter. Stir in
the arrowroot mixture and cook several minutes until the sauce
thickens.

5 Serve immediately, or keep warm in a thermos.

Per tablespoon: *81 calories; 1.36 gm protein; 1.46 gm carbohydrates; 2.08 gm fat;
7.59 mg cholesterol; .05 gm fiber; 23% of calories from fat*

Pineapple Sauce

S erve this sweet and
sour sauce with
Fruit-Stuffed Pork
Tenderloin, roast pork, or
chicken. It keeps well in
the refrigerator for weeks.

Makes 2/3 cup

1 6-ounce can pineapple juice
2 teaspoons cornstarch
1 tablespoon honey
1 tablespoon brown sugar
1 1/2 teaspoons light soy sauce
1 teaspoon seasoned rice vinegar
   (available at Oriental markets)
1/4 teaspoon garlic powder
1/4 teaspoon ground cinnamon
1/8 teaspoon grated orange zest

Whisk together the pineapple juice and cornstarch in a small
saucepan over medium heat. Whisk in all remaining ingredients and
cook gently for several minutes until sauce thickens.

Per tablespoon: *23 calories; 15 gm protein; 0 gm carbohydrates; .01 gm fat; 0 mg
cholesterol; .04 gm fiber; 0% of calories from fat*

Microwave Sauce Moutarde

T his reduced-calorie
mustard sauce goes
well with beef, pork, veal,
chicken, and vegetables.
Try it with Turkey
Tenderloin in Cumin
and Cayenne.

Makes 1 1/4 cups

1/2 cup whipping cream
1/2 cup homemade chicken broth or
   low-sodium instant chicken broth
2 tablespoons reduced-calorie butter
2 tablespoons all-purpose flour
2 tablespoons Dijon mustard
1 raw egg yolk (optional)
1 teaspoon dry vermouth
1/4 teaspoon light salt
1/4 teaspoon white pepper

1 Microwave cream and broth in a 1-quart glass measure on high
power for 1 minute.

2 Whisk in all remaining ingredients. Microwave on high power for 2 minutes.

3 Whisk briskly. Microwave on high power for 1 minute longer. Whisk sauce again. Let stand for 5 minutes. Serve hot or warm.

Per tablespoon: *33 calories; .86 gm protein; 1.12 gm carbohydrates; 2.78 gm fat; 7.97 mg cholesterol; .08 gm fiber; 73% of calories from fat*

Herbed Avocado Cream

This sauce is so tasty I could drink it! Serve it over linguine or your favorite cooked pasta.

1 large peeled, pitted, chunked avocado (about 2 cups)
1/4 cup homemade chicken broth or low-sodium instant chicken broth
2 tablespoons sauterne
1 teaspoon each fresh parsley, basil, and thyme
1/2 teaspoon crumbled, dried tarragon
1/2 teaspoon finely chopped garlic
1/4 teaspoon Lulu's Special Seasoning
1/4 teaspoon white pepper
1/8 teaspoon cayenne pepper
1 teaspoon lemon juice
1 tablespoon reduced-calorie margarine
1/4 cup whipping cream
1/4 cup 2% milk

Makes 1 1/4 cups

1/2 pound cooked pasta

1 Place avocado chunks, broth, wine, all herbs, and lemon juice in the container or a blender or food processor and purée.

2 Melt margarine in a skillet set over medium heat. Whisk in purée, cream, and milk. Heat, but do not boil.

Per tablespoon: *40 calories; .84 gm protein; 2.72 gm carbohydrates; 2.88 gm fat; 4.21 mg cholesterol; .28 gm fiber; 65% of calories from fat*

Jezebel Sauce

S erve this tangy sauce with pork or chicken. I use it as a marinade for baby back ribs. Refrigerated, it stays fresh for months.

Makes 2¹/₂ cups

1 18-ounce jar peach or pineapple preserves
1 18-ounce jar apple jelly
¹/₃ cup dry English mustard
1 5-ounce jar prepared horseradish
1 tablespoon cracked black pepper

Blend all the ingredients listed. Transfer to a jar. Cover and refrigerate.

Per tablespoon: 79 calories; .41 gm protein; 19 gm carbohydrates; .36 gm fat; 0 mg cholesterol; .24 gm fiber; 4% of calories from fat

Microwave White Sauce

W hat is so neat about this sauce is that except for the time it takes you to measure the ingredients, the sauce takes only 3 minutes to cook. You must use a 1-quart microwave-proof vessel or the sauce will overflow. To transform this white sauce into a cheese sauce, merely whisk 1 cup grated cheddar cheese (or whatever kind you like) into the hot sauce.

Makes 1 cup

1 cup 2% milk or skim milk
2 tablespoons reduced-calorie margarine
1 tablespoon all-purpose flour
   Dash cayenne pepper
¹/₄ teaspoon dry English mustard
¹/₄ teaspoon white pepper
¹/₄ teaspoon light salt
1 cup (about 4 ounces) grated cheddar cheese

1 Microwave milk in a 1-quart glass measure for 1 minute on high power.

2 Whisk in milk, margarine, flour, cayenne, mustard, pepper, and salt. Microwave on high power for 2 minutes. Whisk again.

3 Microwave on high power 1 minute longer, then briskly whisk the sauce again. If you are adding cheese, add it now. Let sauce stand 5 minutes, then whisk again.

Per tablespoon: *46 calories; 2.36 gm protein; 1.59 gm carbohydrates; 3.27 gm fat; 8.56 mg cholesterol; .07 gm fiber; 64% of calories from fat*

Tomato Oregano Sauce

I t takes a little time to peel and seed the tomatoes, but things of beauty take time to create. This is a lovely, chunky sauce that would be grand served over any cooked pasta. Or, you could add lean meat or sausage. I created this sauce for Turkey-Stuffed Jumbo Pasta Shells. This sauce can be made ahead of time, and it freezes well.

Makes 2 cups

1 3/4 pounds peeled, seeded, coarsely chopped Roma tomatoes (about 2 cups)
2 tablespoons olive oil
1/2 finely chopped red bell pepper
1/3 cup finely chopped onion
1 teaspoon minced garlic
1/4 cup chili sauce
1/2 cup water
1/2 cup dry red wine
1 tablespoon chopped fresh oregano
1 tablespoon chopped fresh parsley
1 tablespoon brown sugar
1/2 teaspoon cracked black pepper
1/2 teaspoon light salt

Heat oil in a skillet over medium heat and sauté peppers and onion for 5 minutes. Add garlic and sauté 2 minutes longer. Add all remaining ingredients, reduce heat to simmer, and cook sauce, uncovered, for about 1 hour.

Per cup: *284 calories; 2.78 gm protein; 28 gm carbohydrates; 14 gm fat; 0 mg cholesterol; 1.55 gm fiber; 45% of calories from fat*

Eggless Mayonnaise

To date this is the best eggless mayonnaise I have concocted. You can substitute this eggless mayonnaise whenever a recipe calls for light mayonnaise.

Makes 1 1/2 cups

3 teaspoons Dijon mustard
2 tablespoons water
1 tablespoon white wine vinegar
3/4 cup corn oil
1/4 cup olive oil
2 tablespoons chilled evaporated skim milk
1/4 teaspoon light salt
1/8 teaspoon white pepper

1 Blend mustard, water, and vinegar in a blender or food processor. While machine is running add oil in a thin stream alternately with the cold milk. (Add a few drops of milk each time you add 1/4 cup oil.) When all the oils and milk have been used, scrape down the sides of the container.

2 Add salt and pepper and process 30 seconds longer. Keeps 1 to 2 weeks, refrigerated, in a covered container.

Per tablespoon: *104 calories; .52 gm protein; .59 gm carbohydrates; 11 gm fat; .06 mg cholesterol; .09 gm fiber; 98% of calories from fat*

Sour Cream Supreme

Serve this tangy sauce over nachos, steamed green vegetables, or baked potatoes.

Makes 1 cup

3/4 cup 2% milk
1/4 cup light sour cream
2 tablespoons flour
1 tablespoon reduced-calorie butter
1/4 teaspoon light salt
1/8 teaspoon cayenne pepper

1 Place milk in a 2-cup glass measure and microwave on high power for 1 minute.

2 Whisk in the light sour cream, flour, butter, salt, and pepper.

3 Microwave on high power for an additional 2 minutes. Whisk again. Microwave on high 1 minute longer; whisk again. Let sauce stand for 5 minutes before using.

Per tablespoon: *18 calories; .73 gm protein; 1.43 gm carbohydrates; .93 gm fat; .84 mg cholesterol; .01 gm fiber; 47% of calories from fat*

Pesto for Pasta

T oss this uncooked seasoning with cooked pasta, spoon some over a baked potato, or just spread a dab on a slice of fresh sourdough or French bread. It's a healthful seasoning, but highly caloric, so use just a little. To store, pour a thin layer of olive oil over the pesto, and refrigerate in a jar with a tight-fitting lid. The pesto should be as thick as heavy mayonnaise, so don't over-process it.

1 cup loosely packed fresh basil leaves
3 tablespoons chopped fresh parsley
1 tablespoon chopped garlic
1/2 cup olive oil
1/2 cup freshly grated Parmesan cheese
1/3 cup walnuts or pine nuts (pignoli)
1 tablespoon freshly grated Romano cheese (optional—use it if you have it)
1/4 teaspoon light salt
   Fresh cracked black pepper to taste

Makes 1 cup

1 In a food processor fitted with the steel blade, process the basil, parsley, and garlic until finely chopped. (If you don't have a food processor, use a blender.)

2 With the machine running, slowly pour in the oil until well blended.

43

3 Add all remaining ingredients and process briefly to combine. The nuts should be finely chopped but not puréed.

Per tablespoon: 105 calories; 2.83 gm protein; 3.28 gm carbohydrates; 9.7 gm fat; 3.38 mg cholesterol; 1.07 gm fiber; 83% of calories from fat

Light Swiss Cheese Sauce

*E*xcept for the time it takes you to measure the ingredients, this sauce takes 3 minutes to prepare, and turns out perfect every time. This multi-purpose sauce is delicious served over baked or broiled fish, tossed with vegetables such as green peas or cauliflower, or with cooked pasta or baked potatoes.

1 cup 2% milk
2 tablespoons reduced-calorie margarine
2 tablespoons all-purpose flour
1 small clove pressed garlic
2 shakes Tabasco sauce
2 shakes Lulu's Special Seasoning
2 grinds white pepper
1 cup grated low-sodium Swiss cheese

Makes 1 cup

1 Place milk in a 1-quart glass measure and microwave on high power for 1 minute.

2 Whisk in margarine, flour, garlic, Tabasco, special seasoning, and pepper. Microwave sauce on high power for 2 minutes.

3 Whisk briskly; cook sauce on high for another minute, then briskly whisk again. Cook sauce on high for 1 minute longer. Briskly whisk again.

4 Stir in cheese. Let sauce stand 5 minutes. Whisk again. Serve warm.

Per tablespoon: 70 calories; 4.62 gm protein; 2.06 gm carbohydrates; 4.95 gm fat; 14 mg cholesterol; .01 gm fiber; 64% of calories from fat

Chunky Pepper Leek Sauce

A nother zesty, chunky sauce flavored with green bell peppers and leeks, great served as a side dish or over cooked pasta. It is also a perfect filling for omelettes. For variety, I add several types of grated low-fat cheeses to the omelette.

Makes 4 cups

2 tablespoons olive oil
2 tablespoons reduced-calorie margarine
2 tablespoons sauterne
1 large slivered green bell pepper (about 2 cups)
2 cups thinly sliced leeks
1 slivered onion (about 2 cups)
1/2 cup thinly sliced celery
1/2 cup chopped fresh parsley
1 tablespoon light soy sauce
1 tablespoon fresh lemon juice
1 tablespoon Worcestershire sauce
1 teaspoon chopped fresh garlic
1 teaspoon chopped fresh mint
1/2 teaspoon chopped fresh rosemary
1/2 teaspoon light salt
1/4 teaspoon cracked black pepper

1 Heat oil, margarine, and sauterne in a large skillet over medium-high heat. Add peppers, leeks, onion, and celery. Stir and cook about 6 minutes or until the peppers are tender but firm and the onion begins to brown.

2 Stir in all the remaining ingredients and cook 5 minutes longer. Serve hot.

Per cup: *176 calories; 2.7 gm protein; 17.9 gm carbohydrates; 9.76 gm fat; 0 mg cholesterol; 1.76 gm fiber; 50% of calories from fat*

Red Pepper Sauce

S*weet red bell peppers flavor this meatless sauce, best served over any type of cooked pasta. Meat can be added to it—but it's already so tasty, who needs it? The sauce can be frozen.*

Makes 3 1/4 cups

2 tablespoons olive oil
1 large or 2 small seeded, julienned red bell peppers
1/2 cup finely chopped onion
1 28-ounce can whole, peeled, chopped tomatoes, with liquid
1/3 cup dry red wine
1/4 cup chopped fresh parsley
1 tablespoon chopped fresh basil
1 teaspoon chopped fresh mint
1 teaspoon chopped garlic
1 teaspoon sugar
1/2 teaspoon chopped fresh rosemary
1/2 teaspoon light salt
1/4 teaspoon dried oregano
1/4 teaspoon black pepper

1 Heat oil in a large skillet over medium heat. Sauté peppers and onions.

2 Add remaining ingredients and bring to a boil. Reduce heat and simmer covered about 15 minutes.

3 Uncover and continue to cook, stirring occasionally, for about 15 minutes or until sauce thickens slightly.

Per cup: *192 calories; 2.7 gm protein; 17.1 gm carbohydrates; 9.92 gm fat; 0 mg cholesterol; 1.92 gm fiber; 47% of calories from fat*

Superlative
Salads

Bibb Toss

Serves 4

4 cups bite-sized pieces Bibb lettuce
1 wedged tomato (I prefer a Roma or homegrown when available)
1/2 avocado, coarsely diced
1/2 8 1/2-ounce can hearts of palm sliced 1/2 inch thick
1/2 14-ounce can quartered artichoke hearts
Red onion rings to taste
Vegetable Herb Vinaigrette to taste

Place all ingredients in a large glass salad bowl. Toss salad as desired with the vinaigrette.

Per serving: *291 calories; 2.31 gm protein; 8.76 gm carbohydrates; 29 gm fat; 45 mg cholesterol; 1.07 gm fiber; 90% of calories from fat*

Vegetable Herb Vinaigrette

S erve this zesty dressing with Bibb Toss salad, mixed leaf lettuces, or over sliced tomatoes and cucumbers. The refrigerated vinaigrette stays fresh for several weeks. Always shake before using.

Makes 3 cups

1 1/3 cup olive oil
2/3 cup red wine vinegar
1/2 cup coarsely chopped carrots
1/2 cup coarsely chopped celery
1 tablespoon chopped shallot
2 teaspoons chopped fresh basil
2 teaspoons chopped fresh thyme or oregano
1 teaspoon Dijon mustard
1 teaspoon light salt
1/4 teaspoon cracked black pepper
2 raw egg yolks

1 Place all ingredients in your food processor and process at high speed until well blended.

2   Store in lidded container, chill, and serve.

Per tablespoon: *57 calories; .17 gm protein; .22 gm carbohydrates; 6.25 gm fat; 11 mg cholesterol; .02 gm fiber; 99% of calories from fat*

Tortellini Salad

T his salad can be
served just freshly
tossed at room tempera-
ture or well chilled. It's
delicious either way —
and great for entertain-
ing. Roasting the red bell
pepper takes a few
minutes longer, but is
worth the trouble.

1 red bell pepper, halved, seeded,
   and peeled
2 9-ounce packages cheese-filled
   tortellini (one white, one green),
   cooked about 6 minutes or until al
   dente, rinsed in cold water, and
   drained
1 14-ounce can artichoke hearts,
   drained and diced
1/3 cup ripe olives, drained and sliced
1 cup fresh zucchini squash, julienned
1 cup fresh summer yellow squash,
   julienned (I use the 3mm julienned
   blade of my food processor)
   Mustard Vinaigrette to taste
   Fresh grated Parmesan cheese as
   garnish
   Diced fresh tomato as garnish
   Cracked black pepper or garlic
   pepper to taste

Serves 4 to 6

1   Roast the red bell pepper halves covered for 2 to 3 minutes per
    side in a preheated outdoor grill or smoker.

2   In a lidded storage container or in a salad bowl if serving
    immediately, combine and toss until well coated all ingredients.
    Garnish with the cheese, tomato, and pepper. Serve at once or
    cover and chill for later.

Per serving: *247 calories; 9.83 gm protein; 36 gm carbohydrates; 7.97 gm fat; 7 mg cholesterol; 1.94 gm fiber; 29% of calories from fat*

Mushroom Pimiento Vinaigrette

T his is different and tasty. Prepare the dressing ahead of time and toss the salad at the last minute.

Makes 2 1/2 cups

8 ounces cleaned and coarsely chopped fresh mushrooms
1/4 cup chopped canned pimiento
1/4 cup chopped green onion
Mustard Vinaigrette to taste

Just before serving, toss all ingredients together. Serve on crisp red lettuce leaves.

Per tablespoon: *10 calories; .09 gm protein; .37 gm carbohydrates; .91 gm fat; 0 mg cholesterol; .05 gm fiber; 82% of calories from fat*

Colorful Duckling Salad

A lmost too pretty to eat, this gorgeous salad is perfect for entertaining. You do all of the preparation in advance, and assemble the salad at the last moment. Present this unusual salad on a platter or on individual salad plates. Either way it's a knockout.

Serves 4

Thinly sliced cooked roast duckling breast
8 large red leaf lettuce leaves
1 medium head Bibb lettuce torn into bite-size pieces
12 endive leaves
8 tomato wedges
4 medium sliced mushrooms
1 red bell pepper, cut into strips
1 yellow bell pepper (use green if yellow unavailable)
Mustard Vinaigrette to taste

To assemble each salad:

1 On an individual salad plate arrange 2 red leaf lettuce leaves with the outside of the leaves circling the edge of the plate.

2 Pile the Bibb lettuce on top of the red leaf lettuce.

3 Angle 3 endive leaves into the Bibb lettuce so that the endive comes spike-like from the pile of Bibb lettuce.

4 Place slides of duck breast on the Bibb lettuce. Decorate with tomato wedges, mushroom slices, and red and green bell pepper strips.

5 Sprinkle vinaigrette over each salad.

Per serving: *462 calories; 15 gm protein; 6.36 gm carbohydrates; 43 gm fat; 49 mg cholesterol; .95 gm fiber; 84% of calories from fat*

Anchovy Vinaigrette

I serve this anchovy-enriched vinaigrette as I would any other — over a mixture of lettuces or atop an assortment of garden-fresh vegetables. But add a dollop or two of light mayonnaise and this culinary classic is transformed into a luxurious, creamy dressing. Try it over baked potatoes or steamed green beans.

Makes ²/₃ cup

- ¹/₃ cup red wine vinegar
- ¹/₄ cup olive oil
- 1 tablespoon drained and mashed canned anchovy fillets
- ¹/₂ teaspoon chopped fresh garlic
- ¹/₄ teaspoon dried basil
- ¹/₈ to ¹/₄ teaspoon cracked black pepper

Place all ingredients in the container of a blender or in a jar with a tight-fitting lid. Blend until smooth.

Per tablespoon: *47 calories; .17 gm protein; .04 gm carbohydrates; 5.15 gm fat; 0 mg cholesterol; 0 gm fiber; 99% of calories from fat*

Mustardy Yogurt Dressing

T asty on any tossed
green salad and on
fresh vegetables, but try it
on Potato Beet Salad.

Makes 1 cup

1 6-ounce container unflavored
non-fat yogurt
1/2 cup olive oil
2 tablespoons tarragon vinegar
2 teaspoons Dijon mustard
1/2 teaspoon Lulu's Special Seasoning
Cracked black pepper to taste

Place all listed ingredients in either a blender or a 1-quart jar with a tight-fitting lid, and blend until creamy. Chill.

Per tablespoon: 68 calories; .68 gm protein; .98 gm carbohydrates; 7.05 gm fat; .66 mg cholesterol; .03 gm fiber; 93% of calories from fat

Potato Beet Salad
with Mustardy Yogurt Dressing

D rizzle Mustardy
Yogurt Dressing
over the warm potatoes
and beets, allowing the
flavors to blend, and serve
on a bed of red leaf
lettuce. Remember,
leaving 2 inches of beet
stem attached to the beets
when boiling prevents the
color from bleeding.

Serves 4

4 unpeeled medium new potatoes
4 medium beets or 1 16-ounce can
julienne beets
4 to 6 cups torn, chilled red leaf
lettuce
2 peeled and chopped hard-cooked
eggs (if you must, discard the yolk)
1/3 cup chopped green onion
Mustardy Yogurt Dressing to taste

1   Cook potatoes in water for about 15 minutes or until tender. Drain, cool slightly, peel, and slice thinly into rounds.

2   Boil beets in water for about 30 minutes or until tender. Drain, cool slightly, peel, and julienne.

3 Arrange the potatoes on the lettuce. Add beets and sprinkle them with chopped egg and onion. Drizzle with Mustardy Yogurt Dressing.

Per serving: 186 calories; 7.08 gm protein; 34 gm carbohydrates; 3 gm fat; 137 mg cholesterol; 1.5 gm fiber; 15% of calories from fat

Seafood Pasta Salad

T his is a lovely salad medley.

2 cups water
¹/₂ pound squid, cleaned and cut into rounds (about ¹/₂ cup)
1 cup cooked salad shrimp
1 cup cooked bay scallops
3 cups cooked fusilli (corkscrew-shaped pasta)
¹/₂ cup light mayonnaise
¹/₂ cup light sour cream
¹/₃ cup chopped red onion
¹/₃ cup chopped green bell pepper
¹/₃ cup chopped celery
1 teaspoon chopped fresh parsley
¹/₂ teaspoon light salt
¹/₂ teaspoon white pepper
¹/₄ teaspoon dill weed

Serves 6

¹/₄ teaspoon garlic powder

1 Bring 2 cups water to boiling in a small saucepan. Add squid and cook 3 to 5 minutes or until fork tender. Drain and cool.

2 Toss squid, shrimp, scallops, and pasta in a large serving bowl.

3 Blend mayonnaise and all remaining ingredients in a small bowl. Add mayonnaise mixture to seafood mixture, tossing gently to blend.

Per serving: 258 calories; 27 gm protein; 14 gm carbohydrates; 15 gm fat; 92 mg cholesterol; .38 gm fiber; 52% of calories from fat

Tuna Toss

T his makes a light yet filling luncheon salad. Serve with Peach Iced Tea.

Serves 2

2 cups bite-size pieces red or green leaf lettuce
2 cups bite-size pieces romaine lettuce
1/4 cup sliced mushrooms
1/4 cup julienne or thinly sliced carrots
Thinly sliced red onion to taste
1/4 avocado, cubed
1/4 cup chunk light tuna in spring water, drained
1/4 cup chopped Roma tomato
Mustard Vinaigrette or your favorite light salad dressing to taste

Place all ingredients in a large salad bowl and toss gently.

Per serving: *266 calories; 19 gm protein; 17 gm carbohydrates; 13 gm fat; 24 mg cholesterol; 2.06 gm fiber; 45% of calories from fat*

Pure Potato Salad

I served this creamy white salad at my Neiman-Marcus restaurant. You truly taste the pure potato flavor. Serve it warm or chilled with grilled meat or poultry or as part of a salad platter. Waxy red potatoes are a good choice.

Makes 4 cups

1 pound (4 cups) peeled, diced potatoes
1 cup thinly sliced onion (I use the 1 mm slicing blade on my food processor)
1/3 cup light mayonnaise
1/3 cup light sour cream
1/2 teaspoon light salt
1/2 teaspoon Lulu's Special Seasoning
1/4 teaspoon white pepper

1 Place the diced potatoes in a large saucepan with water to cover. Bring potatoes to a boil and boil 10 minutes or until potatoes are tender. Drain. Transfer potatoes to a large bowl.

2 Add and blend in all remaining ingredients. Serve warm or chilled.

Per cup: 157 calories; 3.33 gm protein; 27 gm carbohydrates; 4.66 gm fat; 2.66 mg cholesterol; .56 gm fiber; 27% of calories from fat

Warm Asparagus Pasta Salad with Balsamic Lemon Vinaigrette

*A*uthentic balsamic vinegar is a lengthily–aged fine wine vinegar from Modena in northern Italy.

Serves 4 to 6

2 cups 1 1/2-inch-long julienne strips fresh asparagus (3/4 to 1 pound asparagus)
1 8-ounce package fideo enrollado (curly vermicelli)
3 quarts boiling water
1 tablespoon minced shallot
2 teaspoons grated lemon rind
3 tablespoons balsamic vinegar
1 teaspoon light salt
1 teaspoon fresh ground black pepper
1/2 cup olive oil
1/4 cup grated Parmesan cheese (freshly grated is preferred)

1 Place asparagus in a covered microwave-safe dish. Cover dish and microwave on high for 6 minutes. Let stand covered 5 minutes.

2 Add the vermicelli to 3 quarts boiling water, return to a boil, and boil uncovered for 5 minutes. Drain immediately and then rinse under warm water and drain again.

3 Place all ingredients in a large serving bowl and toss well while the vermicelli and asparagus are still warm. Serve immediately.

Per serving: 227 calories; 4.6 gm protein; 10 gm carbohydrates; 20 gm fat; 3.29 mg cholesterol; .68 gm fiber; 79% of calories from fat

Robert's Favorite Salad

.... easy. You can prepare this salad in a jiffy. I always use Bibb lettuce. All lettuce, regardless of variety, should be rinsed well, drained, and crisped before using. Can we talk tomatoes? In the summer, I grow my own; in the winter, I use Roma, Italian plum, tomatoes.

For each serving:

3 cups bite-size pieces Bibb lettuce, stems discarded
1/4 cup finely chopped Roma tomato
2 tablespoons light mayonnaise
2 teaspoons fresh lemon juice
   Light salt to taste
   Black pepper to taste

Combine all ingredients in a mixing bowl. Toss well. Serve immediately.

Per serving: *80 calories; 3.25 gm protein; 12 gm carbohydrates; 4 gm fat; 4 mg cholesterol; 1.41 gm fiber; 45% of calories from fat*

Rice Vinegar Cucumber Salad

This salad keeps in the refrigerator for days. Feel free to add other vegetables such as cooked pearl onions or cauliflower flowerets to the marinade.

1 large cucumber, peeled and very thinly sliced
1 cup julienne carrots
1/2 onion, very thinly sliced
1 cup seasoned rice vinegar (I like Marukan brand)
1 tablespoon chopped fresh dill or 1/3 teaspoon dried dill weed
1 tablespoon chopped fresh parsley
1 teaspoon fresh lemon or plain thyme or 1/4 teaspoon dried thyme
1 teaspoon cracked black pepper

Makes 4 cups

1   Toss prepared vegetables in a large mixing bowl.

2 Blend remaining ingredients in a jar with a tight fitting lid and pour over vegetables. Pour marinade over vegetables and toss gently.

3 Cover and chill several hours.

Per cup: *18 calories; .38 gm protein; 8 gm carbohydrates; 0 gm fat; 0 mg cholesterol; .34 gm fiber; 0% of calories from fat*

Tangy Sour Cream Dressing

T his reduced-calorie
dressing doubles as
a dip for a platter of low-
calorie raw vegetables.
When I'm dieting, I
drizzle the dressing over a
salad using 2 or 3 types of
lettuce topped with
julienne carrots and
tomato wedges. With it I
eat small amounts of
Grilled Herbed Chicken
Breast. What a delicious
way to lose weight.

Makes 2 1/4 cups

1/2 cup light mayonnaise
1/2 cup light sour cream
1/4 cup 2% milk
2 tablespoons malt vinegar
1/2 teaspoon light salt
1/4 teaspoon Lulu's Special Seasoning
1/8 teaspoon black pepper

Blend all the listed ingredients in a food processor or blender. Pour into a container and tighten lid. Chill and serve.

Per tablespoon serving: *9.74 calories; .26 gm protein; .66 gm carbohydrates; .77 gm fat; .54 mg cholesterol; 0 gm fiber; 71% of calories from fat*

Mustard Vinaigrette

T oss this with
Mushroom Radish
Salad or any tossed green
salad. To blend many of
my salad dressings and
sauces I use a hand-held
electric blender. You can
also use an electric
blender or a mayonnaise
jar with a tight-fitting lid.

Makes 1 cup

2/3 cup olive oil
1/3 cup red wine vinegar
2 teaspoons Dijon mustard
1/2 teaspoon finely chopped shallot
1/2 teaspoon light salt
1/4 teaspoon freshly ground black pepper

Using a blender, food processor, or jar, combine all the ingredients and blend until smooth. Chill and serve.

Per tablespoon: *81 calories; .1 gm protein; .19 gm carbohydrates; 9 gm fat; 0 mg cholesterol; .02 gm fiber; 100% of calories from fat*

Mushroom Radish Salad

A lmost a meal in
itself, make this
hearty salad a day in
advance. I use my food
processor to slice the mushrooms and radishes. You
can substitute mozzarella
or Monterey Jack cheese
for the Mexican
Chihuahua cheese.

Serves 4

8 ounces cleaned, sliced fresh mushrooms
1 6-ounce package sliced red radishes
1/3 cup coarsely chopped green onion
1 tablespoon chopped black olives
1/4 cup chopped fresh parsley
1 1/2 cups grated Chihuahua or mozzarella
1/3 cup Mustard Vinaigrette or to taste
Red leaf lettuce

1 In a large mixing bowl, toss mushrooms, radishes, green onion, olives, parsley, and cheese.

2   Add Mustard Vinaigrette and blend well. Cover and refrigerate.

3   Arrange on red leaf lettuce. Add additional vinaigrette to taste.

Per serving: *352 calories; 23 gm protein; 9.18 gm carbohydrates; 24 gm fat; 0 mg cholesterol; .96 gm fiber; 60% of calories from fat*

Marinated Lentil Salad

T his simple-to-make protein-packed salad is economical as well as nutritious. Refrigerated, it stays fresh for several days. I like to garnish with coarsely diced avocados.

1/2 **pound well-washed lentils**
2 **quarts water**
1 **bay leaf**
1 **peeled clove fresh garlic**
1/2 **cup julienne carrots**
1/2 **cup thickly sliced mushrooms**
1/3 **cup chopped green bell pepper**
1/3 **cup chopped fresh tomato**
1/2 **cup chopped green onion**
2 **tablespoons chopped fresh parsley**
1/2 **teaspoon Lulu's Special Seasoning**
    Mustard Vinaigrette to taste
    Lettuce
    Diced avocado

Makes 5 1-cup servings

1   Place lentils, water, bay leaf, and garlic in a 3-quart saucepan. Heat to boiling. Turn off heat, and let stand 30 minutes. Drain lentils well and transfer to a mixing bowl.

2   Blend lentils with all remaining ingredients, adding Mustard Vinaigrette to taste. Chill salad and serve on a bed of your favorite lettuce. Garnish with avocado.

Per cup serving: *119 calories; 4.48 gm protein; 14 gm carbohydrates; 5.63 gm fat; 0 mg cholesterol; 1.76 gm fiber; 43% of calories from fat*

Chutney Chicken Salad

S weet, bottled commercial chutney is a piquant, but not hot, relish usually made from mangoes, sugar, vinegar, and spices. It complements hot and cold meats. This chicken salad goes nicely with any green salad or fresh fruit salad, or try it as one component of a cold salad platter.

Makes 2 cups

2 cups cooked diced chicken breast
1/4 cup toasted slivered almonds
1/4 cup light mayonnaise
2 tablespoons chutney
1 teaspoon fresh lime juice
1/2 teaspoon curry powder
1/4 teaspoon Lulu's Special Seasoning
1/4 teaspoon white pepper

Blend all the ingredients in a large bowl. Chill until flavors blend.

Per 1/2 cup: 161 calories; 15 gm protein; 9.11 gm carbohydrates; 7.88 gm fat; 39 mg cholesterol; .25 gm fiber; 44% of calories from fat

Garlic French Dressing

G arlic lovers will appreciate this zesty French dressing. I serve it over thick, juicy slices of vine-ripened tomato covered with chopped red onion and chunks of creamy avocado.

Makes 1 cup

1/2 cup olive oil
1 egg
2 tablespoons bottled chili sauce
1 tablespoon fresh lemon juice
1 tablespoon finely chopped fresh garlic
1 tablespoon finely chopped dill pickle
2 teaspoons paprika

Blend all ingredients in a food processor or blender. Chill and serve.

Per tablespoon: 69 calories; .43 gm protein; .99 gm carbohydrates; 7.13 gm fat; 17 mg cholesterol; .02 gm fiber; 93% of calories from fat

Spinach Salad
with Creamy Yogurt Dressing

T his is an
uncomplicated,
quick-to-assemble, and
nutritious salad. The
dressing doubles as a
low-calorie dip for
crudités.

Serves 2

4 cups cleaned, bite-size pieces crisp
   fresh spinach
2 cleaned, sliced fresh mushrooms
1/4 cup chopped green onion
1/4 cup chopped tomato
1/4 cup cubed avocado
   Thinly sliced green bell pepper
1 slice crumbled crisp-cooked bacon
   Yogurt Dressing to taste
   Cracked black pepper to taste

In a large serving bowl, combine and toss all the salad ingredients
with the Yogurt Dressing. Season to taste with pepper and serve.

*Per serving: 96 calories; 6.17 gm protein; 7.46 gm carbohydrates; 6.44 gm fat; 2.64
mg cholesterol; 1.8 gm fiber; 60% of calories from fat*

Yogurt Dressing

Makes 3/4 cup

1/2 cup unflavored non-fat yogurt
1/4 cup light mayonnaise
1 teaspoon ranch-style salad dressing
   mix
1 teaspoon light Italian-style dressing
   mix
1 teaspoon lemon juice
1/4 teaspoon cracked black pepper
1/8 teaspoon paprika

Blend all ingredients. Refrigerate for at least 20 minutes.

*Per tablespoon: 19 calories; .5 gm protein; 1.4 gm carbohydrates; 2.5 gm fat; 2.25
mg cholesterol; 0 gm fiber; 100% of calories from fat*

61

Fajita Salad

F ajitas, or "little skirts," are marinated, grilled, thinly sliced skirt steaks. Although not quite authentic, chicken breasts make a super substitute. Sautéed bell peppers and onions and pico de gallo are traditional accompaniments.

Fajita

1 pound beef skirt steak (or 1 pound boneless chicken breasts)
1/4 cup fresh lemon juice
2 tablespoons soy sauce
1 tablespoon liquid smoke
1/2 teaspoon Lulu's Special Seasoning

1 Trim any fat or stringy membrane from beef.

2 In a medium bowl, blend lemon juice with remaining ingredients. Add beef or chicken and marinate for at least 1 hour, turning once or twice.

3 Ten minutes before you are ready to cook, preheat grill.

4 Over medium heat, grill fajitas until desired degree of doneness.

5 Slice into thin strips going with the grain. Cool and refrigerate.

Salad Preparation

6 cups bite-size pieces curly endive
1/2 tomato, chopped
1/2 cup chopped avocado
1/2 8 1/2-ounce can hearts of palm, cut into 1/2 inch-thick rounds
  Sliced red onion to taste
2 cups cold beef (or chicken) strips (fajitas)
  Vegetable Herb Vinaigrette to taste

Serves 4 to 6

Loosely pile endive on a serving platter almost to edge. Arrange meat or chicken along outside edge of platter. Going toward center of platter arrange rings of chopped tomato, hearts of palm, and avocado. Top with sliced onion.

Per serving: *164 calories; 12 gm protein; 6.55 gm carbohydrates; 9.9 gm fat; 6.6 mg cholesterol; 1.08 gm fiber; 55% of calories from fat*

Tabouli Salad

S oaked bulgur wheat —tabouli—is a Middle East staple. Tabouli has an unusual nut-like flavor which can be mixed with a variety of vegetables to create interesting and nutritious salads. An excellent source of protein, it lends itself to vegetarian-style diets.

Makes 2 cups

³/₄ cup tabouli
1 cup water
¹/₃ cup chopped fresh tomato
¹/₃ cup chopped avocado
¹/₃ cup chopped carrots
3 tablespoons olive oil
2 tablespoons chopped green onion (white and green part)
1 tablespoon fresh lemon or lime juice
1 teaspoon chopped fresh mint
¹/₂ teaspoon Lulu's Special Seasoning
¹/₄ teaspoon garlic powder

1 In a bowl, mix the tabouli with the water, then add all the remaining ingredients. Refrigerate 1 hour or until the liquid is absorbed and the flavors have blended.

2 Serve chilled in a lettuce cup or use to stuff tomatoes or bell peppers.

Per cup: *589 calories; 11 gm protein; 71 gm carbohydrates; 30 gm fat; 0 mg cholesterol; 9.33 gm fiber; 46% of calories from fat*

Shrimp Rémoulade

F rench Rémoulade sauce is merely mayonnaise to which dry mustard, anchovies, capers, and a few other well-chosen ingredients have been added. The result? Magnificent! Serve this as a main course or as a cold appetizer on a bed of lettuce. Large, fresh shrimp are a must. Rémoulade sauce also goes well with cold chicken.

1 pound cooked, shelled, deveined, chilled shrimp
4 small heads cored, crisp iceberg lettuce
Tomato wedges
Avocado wedges
Julienne hearts of palm
Rémoulade Sauce

Serves 4

Use the head of lettuce as your serving container. Pile the shrimp high. Add tomato, avocado, and hearts of palm. Top with the Rémoulade Sauce and dig in!

Per serving: *280 calories; 29 gm protein; 14 gm carbohydrates; 12 gm fat; 173 mg cholesterol; 3.42 gm fiber; 38% of calories from fat*

Rémoulade Sauce

1 1/4 cup light mayonnaise
1/4 cup chopped fresh parsley
2 tablespoons finely chopped onion
1 tablespoon stone-ground mustard
1 tablespoon chopped capers
1 tablespoon white vinegar
1 tablespoon dry sherry
2 teaspoons chopped anchovies
1/2 teaspoon sugar
1/4 teaspoon celery salt

Makes 1 1/2 cups
1/4 teaspoon garlic powder

Blend all listed ingredients. Chill.

Per tablespoon sauce: *21 calories; .17 gm protein; 2.05 gm carbohydrates; 1.8 gm fat; 1.67 mg cholesterol; .03 gm fiber; 79% of calories from fat*

Watercress Salad
with Creamy Garlic Dressing

A perennial aquatic plant, watercress belongs to the mustard family. It's an excellent source of vitamin A and it's low in calories.

Serves 2 to 4

4 cups cleaned, crisped, stemless watercress
1 cup thickly sliced fresh mushrooms
1/2 cup sliced hearts of palm
1/4 cup diced tomato
1/4 cup diced avocado
1 to 2 coarsely diced green onions
Cracked black pepper to taste
Creamy Garlic Dressing

Pile the watercress in a pretty serving bowl or on individual serving plates, then top with the remaining ingredients. Add Creamy Garlic Dressing, and sprinkle to taste with the cracked black pepper. Serve with bagel chips or your favorite low-sodium, low-calorie crackers.

Creamy Garlic Dressing

Serve this zesty dressing over any green salad, or as a dip for raw vegetables.

Makes 2 cups dressing

1 cup low-fat cottage cheese
3/4 cup 2% milk
2 tablespoons light, mild rice vinegar
1 8-ounce pouch light Italian-style salad dressing mix
1 teaspoon chopped fresh garlic
1/4 teaspoon lemon pepper
1/4 teaspoon cracked black pepper
1/8 teaspoon paprika

Process all dressing ingredients in a food processor or blender until smooth. Transfer to a container with a tight-fitting lid. Chill.

Per serving: 322 calories; 29 gm protein; 36 gm carbohydrates; 12 gm fat; 24 mg cholesterol; 4.25 gm fiber; 34% of calories from fat

Curly Endive and Red Cabbage with Garlic Vinaigrette

T his is my rendition
of a different and
delightful salad that I
first ate in a restaurant
called the Alt Herrenberg
in Herrenberg, West
Germany. For variety add
diced tomato, thinly sliced
onion, and diced avocado
to taste.

Serves 2 to 4

4 cups cleaned, bite-size pieces curly
endive (stem removed)
1 cup thinly sliced red cabbage

Garlic Vinaigrette

2/3 cup olive or corn oil
1/3 cup red wine vinegar
1 tablespoon chopped fresh parsley
1 1/2 teaspoons chopped fresh garlic
1/2 teaspoon Lulu's Special Seasoning
1/2 teaspoon light salt
1/2 teaspoon fresh ground or cracked
black pepper

Makes 1 cup dressing

1   In a container with a tight-fitting lid, blend vinaigrette
ingredients. Chill until flavors blend. Keeps for several weeks.

2   When ready to serve, toss endive and cabbage with dressing.
Lightly season with light salt and black pepper if desired.

Per serving: *335 calories; 1.33 gm protein; 3.46 gm carbohydrates; 36 gm fat; 0 mg
cholesterol; .65 gm fiber; 93% of calories from fat*

Beef Salad
with Sweet Pepper Dressing

A great luncheon entree. Accompany with a crusty bread.

1 cup thin strips leftover lean cooked beef (such as eye of round, flank steak, lean brisket, or chuck)
6 to 8 cups crisp mixed lettuce greens (Boston, red leaf, endive, etc.)
1/4 cucumber, very thinly sliced
2 green onions, chopped
1 Roma tomato, thinly wedged
1/2 avocado, cubed
Sweet Pepper Dressing

Salad serves 4

Toasted sesame seeds (optional)

Sweet Pepper Dressing

3 tablespoons light soy sauce
3 tablespoons fresh lemon juice
3 tablespoons olive oil
3 tablespoons peanut oil
1 teaspoon sweet chili sauce

Makes 3/4 cup dressing

1 In a jar with a tight-fitting lid or in the container of a blender combine dressing ingredients well. Chill at least 20 minutes; or longer if desired.

2 In a large salad bowl, combine all the salad ingredients. Toss with Sweet Pepper Dressing.

Per serving: salad with dressing: *216 calories; 19 gm protein; 7.24 gm carbohydrates; 12 gm fat; 58 mg cholesterol; 1.47 gm fiber; 50% of calories from fat*

Per tablespoon dressing: *67 calories; .41 gm protein; .73 gm carbohydrates; 7 gm fat; 0 mg cholesterol; .03 gm fiber; 94% of calories from fat*

Spinach Salad
with Sautéed Chicken Livers

*S erve with French
sourdough bread — so
you can wipe your plate
clean!*

Serves 4 to 6

1 pound chicken livers, rinsed and
  drained
1/4 cup sauterne
1 tablespoon reduced-calorie butter
8 cups cleaned, chilled bite-sized
  pieces fresh spinach
1 to 2 hard-cooked eggs, coarsely
  chopped (optional)
4 to 8 ounces cleaned and thickly
  sliced fresh mushrooms
1 medium green bell pepper, cut into
  thin strips
1/3 cup thinly sliced radishes
Spinich Salad Dressing to taste

1 Braise livers until fully cooked in 1/4 cup sauterne and
tablespoon butter. Cool livers, then chop them coarsely.

2 In a large serving bowl, combine and toss all the salad
ingredients with the dressing and serve at once.

Per serving salad: *192 calories; 22 gm protein; 5.7 gm carbohydrates; 8.53 gm fat;
481 mg cholesterol; 1.01 gm fiber; 40% of calories from fat*

Spinach Salad Dressing

1/2 cup corn oil or olive oil
1 teaspoon fresh garlic, minced
2 tablespoons fresh parsley, chopped
2 tablespoons red wine vinegar
2 tablespoons light sour cream
1/4 teaspoon light salt
1/4 teaspoon dry mustard
1/4 teaspoon sugar
Cracked black pepper to taste

Makes 1 cup

68

In a lidded container, combine and mix together until w
all the dressing ingredients listed. Cover and chill several h
before serving.

Per tablespoon dressing: *64 calories; .15 gm protein; .26 gm carbohydrates; 7.01 gm fat; 0 mg cholesterol; .01 gm fiber; 98% of calories from fat*

Artichoke Chicken Salad

*elicious served with
a fresh fruit salad
and Mushroom Squares.*

D

1 **6-ounce box long-grain and wild rice mix (I like Uncle Ben's brand), cooked in 2 cups of water for 20 to 25 minutes and cooled**
2 **cups diced chicken breast**
1 **6-ounce jar quartered, marinated artichoke hearts**
3/4 **cup light mayonnaise**
1/2 **cup chopped celery**
1/3 **cup chopped green bell pepper**
1/4 **cup chopped green olives**
1/4 **cup chopped green onion**
2 **teaspoons curry powder**

Makes 6 1-cup
servings

1 Gently toss all ingredients.

2 Chill and serve.

Per cup serving: *168 calories; 7.6 gm protein; 15 gm carbohydrates; 9.8 gm fat; 22 mg cholesterol; .95 gm fiber; 53% of calories from fat*

GLORIOUS SOUPS
&
SAVORY
SANDWICHES

Homemade Chicken Stock

E veryone should have a recipe for making a good homemade chicken stock. The procedure is simple; it just takes time. This stock is low in calories, fat, and salt and it enhances the flavor of any dish you use it in. Use the cooked chicken meat for salads, casseroles, and sandwiches.

Makes 3 quarts

7 quarts cold water
1 whole 3- to 3 1/2-pound chicken
6 chicken thighs
2 large, well-washed leeks, coarsely chopped
1 onion, studded with 2 cloves
1 bunch fresh thyme
1 large garlic clove
6 celery stalks with tops
2 large carrots
1 large sprig parsley
12 peppercorns
1 bay leaf

1 Using a stock pot large enough to hold the water, fryer, and thighs, place these 3 ingredients in it, and bring to a boil. Skim off any froth that rises to the top. After the foam ceases to form, turn the heat down to a gentle simmer, add the remaining ingredients, and cook for 2 hours.

2 Remove the fryer and thighs from the stock, allow to cool, and remove meat from bones. Return the bones to pot and simmer 2 hours longer at a barely bubbly stage.

3 Remove from heat and allow the stock to cool, strain the broth through cheesecloth and refrigerate uncovered till grease forms on top. Remove and discard the grease layer on top.

4 If you prefer a stronger stock, return broth to stock pot and reduce by 1/3 using medium heat.

5 Cool and freeze in 1- to 4-cup (one quart) containers, either glass or disposable containers.

Per cup: *20 calories; .53 gm protein; 4.36 gm carbohydrates; .02 gm fat; 0 mg cholesterol; .54 gm fiber; 1% of calories from fat*

Skinny Vegetable Soup

C hock-full of vitamins and fiber, this vegetable soup contains about 55 calories per 8-ounce cup. While I prefer fresh vegetables, for this recipe I have replaced them with the frozen variety for convenience. This soup takes a little longer to prepare, but the results are well worth the time.

Makes 18 1-cup servings

1 cabbage, coarsely chopped (about 4 cups)
2 cups chopped celery
1 cup chopped onion
1 cup chopped green or red bell pepper
10 cups water
1 10-ounce box frozen mixed vegetables
1 10-ounce box frozen yellow squash
1 10-ounce box frozen green beans
1 12-ounce can Hot and Spicy V-8 juice
1/4 cup instant vegetable-flavor bouillon
1/4 cup chopped fresh parsley
2 teaspoons Lulu's Special Seasoning
1 teaspoon summer savory
1/2 teaspoon tarragon
1/2 teaspoon cracked black pepper

1 Place cabbage, celery, onion, and pepper in a large soup kettle and add 10 cups of cold water.

2 Bring to a boil. Boil uncovered, until vegetables are tender, about 20 minutes.

3 Add remaining frozen vegetables, and return soup to a slow boil. Cook for approximately 10 minutes.

4 Add the remaining ingredients. Cover, reduce heat to low, and cook 30 minutes longer.

Per serving: *37 calories; 1.58 gm protein; 8.18 gm carbohydrates; .03 gm fat; 0 mg cholesterol; .91 gm fiber; .72% of calories from fat*

Lemon Chicken Soup

S erved with a sandwich or a crisp salad, this robust, velvety soup is a complete meal. To save time, sauté peppers while you poach the chicken, or prepare chicken in advance. If the red bell pepper is unavailable, substitute a green one. However, the flavor will be more pungent and less sweet.

2 cups low-sodium chicken broth
1 cup water
2 skinless chicken breasts (about 1 pound)
1/2 cup chopped celery
1/2 cup chopped onion
1/2 teaspoon light salt
1/2 teaspoon whole white peppercorns
1/4 teaspoon dried thyme
1 small red bell pepper, seeds and ribs removed, sliced into thin slivers
2 tablespoons melted reduced-calorie margarine
1 tablespoon flour
3 teaspoons long-grain white rice
1 cup half and half (2% milk is O.K, but the soup will have less texture and flavor)
1 tablespoon lemon juice
1/4 teaspoon Lulu's Special Seasoning
1/4 teaspoon white pepper
Chopped fresh parsley (about 2 tablespoons)

Makes 4 1-cup servings

1 In a 2- to 3-quart saucepan, combine and mix together the broth, water, chicken, celery, onion, salt, peppercorns, and thyme. Bring to a boil. Cover, and reduce heat to a simmer. Cook until the chicken is opaque, 15 to 20 minutes. Do not overcook the chicken or it will be tough and stringy. Remove the chicken and allow it to cool. Reserve broth.

2 Using your fingers or a fork, shred the chicken meat. Set aside.

3 Strain and reserve broth. Rinse and dry saucepan.

4 In same saucepan, gently sauté the slivered red pepper in melted margarine until tender. Remove peppers and set aside. Stir the

flour and rice into the saucepan and cook until bubbly. Remove saucepan from heat and gradually stir in the reserved broth. Cook, stirring, until liquid boils. Cover, reduce heat, and simmer about 15 minutes or until rice is tender.

5 Add shredded chicken. Stir in half and half, lemon juice, special seasoning, and pepper and blend well. Cook until hot and serve immediately. Garnish with fresh parsley.

Per serving: 360 calories; 37 gm protein; 8.6 gm carbohydrates; 19 gm fat; 117 mg cholesterol; .31 gm fiber; 48% of calories from fat

Homemade Beef Stock

T his stock, like the chicken stock, is *delicious, nutritious, and low in calories, fat, and sodium. It adds great flavor to the dishes you add it to. The bones in this recipe can be purchased from your favorite meat market. If you cannot secure the veal bones, use 10 pounds of beef bones.*

Makes 3 quarts (12 cups)

5 pounds veal bones
5 pounds beef bones
2 pounds beef stew meat
1 pound salt pork
2 onions, each peeled and studded with 2 cloves
2 large carrots, peeled
8 quarts water
2 bay leaves
$^1/_2$ teaspoon black peppercorns
$^1/_2$ teaspoon thyme
4 stalks celery with tops
1 leek, coarsely chopped
2 cloves garlic
1 large sprig parsley
2 whole tomatoes

1 Preheat oven to 350°.

2 With a hammer, crack the large bones, place them in a large heavy browning pan, and brown the bones in the preheated 350° oven for 30 minutes. Add the onions and carrots and brown 30 minutes longer. Drain off any fat and discard.

3 Then transfer browned bones and vegetables to a large stock pot, add 8 quarts of water, bring to a boil, reduce heat and simmer for one hour, having the pot partially covered with a lid.

4 Add all remaining ingredients and simmer for 5 hours, removing any froth that rises to the top.

5 Remove from heat and allow the stock to cool. Strain the broth through cheesecloth and refrigerate uncovered till grease forms on top. Remove and discard the grease layer on top.

6 If you prefer a stronger stock, return broth to stock pot and reduce by ⅓ using medium heat.

7 Cool and freeze in 1- to 4-cup containers.

Per cup: *25 calories; .79 gm protein; 5.49 gm carbohydrates; .02 gm fat; 0 mg cholesterol; .61 gm fiber; .72% of calories from fat*

Sherried Carrot Soup

This puréed soup is a nice complement to your favorite sandwich. To make in advance, add everything except half and half. Purée, cool, and refrigerate soup. Just before serving, add half and half and gently reheat to a simmer.

Serves 4

2 cups chopped onions
3 tablespoons reduced-calorie butter or margarine
4 cups thinly sliced carrots
½ teaspoon Lulu's Special Seasoning
½ teaspoon light salt
½ teaspoon ground ginger
¼ teaspoon cinnamon
3 cups low-sodium chicken broth
½ cup half and half
¼ cup dry sherry
Fresh cracked black pepper to taste
Chopped fresh parsley (optional)

1 In a 2-quart saucepan over medium heat, sauté the onions in the butter until soft. Mix in carrots, special seasoning, salt, ginger, cinnamon, and broth.

2 Bring to a boil; then reduce heat. Cover and simmer until carrots are tender, about 20 minutes.

3 In a blender purée in 2 batches until smooth.

4 Return puréed soup to the saucepan and add cream, sherry, and pepper.

5 Reheat to a simmer and serve piping hot. If desired, sprinkle soup with fresh parsley.

Per serving: 221 calories; 5.64 gm protein; 26 gm carbohydrates; 8.39 gm fat; 11 mg cholesterol; 2.74 gm fiber; 34% of calories from fat

Curry Onion Soup

T his fragrant soup is low in fat and sodium. Because I like its snappiness, I use hot, West-Indian-style curry powder in this recipe.

Makes 4 1-cup servings

4 cups low-sodium beef broth
2 cups thinly sliced onions
1/2 bay leaf
1 tablespoon light sour cream
1/2 teaspoon Lulu's Special Seasoning
3/4 teaspoon hot West-Indian-style curry powder
Chopped fresh parsley for garnish

1 In a soup kettle cook the broth, onions, and bay leaf over medium-high heat until the onions are tender. Discard the bay leaf. Purée soup in 2 batches and return to soup kettle. If you try to purée all of the soup at once, it will overflow the food processor's canister.

2 Add the seasoning and curry. Heat, garnish, and serve hot.

Per serving: 51 calories; 4 gm protein; 6.75 gm carbohydrates; 1.75 gm fat; 1.25 mg cholesterol; .44 gm fiber; 30% of calories from fat

Favorite Cioppino

C ioppino is a light
and luscious
Portuguese shellfish stew.
Even though I prefer to
use fresh Italian-style
Roma tomatoes, feel free
to substitute the canned
variety. Serve this stew
with Bibb Toss with
Vegetable Herb
Vinaigrette. Accompany
with sourdough or French
bread. Cioppino is even
better the second day.

¼ cup olive oil
1 cup ¼-inch-thick sliced onions
2 teaspoons finely chopped fresh garlic
3 pounds fresh Roma tomatoes, peeled and chopped with their juices or 2 16-ounce cans undrained Italian-style tomatoes with basil
¼ cup chopped fresh parsley
1 teaspoon light salt
¼ teaspoon dried oregano
¼ teaspoon saffron
⅛ teaspoon cayenne pepper
2 cups dry white wine
3 tablespoons tomato paste
2½ pounds boneless snapper, redfish, bass, or rockfish, rinsed and patted dry (whatever fish fillet you select must be 1-inch thick or it will cook into oblivion)
12 large (16-20 per pound) raw shrimp, shell removed, cleaned
18 littleneck or cherrystone clams, cleaned
2½ to 3 pounds Dungeness or Alaskan King crab legs and claws in shell, cut into 3-inch sections for easy picking (cut shell with scissors to avoid a mess at the table)

Serves 6

1 Heat the oil in a heavy 4 to 6 quart kettle over medium heat. Add the onions and garlic and cook until onions are tender. Add the tomatoes, parsley, salt, oregano, saffron, and cayenne. Cook uncovered over low heat, for 15 minutes, stirring occasionally.

2 Blend in wine and tomato paste. Bring to a simmer, then add all the fish and shellfish. Cook uncovered for 30 to 40 minutes without stirring.

3 Serve right from the pot or transfer to a tureen.

Per serving: 593 calories; 80 gm protein; 18 gm carbohydrates; 16 gm fat; 228 mg cholesterol; 1.13 gm fiber; 23% of calories from fat

Potato Leek Soup

Leeks, a mild member of the onion family, flavor this soup treat that everyone will enjoy. Be sure to strain the soup, because the leeks can be tough. Served cold, leek and potato soup is called vichyssoise.

Makes 5 1-cup servings

1¹/₂ cups minced leeks (white part only)
¹/₂ cup chopped onions
1 teaspoon finely chopped garlic
¹/₄ cup reduced-calorie butter or margarine
4 cups low-sodium chicken broth
2 cups peeled and diced potatoes
¹/₂ cup whipping cream
¹/₂ cup 2% milk
¹/₂ teaspoon light salt
¹/₂ teaspoon Lulu's Special Seasoning
¹/₈ to ¹/₄ teaspoon black pepper
Chopped green onion (optional)

1 In a large kettle over medium heat, sauté leeks, onions, and garlic in butter or margarine until tender.

2 Add broth and potatoes, cooking until potatoes are tender.

3 Purée mixture in a food processor or blender.

4 Return purée to pan. Add cream, milk, and seasonings. Heat to simmer (do not boil).

5 Let cool and refrigerate for 24 hours. Serve hot or cold garnished with chopped green onions.

Per serving: *228 calories; 5.73 gm protein; 24 gm carbohydrates; 13 gm fat; 28 mg cholesterol; 1.32 gm fiber; 51% of calories from fat*

Artichoke Cheese Chowder

T his is luscious but light. *Great soup for entertaining!*

Makes 5 1-cup servings

2 tablespoons reduced-calorie butter
1 tablespoon finely chopped shallots
1/4 cup flour
2 cups low-sodium chicken broth
1 cup whipping cream or crema mexicana
1 cup evaporated skim milk
1 13 3/4-ounce can artichoke hearts, drained and puréed
4 ounces grated farmer's cheese
2 tablespoons sauterne
1 teaspoon Lulu's Special Seasoning
1/2 teaspoon light salt
1/4 teaspoon white pepper
1/8 teaspoon cayenne pepper

1 In a pot over medium heat, melt the butter. Add the shallots and cook until they are tender.

2 Add the flour and stir constantly until it forms a paste. Using a wire whisk, gradually add the broth and stir until the broth is well mixed and thickens, about 5 minutes.

3 Whisk in all the remaining ingredients, reduce heat to low, and cook, stirring constantly, until well heated and the cheese has melted, about 10 minutes. Serve at once garnished with either fresh chopped parsley or paprika.

Per serving: *333 calories; 15 gm protein; 21 gm carbohydrates; 22 gm fat; 67 mg cholesterol; .86 gm fiber; 58% of calories from fat*

Smoked Corn and Chicken Chowder

G rilled or smoked chicken and smoked ham flavor this fast and fabulous soup made with low-fat chicken broth. To develop the soup's unique flavor, use my recipe for Grilled Herbed Chicken Breasts to marinate the chicken prior to cooking.

Makes 8 1-cup servings

1 pound smoked or grilled boneless, skinless chicken breast
3 tablespoons reduced-calorie butter or margarine
1/2 cup finely diced celery
1/2 cup finely diced red bell pepper
1/3 cup diced fresh green onion
1/4 cup finely diced smoked ham (I use smoked pork loin chops)
1/4 cup chopped fresh parsley
1 jalapeño pepper, deseeded and finely chopped
1 1/2 teaspoons finely chopped garlic
4 cups low-sodium chicken broth
2 tablespoons arrowroot dissolved in 3 cups hot water
1 10-ounce package frozen cut corn
2 tablespoons fresh lemon juice
1 tablespoon chopped fresh cilantro leaves
1 teaspoon light salt
1/2 teaspoon Lulu's Special Seasoning
2 shakes Tabasco sauce
Fresh ground or cracked black pepper to taste

1 Using a fork, shred the chicken breast and set aside. Meanwhile, in a large soup kettle over medium heat, melt the butter or margarine. Add the celery, bell pepper, green onion, and ham, cooking until the vegetables are tender, about 3 to 5 minutes. Add the parsley, jalapeño, and garlic. Cook 1 minute longer, stirring occasionally.

2 Add all remaining ingredients. Stirring occasionally, simmer soup 20 minutes or until soup is hot and flavors have had time to mingle.

Per serving: *162 calories; 18 gm protein; 6.27 gm carbohydrates; 7.4 gm fat; 41 mg cholesterol; .260 gm fiber; 41% of calories from fat*

Three Lentil Soup

The red, yellow, and brown lentils I use create a colorful, chunky soup, and the buffet-style garnishes forever fascinate my guests. Even if you omit the pork, this is still a nourishing vegetarian soup. This freezes well.

Makes 8 1-cup servings

3/4 pound smoked pork loin chops or any lean well-trimmed piece of smoked pork, diced. (You should have about 1 cup lean, diced, smoked pork)
1 tablespoon chopped fresh parsley
1 teaspoon minced fresh garlic
1 cup each of coarsely chopped carrots, celery, and onions
1 14 1/2-ounce can peeled tomatoes
4 cups water
2 packages low-sodium instant beef broth
1/2 cup each of red, yellow, and brown lentils, rinsed
1 teaspoon light salt
1/4 teaspoon black pepper
Shredded lettuce (optional)
Diced tomatoes (optional)
Diced avocado (optional)
Chopped green onion (optional)

1 In a 3-quart saucepan over medium heat, sauté the diced pork, parsley, and garlic until lightly browned.

2 In a food processor, purée carrots, celery, onions, and tomatoes. Add the puréed vegetables and all remaining ingredients to sautéed pork mixture.

3 Bring soup to a boil. Reduce heat to simmer, and cook until lentils are tender but firm; about 20 minutes.

4 Serve hot. Garnish with shredded lettuce, diced tomatoes, diced avocado, chopped green onion, or your favorite grated low-fat cheese.

Per serving: 162 calories; 18 gm protein; 12 gm carbohydrates; 5.24 gm fat; 43 mg cholesterol; 1.44 gm fiber; 29% of calories from fat

Tomato and Red Bell Pepper Soup

*T*o serve, place thin
slices of avocado or
pieces of cooked asparagus
spears (or both) in the
bottom of each bowl. Then,
pour in the hot soup, and
garnish with a teaspoon of
crème fraîche and fresh
sprig of basil or mint.

Makes 4 1-cup
servings

2 tablespoons oil
1 cup coarsely chopped onion
2 cups peeled, deseeded, and
   coarsely chopped fresh tomatoes
   or 1 1-pound can Italian-Style
   Tomatoes (I use Progresso Peeled
   Italian-Style Tomatoes with Basil)
1 1/2 cups low-sodium chicken broth
2 large peeled and chopped red bell
   peppers
1 tablespoon chopped fresh garlic
1/2 cup light cream
1/4 cup 2% milk
1/3 cup low-sodium chicken broth
   (additional)
1/2 teaspoon light salt
1/2 teaspoon dried basil
8 to 10 drops Tabasco sauce
   crème fraîche (optional)
   Mint sprigs (optional)

1 In a large saucepan, heat over medium heat. Add onions and cook until tender.

2 Add the tomatoes and cook for 10 to 15 minutes, stirring occasionally.

3 Add the 1 1/2 cups chicken broth, peppers, and garlic, and simmer for about 30 minutes. Transfer mixture into a food processor or electric blender and purée.

4 Return the purée back to the saucepan. Add all remaining ingredients, and cook, stirring occasionally until hot.

5 Garnish with a dab of crème fraîche and a sprig of fresh mint.

Per serving: 166 calories; 4.75 gm protein; 12 gm carbohydrates; 11 gm fat; 12 mg cholesterol; 1.23 gm fiber; 60% of calories from fat

Fresh Tomato
Leek Soup with Curry

S mooth as satin, this fresh tomato soup is high in flavor but low in calories. When good, fresh tomatoes are not abundant, canned peeled tomatoes can be substituted. This soup freezes well.

2 tablespoons olive oil
1 slice bacon, finely chopped
1/2 cup finely chopped onions
1/2 cup finely chopped carrots
1/4 cup chopped leeks (white and tender green parts)
3 tablespoons finely chopped celery
1/2 cup tomato sauce
2 cups peeled, seeded, and finely chopped fresh tomatoes
2 teaspoons chopped fresh basil
1 teaspoon chopped fresh oregano
1/4 teaspoon summer savory
4 cups low-sodium chicken broth
1 teaspoon sugar substitute
1/2 teaspoon light salt
White pepper to taste
1/4 cup dry vermouth
1 tablespoon plus 1 teaspoon hot curry powder (taste soup after you have added the 1 tablespoon and if that is enough curry for your taste, omit the 1 teaspoon)
1/3 cup whipping cream
Fresh mint sprigs (optional)

Makes 6 1-cup servings

1 In a large soup kettle over medium heat, heat oil. Add bacon, onions, carrots, leeks, and celery. Cook, stirring frequently, about 10 minutes or until vegetables are tender.

2 Stir in tomato sauce and cook 10 minutes longer.

3 Add all remaining ingredients, except whipping cream. Simmer for another 10 minutes. In a food processor or blender purée soup in 2-cup batches. Strain soup and pour back into pot. Stir

in cream and heat until hot. Serve immediately. Garnish with
fresh mint sprigs.

Per serving: *127 calories; 3.55 gm protein; 6.13 gm carbohydrates; 9.9 gm fat; 15 mg
cholesterol; .63 gm fiber; 70% of calories from fat*

Red Pepper Gazpacho

G *azpacho, meaning
"soaked bread," is
the famed cold vegetable
soup of southern Spain.
This low-calorie soup
always tastes better the
next day.*

**Makes 5 1-cup
servings**

1 slice white bread or 1/2 cup fresh
   white breadcrumbs
1/2 cup cold water
1 pound diced, ripe, fresh Roma
   tomatoes
2 medium deseeded and diced red
   bell peppers
1/2 cup chopped green onions
1/2 cup peeled and diced cucumber
1 teaspoon chopped garlic
1/4 cup Hot and Spicy V-8 juice
1/4 cup olive oil
3 tablespoons red wine vinegar
1 teaspoon light salt
1/2 teaspoon cracked black pepper
1/8 teaspoon cayenne pepper
   Chopped green onion (optional)
   Chopped hard cooked eggs
   (optional)
   Diced cucumber (optional)
   Diced green pepper (optional)
   Diced tomato (optional)
   Diced avocado (optional)

1 In a food processor or blender, crumb the bread. You should
have 1/2 cup crumbs. Soak crumbs in the 1/2 cup of cold water for
15 minutes. Drain. Prepare purchased crumbs identically.

2   Return crumbs to food processor or blender. To crumbs, add tomatoes, red pepper, green onion, cucumber, and garlic and process until almost smooth. While the machine is running, slowly add the V-8 juice, olive oil, and vinegar.

3   Pour soup into lidded storage container, season with salt, pepper, and cayenne and chill several hours.

4   Serve with bowls of the following garnishes: chopped green onion, chopped hard cooked eggs, diced cucumber, diced green pepper, diced tomato, and diced avocado.

Per serving: *165 calories; 2.63 gm protein; 13 gm carbohydrates; 11 gm fat; .500 mg cholesterol; 1.24 gm fiber; 60% of calories from fat*

New England Fish Chowder

T his chowder is a *favorite on the East coast. Use only cod or haddock.*

Makes 6 1-cup servings

1 slice lean bacon, chopped (optional)
1/4 cup smoked ham, well-trimmed
1 cup chopped onion
1 bay leaf
1 cup bottled clam juice plus 1 cup water (or 2 cups fish stock)
1 pound new potatoes, unpeeled and diced
1 pound cod or haddock
1 1/2 cups 2% milk
1 cup half and half
1/2 to 1 teaspoon light salt
1/8 to 1/4 teaspoon ground black pepper
Fresh chopped parsley

1   In a large soup pot over medium-high heat, fry the bacon until it is partially cooked. Add the smoked ham, onion, and bay leaf. Cook until onion is soft but not browned.

2   Stir in the clam juice and water (or fish stock) and potatoes. Simmer, covered, until potatoes are tender, about 15 minutes.

3   Add fish, milk, cream, and simmer for 3 to 5 minutes or until the fish begins to flake. Remove bay leaf, season with salt and pepper, sprinkle with the fresh parsley, and serve at once.

Per serving: *332 calories; 27 gm protein; 29 gm carbohydrates; 11 gm fat; 23 mg cholesterol; .5 gm fiber; 29% of calories from fat*

Creamy Brie Soup

I f you are a Brie lover as I am, treat yourself! It is divine.

2 tablespoons reduced-calorie margarine
$^1/_3$ cup finely chopped carrots
$^1/_3$ cup finely chopped celery
$^1/_4$ cup flour
2 cups low-sodium instant chicken broth
1 cup whipping cream or crema mexicana
1 cup evaporated skim milk
2 tablespoons dry white wine
$^1/_2$ teaspoon Lulu's Special Seasoning
$^1/_2$ teaspoon light salt
$^1/_8$ teaspoon cayenne pepper
1 cup cubed Brie (remove and discard the white surface coating)
Chopped fresh parsley

Makes 4$^1/_2$ 1-cup servings

1   In a pot over medium heat melt the margarine; add the carrots and celery and cook until the vegetables are tender.

2   Add the flour and stir constantly until it forms a paste. Using a wire whisk, gradually add the broth, cream, evaporated milk, wine, special seasoning, salt, and cayenne. Mix well, reduce heat slightly, and cook until soup thickens (approximately 15 minutes),

whisking it every 5 minutes. Turn off the heat, stir in Brie, and allow it to melt. Blend in the melted Brie with the wire whisk.

3 Garnish with the fresh chopped parsley and serve piping hot.

Per serving: 397 calories; 15 gm protein; 15 gm carbohydrates; 30 gm fat; 98 mg cholesterol; .31 gm fiber; 68% of calories from fat

Crab Vegetable Bisque

This colorful and tasty creamy bisque is full of vegetables and crabmeat. It is very easy to prepare. It tastes even better the next day and it freezes well. A bisque is a shellfish-based cream soup.

Makes 5 1/2 1-cup servings

1 10-ounce box frozen mixed vegetables
1/2 cup chopped green onions
1/2 cup chopped fresh tomato
1/3 cup unbleached flour
1 tablespoon chopped fresh parsley
1 teaspoon summer savory
1/2 teaspoon Tabasco sauce
1/4 teaspoon light salt
    Cracked black pepper to taste
2 cups low-sodium chicken broth
1 1/2 cups 2% milk
1 cup fresh crabmeat or 1 6-ounce can white crab meat
2 tablespoons sauterne
1 cup grated sharp cheddar cheese
3 ounces light cream cheese
2 teaspoons Dijon mustard

1 In a pot, combine together the mixed vegetables, onions, tomatoes, flour, parsley, savory, Tabasco, salt, and pepper, stirring until all is coated with the flour.

2 Stir in the broth, milk, crabmeat, and wine. Bring to a boil and cook about 5 minutes or until the bisque thickens. Reduce the

heat, blend in all the remaining ingredients, and cook until the vegetables are tender. Serve hot.

Per serving: *287 calories; 20 gm protein; 20 gm carbohydrates; 13 gm fat; 62 mg cholesterol; .99 gm fiber; 42% of calories from fat*

Shrimp and Corn Chowder

T his hearty, satisfying soup is different and one of my favorites. It is great served with a Muffaletta Sandwich.

2 tablespoons reduced-calorie butter or margarine
1/3 cup finely chopped celery
1/3 cup finely chopped onion
1 10-ounce box frozen whole kernel corn
2 cups low-sodium instant chicken broth
1 cup whipping cream
1 cup 2% milk
1 cup shrimp pieces (shell off and deveined)
1/4 cup tomato sauce
1 bay leaf, broken into several large pieces
1 tablespoon chopped fresh parsley
1/2 teaspoon Tabasco sauce
1/2 teaspoon Lulu's Special Seasoning
1/4 teaspoon light salt
1/8 teaspoon cayenne pepper

Makes 4 1/2 1-cup servings

1 tablespoon cornstarch dissolved in 2 tablespoons cold water

In a large pot sauté the onion, celery, and shrimp over medium heat in the melted butter until the vegetables are tender and the shrimp pieces are cooked. Add all remaining ingredients. Mix well. Reduce heat and simmer for 20 minutes. Serve hot.

Per serving: *326 calories; 18 gm protein; 18 gm carbohydrates; 12 gm fat; 139 mg cholesterol; .44 gm fiber; 58% of calories from fat*

Soup Cancún

This Southwest-style soup takes a little preparation time but it is well worth the extra effort. It makes a beautiful presentation.

8 cups low-sodium chicken broth
2 cubes chicken broth (I prefer Knorr Swiss)
1 bunch fresh cilantro, stems removed and coarsely chopped
2 boneless, skinless chicken breasts, cut into 1-inch strips
1 ear of fresh corn, cut into 6 rounds
1 jalapeño pepper, seeds removed, chopped
1 tablespoon ground cumin
1 tablespoon reduced-calorie butter or margarine
2 medium onions, one finely chopped, one coarsely chopped
1 red bell pepper, ribs and seeds removed, cut into 1/4-inch strips
1 teaspoon chopped fresh garlic
2 finely diced tomatoes
1 poblano pepper, seeds removed, cut into large pieces
1 Anaheim pepper, seeds removed, sliced into 1/4-inch-wide circles
4 seedless black olives, sliced
1/2 teaspoon sugar
4 tablespoons fresh lime juice
4 corn tortillas, cut into 1/4-inch-side strips, fried until crisp
6 slices avocado
6 slices fresh lime
1 tablespoon crème fraîche for each bowl of soup as garnish (optional)

Serves 6

1 In a large saucepan over high heat, bring the chicken broth and cubes to a boil. Add half the chopped cilantro plus all the chicken, corn, jalapeño, and cumin and cook until chicken and corn are done, about 8 to 10 minutes. (Remainder of cilantro is used to garnish soup.) Remove the chicken and corn so they will not overcook. Reserve broth.

2 Meanwhile in a large skillet melt the butter over medium-high heat and add the 1 finely chopped onion, red pepper, and garlic. Cook, stirring frequently, until vegetables are wilted. Do not brown. Add tomatoes and cook 5 minutes longer.

3 To the broth add the tomato mixture, the coarsely chopped onion, poblano and Anaheim peppers, olives, and sugar. Cook until the onions and peppers are soft, but not mushy.

4 Turn off the heat, stir in the lime juice, and pour the soup into 6 large serving bowls. Be sure that each bowl has chicken, corn, and all varieties of peppers.

5 Garnish each bowl with strips of fried tortilla, slices of avocado and lime, and if you wish, 1 tablespoon of crème fraîche. Sprinkle top with reserved chopped cilantro and serve hot.

Per serving: *195 calories; 13 gm protein; 18 gm carbohydrates; 9.34 gm fat; 21 mg cholesterol; 1.39 gm fiber; 43% of calories from fat*

Muffaletta Sandwich

Y ou will find wonderful muffalettas in New Orleans. The two keys to a tasty muffaletta are the sourdough bread used to make the round sandwich and the Olive Salad used inside. This sandwich, broiled to melt the cheese, is served warm with a salad or a cup of soup.

1 round sourdough bun
1 rounded tablespoon Olive Salad at room temperature
3 wafer-thin slices ham
3 wafer-thin slices salami
3 wafer-thin slices skim-milk mozzarella

Makes 1 sandwich

1 Preheat broiler.

2 Slice the bun in half and spread one side with the olive salad. On the other side of the bun arrange the ham, salami, and cheese. Place bun cheese side up under the broiler until cheese melts. Put sandwich together and serve hot.

Per sandwich: *556 calories; 42 gm protein; 31 gm carbohydrates; 28 gm fat; 111 mg cholesterol; .27 gm fiber; 45% of calories from fat*

Olive Salad

U se on other sandwiches and to garnish salads.

1 18-ounce bottle pitted green salad olives, drained and finely chopped
1 4 1/2-ounce can pitted, finely chopped ripe olives
2 medium carrots, peeled and sliced
6 stalks celery, peeled and sliced
1 5-ounce jar white cocktail onions, drained and rinsed (mash some of the onions but leave most of them whole)
1/3 cup olive oil
1 tablespoon fresh lemon juice
1 teaspoon oregano
1 teaspoon finely chopped fresh garlic

Makes 6 cups

1 Using a food processor, chop the green and ripe olives and empty into a 1-quart container with a tight-fitting lid. Chop the carrots and celery and empty into the container.

2 Add all remaining ingredients. Mix well, and let stand overnight at room temperature, then refrigerate. Refrigerated, this salad keeps for 6 weeks.

Per ¹/2 cup: *82 calories; .53 gm protein; 3.07 gm carbohydrates; 7.73 gm fat; 0 mg cholesterol; .54 gm fiber; 85% of calories from fat*

Ham and Cheese on Sourdough

F *rancisco Extra Sourdough bread is what makes this hot sandwich special. If that is unavailable, choose any other light, airy-textured, sliced sourdough bread.*

Serves 1 to 2

Light mayonnaise to taste
Dijon mustard to taste
2 slices Francisco Extra Sourdough Bread
1 to 2 slices cooked ham
Thinly sliced onions to taste (optional)
Cracked black pepper to taste
¹/3 cup grated cheddar cheese
¹/3 cup grated farmer's, or any low-fat, cheese

1 Preheat broiler.

2 Lightly spread the mayonnaise and mustard on the inside slices of the bread, add ham and onions, and sprinkle to taste with cracked black pepper.

3 Close sandwich. Blend cheeses and pile on top of the sandwich. Broil until cheeses are melted and bubbly. Serve at once.

Per serving: *206 calories; 13 gm protein; 15 gm carbohydrates; 10 gm fat; 38 mg cholesterol; .1 gm fiber; 44% of calories from fat*

French Bread Spinach and Ham Hero

This sandwich is a treat. Use a quality loaf of French or sourdough bread.

1 10-ounce package frozen chopped spinach, thawed if possible
1/3 cup chopped onion
1/2 teaspoon Lulu's Special Seasoning
1/4 teaspoon or more fresh ground pepper
1 loaf French or sourdough bread
Pesto for Pasta sauce to taste
1 4-ounce package 97% fat-free thinly sliced ham
Fresh ground pepper to taste

Serves 4

1 Preheat oven to 350°.

2 Place spinach and onion in a small saucepan with water to cover and cook until the spinach is done, about 5 minutes if spinach has been thawed. Drain spinach and onion very well, using a spoon to press out any excess water. Stir in the special seasoning, the black pepper, and set aside.

3 Slice the bread into 1-inch-thick diagonal slices, but do not cut all the way through. Lightly spread the pesto sauce on both sliced sides. Add a slice of ham, and a thin layer of cooked spinach mixture. Place the loaf on a piece of foil, bringing the foil half way up the sides of the loaf.

4 Bake in the preheated 350° oven until the loaf is heated through, about 15 to 20 minutes. You can totally seal the stuffed loaf in foil, but, if you do, the crust will not be crisp.

Per serving: 442 calories; 22 gm protein; 65 gm carbohydrates; 11 gm fat; 16 mg cholesterol; 3.65 gm fiber; 22% of calories from fat

Ham and Avocado Baguette

T his sandwich is different, easy to assemble, and good! If you can't find a cheese garlic baguette, substitute a loaf of plain French bread or bake a loaf of crusty French bread from a can.

Serves 4

1 cheese garlic baguette cut in half lengthwise
Light cream cheese
1/4 ripe mashed avocado
Pesto for Pasta sauce (or mix equal parts light mayonnaise and Dijon mustard)
97% fat-free sliced ham, squares cut in half
Julienned or shredded carrots
Thinly sliced tomato
Thinly sliced onion
Cracked black pepper to taste
Parsley Plus

1 Spread a thin layer of cream cheese and mashed avocado on one side of the bread. Each layer should be thin and cover the entire length of the bread.

2 Spread the other side with a thin layer of Pesto for Pasta sauce, or if you have none on hand, spread the mayonnaise mustard combo on this side.

3 Top with thin layers of ham, carrots, tomato, and onions. Sprinkle to taste with the pepper and Parsley Plus.

4 Close and cut the sandwich into 5-inch-long sections.

Per serving: *429 calories; 17 gm protein; 65 gm carbohydrates; 11 gm fat; 14 mg cholesterol; 3 gm fiber; 23% of calories from fat*

Sandwich Olé

What could be better than a Southwestern-style, streamlined BLT with grilled chicken? A socko-sandwich, serve it with soup or a chilled platter of seasonal fruit. Pico de Gallo is a must.

Makes 1 sandwich

1 slice bacon
¹/₈ thinly-sliced ripe avocado
1 tablespoon crumbled low-fat farmer's cheese
2 to 4 thin slices deseeded poblano pepper
2 slices sourdough French bread or 2 slices 40-calorie bread
4 thin slices grilled chicken breast
Sliced tomatoes and lettuce as desired
Cracked black pepper to taste

1 Microwave bacon and set aside.

2 Arrange avocado, cheese, and poblano pepper on one slice of bread. Microwave on high power for 30 seconds and transfer to a serving plate.

3 Sparingly spread the slice with light mayonnaise. Add chicken, bacon, tomatoes, lettuce, and pepper. Close sandwich.

Per sandwich: 636 calories; 70 gm protein; 29 gm carbohydrates; 25 gm fat; 179 mg cholesterol; .660 gm fiber; 35% of calories from fat

SPLENDID SOUFFLÉS, FRITTATAS, & OMELETTES

Corn Broccoli Soufflé

T his soufflé is fool-
proof. Perfect for a
light brunch, it will
delight you and your
guests. I have used egg
yolks; however, you could
substitute the equivalent
of 2 egg yolks using egg
substitute.

Serves 4 to 6

Non-stick coating spray
Uncooked corn scraped from the
  ear or 1/2 cup frozen corn kernels
2 cups cooked fresh broccoli
  flowerets, processed in a food
  processor or blender (about 1 cup
  processed)
2 tablespoons reduced-calorie butter
  or margarine
2 tablespoons minced fresh shallots
2 tablespoons flour
1/2 cup each of half and half and 2%
  milk, warmed
2 tablespoons shredded Parmesan
  cheese
1 tablespoon fresh lemon juice
1 teaspoon Parsley Plus
1/4 teaspoon cayenne pepper
1/2 teaspoon light salt
2 egg yolks
4 egg whites at room temperature

1 Preheat oven to 325°.

2 Spray a 1 1/2-quart soufflé dish with non-stick cooking spray.
Have ready a larger pan that can accommodate the soufflé dish.

3 Cover the bottom of the soufflé dish with the cut corn and
sprinkle with fresh ground black pepper to taste. Set the dish in
larger pan filled with very hot, but not boiling, water. This water
allows the soufflé to cook evenly.

4 In a small skillet over medium heat, melt the butter, add the
shallots, and sauté until shallots are tender, about 2 minutes.
Sprinkle in the flour, whisking until smooth. Slowly whisk in
the cream and milk. Cook, stirring constantly until white sauce
is smooth. Remove from heat and whisk in the Parmesan, lemon

juice, parsley plus, cayenne, salt, and egg yolks. Blend in the broccoli purée and cool.

5 Using your food processor or electric beaters, beat the egg whites until they are stiff.

6 Gently fold the stiffly beaten egg whites into the broccoli mixture, then pour this into the soufflé dish. Place it in the preheated 325° oven and bake 40 to 50 minutes or until the soufflé is browned and set. Serve immediately.

Per serving: 139 calories; 7.55 gm protein; 12 gm carbohydrates; 7.13 gm fat; 101 mg cholesterol; .85 gm fiber; 46% of calories from fat

Egg Substitute

C ommercial egg substitutes are excellent, but they can be costly and they are some- times unavailable. Here is my made-from-scratch egg substitute recipe. One- fourth cup is equal to one egg. Egg substitute can be frozen in small containers until needed.

4 egg whites, at room temperature
2 teaspoons non-fat dry milk solids
1 tablespoon corn or safflower oil

Makes ¹/₂ cup

1 Place all ingredients in a blender and blend.

2 Store in a lidded container or freeze until needed.

Per ¹/₂ cup: 221 calories; 16 gm protein; 5.17 gm carbohydrates; 14 gm fat; 1.87 mg cholesterol; 0 gm fiber; 57% of calories from fat

Fettucine Soufflé

For variety, vegetables can be added to the soufflé and for the vegetarian, the ham can be deleted. This is a creative way to use leftover chopped vegetables.

Serves 4

6 ounces uncooked fettucine
Non-stick cooking spray
1¹/₃ cup 2% milk
2 tablespoons reduced-calorie margarine
¹/₂ cup grated Parmesan cheese
¹/₂ cup grated Swiss cheese
¹/₄ cup crumbled Gorgonzola or blue cheese
¹/₂ cup chopped ham (I use the 97% fat-free variety)
¹/₂ teaspoon Lulu's Special Seasoning
¹/₄ teaspoon white pepper
¹/₈ teaspoon cayenne pepper
2 egg yolks, slightly beaten
4 egg whites

1 Cook fettucine al dente. Drain well.

2 Preheat oven to 375° and spray a 2-quart casserole with non-stick cooking spray.

3 Heat milk to boiling.

4 Add the margarine, 3 cheeses, ham, seasonings, and egg yolks to the cooked fettucine.

5 In a clean dry bowl, using clean dry beaters, beat egg whites until stiff but not dry. Gently fold beaten egg whites into fettucine mixture. Turn fettucine mixture into prepared 2-quart soufflé dish.

6 Bake in the preheated 375° oven for 30 to 35 minutes or until top is golden brown.

Per serving: *346 calories; 25 gm protein; 12 gm carbohydrates; 22 gm fat; 190 mg cholesterol; .19 gm fiber; 57% of calories from fat*

Light Cheese Soufflé

U sing substantially less fat and two fewer egg yolks than a traditional soufflé, this speedy, streamlined version contains a microwaved white sauce along with a trio of cheeses. If desired, you can hold the soufflé mixture for one hour at room temperature before baking. For this recipe you will need 6 individual 4-inch-wide soufflé dishes.

Serves 6

1 cup 2% milk
2 tablespoons reduced-calorie margarine
2 tablespoons flour
Dash of cayenne pepper
1/4 teaspoon dry English mustard
1/4 teaspoon white pepper
1/4 teaspoon light salt
4 egg yolks, beaten
1 cup grated cheddar cheese
6 egg whites, at room temperature
1/8 teaspoon cream of tartar
Grated Parmesan and Romano cheese to dust soufflé dishes

1 Preheat oven to 400°.

2 Spray 6 individual 4-inch-wide soufflé cups with non-stick cooking spray.

3 Place milk in a 1-quart glass measure and microwave for 1 minute on high power. To warm milk, add margarine, flour, cayenne, mustard, white pepper, and salt. Blend the ingredients using a wire whisk. Microwave sauce on high power for 2 minutes. Whisk sauce briefly. Return sauce to microwave and cook on high power for 1 minute longer. Remove from microwave and briskly whisk sauce again. Quickly whisk beaten egg yolks and cup of grated cheddar cheese sauce until well blended. Set aside.

4 In a large mixing bowl, using electric beaters, beat egg whites until frothy. Add cream of tartar and continue beating until egg whites hold stiff peaks. Gently fold the sauce into the beaten whites, just until blended. (There still may be streaks.)

5 Coat the inside of each prepared cup with grated Parmesan and Romano cheese and fill 3/4 inch full with egg mixture.

6 Bake in preheated 400° oven for 15 to 20 minutes or until the soufflés have risen at least 1½ inches above the top of the cups and the top is golden brown.

Per serving: *180 calories; 11 gm protein; 4.15 gm carbohydrates; 13 gm fat; 204 mg cholesterol; .030 gm fiber; 65% of calories from fat*

Cheesy Rice Soufflé

W*hat a wonderful way to use up leftover rice. You can use one or a combination of rice. Serve it at once, for, like most soufflés, it falls quickly.*

Non-stick cooking spray
2 tablespoons reduced-calorie butter or margarine
3 tablespoons all-purpose flour
1 cup 2% milk
¼ teaspoon dry mustard
⅛ teaspoon cayenne pepper
⅔ cup grated cheddar cheese
⅓ cup grated skim mozzarella cheese
2 tablespoons grated Parmesan or Romano cheese
1 cup cooked rice, cooked without salt or fat
4 room temperature egg whites, in a medium glass or metal bowl

Serves 4 to 6

1 Preheat oven to 325°.

2 Spray a 1½-quart soufflé dish with non-stick cooking spray.

3 Melt the margarine or butter in a skillet over medium heat.

4 Add the flour and, stirring constantly, cook the roux until it bubbles and becomes thick and smooth, about 5 minutes.

5 Add the milk, mustard, and cayenne. Stirring constantly, cook until the sauce thickens, about 5 minutes. Remove pan from the

heat. Stir in the 3 cheeses until they melt and blend into the sauce. Add the cooked rice.

6   Using clean beaters, beat the egg whites until stiff, but not dry. Gently fold whites into the rice mixture.

7   Turn rice mixture into the prepared soufflé dish and bake in the preheated 325° oven for about 20 to 30 minutes or until the soufflé is set and the top is golden brown.

Per serving: 230 calories; 14 gm protein; 16 gm carbohydrates; 12 gm fat; 29 mg cholesterol; .46 gm fiber; 45% of calories from fat

Cheesy Broccoli Quiche

*M*ade from egg sub-
stitute, this pretty
*quiche is ideal for the
vegetarian or the
cholesterol-conscious. If
you do not have Mexican
Chihuahua cheese,
substitute mozzarella or
Monterey Jack.*

Serves 4

1 baked pie shell
1 1/2 cups coarsely chopped broccoli
1/2 cup grated Chihuahua cheese
1/2 cup grated cheddar cheese
1 cup loosely packed thinly sliced onion
1/2 cup shredded or julienned carrots
1/2 cup fresh sliced mushrooms
1/4 cup thinly slivered poblano pepper
1/4 cup chopped tomatoes
1 12-ounce can evaporated skim milk
Egg substitute to equal 3 eggs
1/4 teaspoon Lulu's Special Seasoning
1/4 teaspoon garlic pepper
1/4 teaspoon Szechuan seasoning
1/8 teaspoon cayenne pepper

1   Preheat oven to 350°.

2   Evenly sprinkle the broccoli, both cheeses, onions, carrots, mushrooms, peppers, and tomatoes into the baked pie shell.

3 In a bowl or large measuring cup, blend the remaining ingredients and pour into the filled shell.

4 Bake in preheated 350° oven for about 35 minutes or until custard is firm when the quiche is jiggled.

Per serving: 227 calories; 11 gm protein; 18 gm carbohydrates; 13 gm fat; 8.11 mg cholesterol; 1.12 gm fiber; 52% of calories from fat

Vegetarian Quiche

*ppetizing and color-
ful, this nutritious,
protein-packed quiche is
also quick and easy to
prepare. Try it for a
Sunday supper with warm
whole wheat tortillas and
a glass of dry white wine.*

Serves 4 to 6

1 **9-inch deep-dish pastry shell, thawed**
1/3 **cup chopped green onions**
1 **teaspoon finely chopped fresh garlic**
1 **14 1/2-ounce can whole peeled tomatoes (do not drain)**
2 **tablespoons chopped fresh parsley**
1/2 **teaspoon dried thyme**
1/8 **teaspoon cayenne pepper**
Cracked black pepper to taste
2 **cups crumbled farmer's cheese, (or any other white skim-milk cheese)**
3 **eggs**
1/4 **cup sliced pitted black olives**

1 Thaw pastry shell.

2 Adjust oven rack to lowest position. Preheat to 450°.

3 Place green onions, garlic, tomatoes, parsley, thyme, and cayenne and black peppers in a large skillet and bring to a boil. Cover, reduce heat, and simmer for 15 minutes. Remove from heat and cool slightly.

4 Meanwhile, sprinkle cheese evenly over the bottom of the thawed pastry shell and set aside.

5 In a mixing bowl beat eggs. Gradually beat in cooled tomato mixture. Stir in olives and pour mixture over cheese-filled pastry shell.

6 Bake at 450° for 10 minutes. Reduce heat to 350° and continue baking until crust is brown and custard is set (approximately 10 minutes longer). Quiche is done when the point of a knife inserted near the center of the custard comes out clean. Let stand about 5 minutes before cutting into wedges.

Per serving: 441 calories; 29 gm protein; 20 gm carbohydrates; 29 gm fat; 177 mg cholesterol; 1.27 gm fiber; 59% of calories from fat

Cheese Olive Pie

Serve this tasty, easy, and colorful pie for breakfast, brunch, lunch, or dinner. Dress it up or down. Use any cheese you choose, as long as it's low-fat. A combination of cheeses would be interesting.

Serves 4–6

1 unbaked 9-inch pie crust
1 tablespoon reduced-calorie butter or margarine
1/2 chopped medium zucchini
4 chopped green onions
1 1/2 cups diced processed low-fat cheese spread
Egg substitute to equal 4 eggs
1/2 cup 2% milk
1/4 cup bottled picante sauce
1/4 cup sliced black olives
1/2 teaspoon light salt
1/2 teaspoon ground black pepper

1 Preheat oven to 350°.

2 In a saucepan melt the butter or margarine over medium heat. Add the zucchini and green onion and sauté for 2 minutes, stirring occasionally.

3 Place the sautéed vegetables in the pie crust and sprinkle with the cheese.

4   In a small bowl combine all the remaining ingredients, and pour over the sautéed vegetables and cheese.

5   Bake the pie in the preheated 350° oven for 45 to 50 minutes or until the center of the pie is not quite fully set. The pie is done when the point of a knife inserted near the center of the pie comes out clean. Let stand 10 minutes and the center will firm up. Do not overcook. I suggest that you start watching how the custard is setting up after about 30 minutes of baking time.

Per serving: *482 calories; 23 gm protein; 23 gm carbohydrates; 34 gm fat; 430 mg cholesterol; 1.24 gm fiber; 63% of calories from fat*

Triple-Cheese Omelette with Sautéed Onion Rings

*Y*ou can use whatever brand of cholesterol-free, 99% real egg product you prefer. One 8-ounce carton of my favorite brand contains 100 calories, no fat, and 320 milligrams of sodium. I thaw a carton overnight in the refrigerator for next day use. To prevent sticking, be sure that the margarine is bubbly and hot before you add the seasoned eggs.

Sautéed Onions

½   medium onion sliced in ¼-inch-thick rounds, separated into rings
1   tablespoon reduced-calorie margarine
1   teaspoon Worcestershire sauce
    Garlic pepper to taste

1   Adjust rack 6 inches from broiler. Preheat broiler.

2   In a small skillet place onion rings, margarine, Worcestershire sauce, and garlic pepper. Cook over medium heat until onions are tender but not mushy. If made in advance, onions can be reheated before incorporating into omelette.

Omelette

Non-stick cooking spray
1 tablespoon reduced-calorie margarine
1 8-ounce carton commercial egg substitute (I prefer Egg Beaters)
1 teaspoon chopped fresh parsley
1/8 teaspoon Lulu's Special Seasoning
1/8 teaspoon summer savory
Cracked black pepper to taste
Dash of Tabasco sauce
Dash of Worcestershire sauce
1/4 cup chopped fresh tomatoes
2 large mushrooms, cleaned and sliced
1/3 cup grated skim-milk mozzarella
1/4 cup grated cheddar cheese (optional)
1 tablespoon shredded Romano cheese (optional)

Serves 2

1 Generously spray a 10-inch heavy, oven-proof skillet or omelette pan with non-stick cooking spray. Melt margarine over medium heat until bubbly.

2 Meanwhile, to egg substitute in carton add the parsley, special seasoning, summer savory, pepper, Tabasco, and Worcestershire. Using a fork, mix well right in the carton.

3 Pour seasoned egg mixture into the skillet. Add tomatoes, mushrooms, and cheeses, and cook about 5 minutes.

4 Hold skillet 3 to 4 inches below broiler and broil 2 to 3 minutes or until cheese melts. Remove from broiler. Using a spatula, fold omelette in half and slide omelette from the skillet onto a warm plate. Sprinkle the top with sautéed onion rings.

Per serving: *366 calories; 26 gm protein; 14 gm carbohydrates; 22 gm fat; 19 mg cholesterol; .59 gm fiber; 54% of calories from fat*

Leafy Spinach Cheese Omelette

This elegant light-cream-cheese-filled omelette is made with seasoned egg substitute. The spinach leaves create a dramatic presentation. The beer gives the omelette "a lift."

Serves 1 to 2

Non-stick cooking spray
1 tablespoon reduced-calorie butter or margarine
8 to 12 fresh well washed spinach leaves, stems removed
Egg substitute to equal 3 eggs
1 tablespoon chopped fresh parsley
2 teaspoons shredded or grated Parmesan cheese
1/4 teaspoon Lulu's Special Seasoning
1/4 teaspoon summer savory
1/4 teaspoon fresh ground pepper or bottled cracked pepper
1/8 teaspoon cayenne pepper
2 teaspoons beer (do not use dark)
2 2-by-1/2-inches each light cream cheese slices

1 Spray an 8 1/2-inch non-stick skillet with non-stick cooking spray. Add and melt the butter, then line the bottom of the skillet with the spinach leaves. Have a warm serving plate ready.

2 In a bowl, blend the egg substitute, parsley, Parmesan, special seasoning, summer savory, black pepper, and cayenne.

3 Briefly cook spinach until the leaves are dark and limp.

4 Add beer to egg substitute mixture and immediately pour egg mixture over spinach. Cover and cook 5 minutes, checking every 2 minutes. When eggs on the sides are set but the omelette center is still liquid, place the cream cheese in the middle of the omelette. Grasp pan's handle firmly and gently tilt skillet up and away from the skillet handle. Using a spatula or fork, flip over about 1/3 of the omelette. As you turn out the omelette, tilt pan at a 90° angle. The omelette will make a second fold as it slides from the skillet onto the warm serving plate. The omelette's "seam" will be on its under-side. Let stand 5 minutes, then serve.

Per serving: *304 calories; 19 gm protein; 9.04 gm carbohydrates; 22 gm fat; 478 mg cholesterol; 1.59 gm fiber; 65% of calories from fat*

Eggs Rachel

S erve at brunch, lunch, or any time you want to eat something light, lovely, and delicious. You can use just egg substitute and if so, use the equivalent of 2 eggs.

Serves 4

4 frozen tart shells (your favorite brand)
3/4 cup fresh sliced mushrooms
2 tablespoons reduced-calorie butter or margarine
1 tablespoon flour
3/4 cup 2% milk
1 1/2 tablespoons sherry
1/4 teaspoon light salt
1 tablespoon reduced-calorie butter or margarine (additional)
2 eggs or egg substitute to equal 2 eggs
1/2 cup light sour cream
1/4 cup finely chopped green onion tops
1/4 teaspoon black pepper
Strawberries (optional)
Cherry tomatoes (optional)
Avocado wedges (optional)

1 Preheat oven and bake tart shells according to package directions.

2 In a 1-quart saucepan over medium heat, melt the 2 tablespoons butter or margarine and sauté the mushrooms. Whisk in the flour, then the milk, sherry, and salt. Stirring constantly, cook until sauce thickens, about 5 minutes. Set sauce aside.

3 In a medium skillet over low to medium heat, melt the remaining 1 tablespoon of butter. Add the eggs or egg substitute, sour cream, green onions, and pepper. Scramble eggs softly; do not overcook.

4 Fill each baked shell with the scrambled eggs and top with mushroom sauce. Garnish plate with whole strawberries, cherry tomatoes, or wedges of ripe avocado.

Per serving: *399 calories; 7.89 gm protein; 45 gm carbohydrates; 20 gm fat; 153 mg cholesterol; .64 gm fiber; 45% of calories from fat*

Lulu's Favorite Vegetarian Frittata

A *pleasing combina-tion of eggs, spinach, fresh vegetables, and angel hair pasta, this frittata is perfect for any meal. Serve with garlic toast, Bibb Toss, and chilled white Zinfandel or sauterne.*

1/2 a 9-ounce package of angel hair pasta
1 tablespoon reduced-calorie butter or margarine
1/3 cup frozen corn kernels
12 thin sliced poblano pepper rings
1/4 cup chopped green onions
1 teaspoon finely chopped fresh garlic
1/2 cup egg substitute (about 5 eggs)
1/4 cup half and half
1/2 teaspoon Lulu's Special Seasoning
1/4 teaspoon summer savory
1/4 teaspoon freshly ground black pepper
1/4 teaspoon Szechuan seasoning
1/4 teaspoon cayenne pepper
   Non-stick cooking spray
2 tablespoons olive oil
2 ounces (about 1 cup) fresh spinach, cleaned and stems removed
3 ounces smoked Gouda or Edam or your favorite semi-soft cheese

2 tablespoons sliced black olives
12 to 14 thin slices Roma tomato
(enough to garnish the top)
1 to 2 tablespoons freshly shredded
Parmesan or Romano cheese
(optional)
Fresh rosemary or tarragon
(optional)

Serves 4 to 6

Fresh melon slices (optional)

1 Cook pasta al dente. Drain well and reserve.

2 Preheat oven to 350°. Have a warm serving platter ready.

3 In a small skillet, over medium heat melt the butter and add the corn, pepper rings, green onion, and garlic. Sauté for about 3 minutes. Do not overcook. Remove from heat and set aside.

4 Meanwhile, in medium bowl, blend the egg substitute, half and half, special seasoning, summer savory, black pepper, Szechuan seasoning, and cayenne. Set aside.

5 In a 10-inch ovenproof skillet sprayed with non-stick cooking spray, gently heat the oil. Add the spinach. Cover pan and, over medium heat, cook the spinach until it is limp but still bright green. The spinach is the bottom layer of the frittata.

6 Over low heat layer on the sautéed corn and pepper mixture, the cooked pasta, the smoked cheese, and the olives. Pour the egg substitute mixture over vegetable layers. Top the frittata with the sliced tomatoes and sprinkle with the shredded cheese. Cook over low heat until the frittata is almost set.

7 Place skillet in preheated 350° oven for 5 minutes or just until the eggs are set. Shake the pan to loosen the omelette, then slide it onto a serving platter, and garnish with herbs and fresh fruit.

Per serving: *198 calories; 8.6 gm protein; 10 gm carbohydrates; 12 gm fat; 16 mg cholesterol; 1.06 gm fiber; 53% of calories from fat*

111

Tomato and Green Bean Frittata

Frittata, an open-face Italian omelette, can contain a wide variety of fillings. This appealing frittata features herbed green beans and cooked spaghetti.

Serves 4 to 6

3 tablespoons reduced-calorie butter or margarine
1 tablespoon olive oil
4 ounces diagonally sliced (1 inch) frozen deluxe petite green beans
2/3 cup slivered red bell pepper
3/4 cup diced tomatoes
1/4 cup diced green onion (white part only)
1 teaspoon minced garlic
1 1/2 cup cooked, well-drained thin spaghetti
Egg substitute to equal 4 eggs
1/4 cup 2% milk
1/4 cup shredded Parmesan cheese
1 teaspoon dried oregano
1/2 teaspoon light salt
1/2 teaspoon sugar
1/4 teaspoon fresh ground pepper
1/4 teaspoon summer savory
Parsley (optional)
Cilantro (optional)
Fresh whole strawberries (optional)

1 Preheat oven to 350°. Have a warm serving platter ready.

2 In a 10-inch ovenproof skillet sprayed with non-stick cooking spray, melt the butter and oil. Over medium heat, sauté the green beans, bell pepper, tomatoes, onion, and garlic for 5 to 7 minutes. Stir in the cooked spaghetti.

3 In a medium bowl beat together the egg substitute, milk, cheese, oregano, salt, sugar, pepper, and summer savory.

4 Pour eggs into skillet and mix gently. Reduce heat to low, and cook about 5 minutes.

5 Place pan in preheated 350° oven for 5 to 10 minutes or just until eggs are set. Do not overcook.

6 Loosen omelette and slide onto serving platter. Garnish with sprigs of parsley or cilantro leaves and fresh whole strawberries.

Per serving: *202 calories; 13 gm protein; 4.98 gm carbohydrates; 14 gm fat; 400 mg cholesterol; .47 gm fiber; 62% of calories from fat*

Zapata Frittata

M*y frittata with a Mexican twist. Serve with my Pico de Gallo.*

2 tablespoons reduced-calorie butter or margarine
1 tablespoon olive oil
1 link of chorizo sausage (remove casing)
¹/2 cup finely diced red bell pepper
¹/2 cup fresh or frozen petite green beans
¹/4 cup finely chopped green onions
1 deseeded and chopped jalapeño pepper
1 teaspoon minced garlic
¹/2 cup egg substitute
¹/4 cup half and half
¹/2 teaspoon Lulu's Special Seasoning
¹/2 teaspoon sugar
¹/4 teaspoon black pepper
¹/8 teaspoon dried thyme
¹/2 of a 9-ounce package angel hair pasta, cooked
1 cup grated Chihuahua cheese or Monterey Jack cheese to sprinkle on top

Serves 4 to 6

1 Preheat oven to 350°.

2 In a 10-inch ovenproof skillet over medium-low heat, melt the butter. Add the oil, sausage, bell pepper, green beans, onions, jalapeño, and garlic and cook for 5 to 8 minutes or until the vegetables are tender, but still have a firm texture.

3 Meanwhile in a bowl, combine and mix well the egg substitute, cream, special seasoning, sugar, pepper, and thyme.

4 While still cooking, in this sequence, cover the sautéed sausage and vegetables with the cooked pasta, pour the egg substitute mixture over the pasta, then top with the grated cheese and cook until the frittata is almost set.

5 Place the skillet in a preheated 350° oven for 5 minutes longer or just until the eggs are set. Loosen the omelette and slide it onto a serving platter and garnish with tomato and avocado slices and fresh cilantro.

Per serving: *172 calories; 6.74 gm protein; 13 gm carbohydrates; 11 gm fat; 12 mg cholesterol; .6 gm fiber; 56% of calories from fat*

Classic Crêpes

T oday you can buy
an electric crêpe
cooker, but I think a large
heavy skillet is just as
easy: it just takes a little
practice. You rest the crêpe
batter to allow flour
particles time to swell and
to soften. The result is a
lighter textured crêpe.

1 cup 2% milk
3/4 cup flour
2 eggs
1/4 teaspoon light salt

Makes 1 1/2 cup batter

1 In your blender combine all the ingredients listed and blend until smooth, about 45 seconds. Let the batter rest for 15 minutes.

2 Spray an 8-inch or larger nonstick heavy skillet with non-stick cooking spray and, over medium heat, pour 1/4 cup batter into the skillet, quickly tilting the skillet in all directions so batter covers the bottom of the pan in a thin film. The crêpe is ready to turn when it is lightly browned and can be shaken loose from the skillet. Carefully flip crêpe using a spatula and cook 30 seconds longer. (This side is rarely more than spotty and is the side on which the filling is placed.) Slide crêpe onto plate and repeat procedure 5 more times.

3 Once crêpes have cooled, stack crêpes between layers of waxed paper to prevent sticking and cover. Will hold in refrigerator for several days.

1/4 cup of batter makes 6 7 1/2-inch crêpes
2   tablespoons of batter makes 12 4 1/2-inch crêpes
1   tablespoon of batter makes 24 3 1/2-inch crêpes

Per 7 1/2-inch crêpe: *17 calories; .81 gm protein; 2.22 gm carbohydrates; .49 gm fat; 16 mg cholesterol; .03 gm fiber; 27% of calories from fat*

Seafood Crêpes

A dynamite dish for entertaining! If you are not in the mood to prepare crêpes, serve seafood over cooked pasta or over a bed of white, brown, or wild rice, or a combination of all three.

Serves 4

3 tablespoons reduced-calorie butter or margarine
2 tablespoons dry vermouth
1 tablespoon dry sherry
1 tablespoon finely chopped shallots
1/2 pound (21 to 25 per pound) peeled and deveined shrimp
1/2 pound (10 to 20 per pound) sea scallops
6 ounces (1 cup) King crabmeat
1/2 cup half and half
1/2 cup 2% milk
2 tablespoons plain non-fat yogurt
1/2 teaspoon Lulu's Special Seasoning
1/4 teaspoon summer savory
1/4 teaspoon Parsley Plus
1/4 teaspoon ground white pepper
1/8 teaspoon Tabasco sauce
1/4 teaspoon arrowroot
4 7 1/2-inch crêpes
Hollandaise Sauce to taste

1 Preheat broiler. Drain crabmeat on a paper towel and place in a medium bowl.

2 Melt the butter or margarine in a heavy skillet over medium heat. Add the vermouth, sherry, and shallots, and sauté for 2 to 3 minutes. Add the shrimp, and cook for 2 minutes. Add the scallops and cook for 2 to 3 minutes longer, stirring occasionally. With a slotted spoon, transfer shrimp and scallops to a medium bowl. Stir in crabmeat. Keep warm.

3 To the skillet, add all remaining ingredients, except the arrowroot. Cook until the sauce thickens by reduction, about ten minutes. Whisk in the arrowroot, stir the seafood back to the sauce, cooking gently until thoroughly heated.

4 Fill the crêpes evenly with the sautéd seafood and roll up. Top with Hollandaise Sauce. Place dish 5 to 6 inches from broiler for 2 to 3 minutes or until sauce bubbles. Serve hot.

Per serving: *358 calories; 37 gm protein; 11 gm carbohydrates; 12 gm fat; 188 mg cholesterol; .06 gm fiber; 31% of calories from fat*

Chicken and Tomato Crêpes

U se the recipe for Classic Crêpes. When the seasonal supply of fresh tomatoes is exhausted, use Progresso's Peeled Tomatoes with Basil. You can bake, boil, or microwave the chicken breasts. Top the filled and rolled crêpe with Hollandaise Sauce or a dollop of light sour cream.

Makes 4 crêpes

2   tablespoons reduced-calorie butter or margarine
1   tablespoon minced shallots
2   tablespoons sauterne or dry white wine
2   cups fork-shredded cooked chicken meat (the meat off about 2 ounces raw chicken breasts)
1   cup peeled and coarsely chopped fresh tomatoes
1/4 cup 2% milk
1/4 cup whipping cream
1/4 teaspoon Lulu's Special Seasoning
1/4 teaspoon light salt
1/8 to 1/4 teaspoon white pepper
4   medium 4 1/2-inch diameter crêpes (or 2 large 7 1/2-inch) Hollandaise Sauce to taste
1   to 2 tablespoons grated reduced-calorie cheese (I prefer mozzarella) Pinch of shredded Parmesan cheese (optional)

1 Preheat broiler.

2 Melt the butter in a large skillet over medium heat. Add the shallots and wine, sautéing until the shallots are tender.

3 Stir in the shredded chicken, tomatoes, milk, cream, special seasoning, salt, and pepper. Cook gently until the liquid evaporates and filling is thick enough to stay inside the rolled crêpe. Place equal amounts of filling on each crêpe, and roll up.

4 Fill the crêpes evenly with the mixture. Lightly wrap the crêpes with Hollandaise Sauce or glaze with light sour cream. Sprinkle crêpes with the grated reduced-calorie cheese and a pinch of Parmesan.

5 Lightly brown under the broiler. Serve at once.

Per crêpe: *151 calories; 7.63 gm protein; 5.85 gm carbohydrates; 10 gm fat; 61 mg cholesterol; .2 gm fiber; 60% of calories from fat*

POULTRY & GAME:

THE LIGHT TOUCH

Chicken Breasts
in Madeira Cream Sauce

Absolutely *melts in your mouth. But remember, do not over-cook the chicken breasts or they will be tough and stringy. In place of the chicken breast you can use ½ to 1 pound veal scallops.*

Serves 4

4 boneless chicken breasts
  Seasoned flour (See Step 1)
2 tablespoons reduced-calorie butter
  or margarine
1/4 cup chopped shallots
  Cracked black pepper to taste
4 to 8 ounces thickly sliced
  mushrooms
1/2 cup low-sodium chicken broth
3 tablespoons Madeira
3 tablespoons crema mexicana, crème
  fraîche, or whipping cream
1/4 teaspoon Lulu's Special Seasoning
  Chopped fresh parsley to taste
  (optional)

1 Place chicken breasts on cutting board and pound with a mallet to about ¼-inch thickness. If you use the veal, it is already ready to be floured. Lightly sprinkle the surface of the chicken with seasoned flour (I keep ½ cup flour seasoned with ¼ teaspoon light salt and ⅛ teaspoon ground black pepper in a shaker for ready use).

2 In a skillet over medium-high heat, melt the butter. Add the shallots and chicken or veal, and cook 3 to 5 minutes per side or until done. Transfer meat to warm serving platter. Sprinkle to taste with cracked black pepper.

3 Add the mushrooms, broth, wine, cream, and special seasoning. Cook until the liquid is reduced by half and the sauce has thickened.

4 Pour the sauce over the meat and serve immediately.

Per serving: *320 calories; 43 gm protein; 9.16 gm carbohydrates; 11 gm fat; 122 mg cholesterol; .77 gm fiber; 31% of calories from fat*

Ginger-Lime Chicken Breast

A mainstay of Chinese cuisine, ginger root is the base for the citrus sauce that accompanies these luscious, low-calorie chicken breasts. Serve with Potato Beet Salad and sautéed summer squash. Compatible wines include Sauvignon Blanc, Montrachet, or other dry white wines. Refrigerate leftover ginger in a plastic bag.

4 to 6 skinless chicken breasts
1/2 cup lime marmalade (I use Rose's)
1/2 cup red currant jelly
2 teaspoons arrowroot dissolved in 1 tablespoon hot water
2 tablespoons soy sauce
2 tablespoons dry sherry
1/2 teaspoon Lulu's Special Seasoning
1/2 teaspoon finely chopped fresh ginger
1/2 teaspoon finely chopped garlic
1 tablespoon fresh orange juice
1 tablespoon reduced-calorie butter or margarine

Serves 4 to 6

1 Preheat oven to 350°.

2 Wash and dry chicken breasts and place them in a glass baking dish.

3 In a saucepan, blend all sauce ingredients.

4 Over medium heat cook the sauce until the jellies melt and the marinade thickens. Makes 1 cup of sauce.

5 Pour marinade over the chicken and bake for 30–45 minutes in the preheated 350° oven or until breasts are done, basting several times during baking.

6 For a more well-defined glaze, briefly place the breasts under a preheated broiler, basting several times.

Per serving: *249 calories; 30 gm protein; 11 gm carbohydrates; 8.4 gm fat; 83 mg cholesterol; 0 gm fiber; 30% calories from fat*

121

Chicken and Pasta Primavera

For an ample meal, serve with a light lettuce salad and crusty French bread. To save time, buy a pre-cooked chicken: it takes mere minutes to debone and dice.

Serves 4 to 6

3 boneless chicken breasts, cut into slivers or chunks (about 1 1/2 cups)
4 to 6 ounces fresh mushrooms, sliced
1 cup fresh broccoli florets
1 cup julienned carrots
1 cup julienned yellow squash
1/2 teaspoon chopped fresh garlic
4 tablespoons reduced-calorie butter or margarine
2 cups white wine sauce
1 12-ounce package colored, flavored rotelli

White Wine Sauce

1/4 cup reduced-calorie butter or margarine
1/4 cup all-purpose flour
3/4 cup 2% milk
1/2 cup broth from sautéed chicken and vegetables
1/2 cup half and half
1/4 cup dry white wine
1/4 teaspoon Lulu's Special Seasoning
1/4 teaspoon light salt
1/2 teaspoon white pepper
1/3 cup grated Parmesan or Romano cheese

1 In a large skillet over medium heat, sauté the chicken, mushrooms, broccoli, carrots, squash, and garlic in 1/4 cup butter or margarine. Set aside and keep warm.

2 Meanwhile, to make the sauce, melt the butter or margarine in a skillet over medium heat. Add the flour and, stirring constantly, cook the flour until it bubbles and becomes thick and smooth, about 5 minutes. Add milk, broth, half and half, wine, special seasoning, salt, and pepper. Stirring constantly, cook until sauce

thickens, about 5 minutes. Remove from the heat and stir in the grated cheese.

3 Cook rotelli al dente. Drain and place in a large serving bowl. Add sautéed chicken, vegetables, and white wine sauce. Mix well to combine. Serve hot.

Per serving: *289 calories; 22 gm protein; 20 gm carbohydrates; 12 gm fat; 56 mg cholesterol; 1.23 gm fiber; 37% of calories from fat*

Sautéed Chicken Breast

One of my short-cut marinades, it's for those days when you get home from work and you want an almost ready-made meal. The herbs are already in the bottle for you.

Serves 4

4 boneless, skinless chicken breasts
1/2 cup commercial light Italian salad dressing
1 tablespoon light soy sauce
2 teaspoons fresh lemon juice
1 teaspoon lemon pepper
2 tablespoons reduced-calorie butter or margarine
2 teaspoons white wine Worcestershire sauce

1 Marinate the chicken breast for at least 10 minutes per side or overnight in the salad dressing, soy sauce, lemon juice, and lemon pepper.

2 Over medium-high heat, in a large heavy skillet, sauté the breasts about 3 minutes per side or until lightly browned. Do not overcook or chicken will be tough. Transfer to a platter and keep warm.

3 To the skillet add the butter or margarine and Worcestershire. Heat sauce thoroughly and pour over the sautéed chicken.

Per serving: *386 calories; 30 gm protein; 3.2 gm carbohydrates; 28 gm fat; 83 mg cholesterol; .02 gm fiber; 65% of calories from fat*

Chicken Breast Marsala

As delicious as it is easy to prepare. If you wish, use veal instead of chicken. The mush-rooms are optional.

Serves 4

4 skinless, boneless chicken breasts
1/2 cup all-purpose flour
1/2 teaspoon Lulu's Special Seasoning
1/4 teaspoon light salt
1/4 teaspoon ground black pepper
2 tablespoons reduced-calorie margarine
2 tablespoons olive oil
Cracked black pepper to taste
1/2 cup Marsala
1/2 cup low-sodium beef broth
8 ounces cleaned and thickly sliced fresh mushrooms

1 Pound breasts 1/4-inch thick with a metal meat mallet.

2 In a bowl blend the flour, special seasoning, and ground pepper. Dip each breast in the seasoned flour, lightly coating both sides.

3 Over medium heat, heat the margarine in a large skillet; add oil until foamy. Add chicken and brown about 3 minutes on each side. Transfer chicken to a serving plate and sprinkle with cracked pepper to taste. Keep warm.

4 Increase heat to medium-high. Add the Marsala, broth, and mushrooms. Boil and stir until the liquid in the skillet is reduced by half.

5 Reduce heat to low. Return chicken to skillet, and simmer uncovered 10 minutes. Serve at once with the sauce and mushrooms poured over the chicken.

Per serving: 432 calories; 50 gm protein; 16 gm carbohydrates; 15 gm fat; 128 mg cholesterol; .94 gm fiber; 31% of calories from fat

Chicken Breasts Sautéed in Basil Cream

S erve this with Spinach Madeleine and a salad of your choice.

¹/₂ cup chopped fresh Roma tomato
¹/₄ cup crema mexicana or whipping cream
¹/₄ cup 2% milk
2 tablespoons brandy
¹/₂ teaspoon Lulu's Special Seasoning
Cracked black pepper to taste
4 5-ounce chicken breasts, rinsed and dried
2 tablespoons reduced-caloric butter or margarine
Garlic pepper to taste
2 green onions, chopped
2 tablespoons chopped fresh parsley
2 teaspoons chopped fresh basil

Serves 4

1 In a blender purée the tomato, cream, milk, brandy, special seasoning, and pepper. Set aside.

2 In a medium skillet, melt butter or margarine over medium heat. When butter is hot sauté chicken for about 10 minutes on each side, turning as needed. Do not overcook. While they are cooking, sprinkle each breast to taste with garlic pepper. Transfer chicken to a warm plate and keep warm.

3 Pour reserved mixture into the hot butter. Add the green onions, parsley, and basil. Cook, stirring occasionally, over medium heat for 5 minutes or until the cream thickens. Pour at once over the cooked chicken breasts and serve at once over the rice.

Per serving: 359 calories; 43 gm protein; 2.6 gm carbohydrates; 18 gm fat; 136 mg cholesterol; .16 gm fiber; 45% of calories from fat

Grilled Chicken Fajita Quesadillas

A quesadilla is the Mexican equivalent of an American grilled cheese sandwich. In this interpretation, pan-grilled flour tortillas are filled with marinated charbroiled strips of chicken (fajitas), grated Monterey Jack and cheddar cheeses, diced green onions, and tomatoes. Accompany with guacamole, light sour cream, my Pico de Gallo, shredded lettuce, and Fiesta Red Rice.

Serves 4

Chicken Fajitas

1 pound boneless, skinless chicken breasts
2 tablespoons chopped fresh parsley
2 tablespoons finely chopped onion
2 tablespoons each of fresh lemon and lime juice (you can use 1/4 cup lemon juice if you have no limes, but I prefer both)
2 tablespoons olive oil
1 tablespoon finely chopped fresh jalapeño pepper
1 teaspoon chopped fresh garlic
1 teaspoon liquid smoke
1 teaspoon Worcestershire sauce

1 In a medium glass bowl, blend ingredients, including the chicken. Cover and marinate for at least 2 hours, longer if possible.

2 Ten minutes before you are ready to cook, preheat grill. Grill the chicken until done and prepare to assemble the quesadillas.

For Each Quesadilla:

Strips of grilled chicken
1 7-inch flour tortilla
2 thin slices Roma tomato
Finely minced green onion to taste
2 tablespoons grated Monterey Jack cheese or mozzarella
2 tablespoons grated cheddar cheese
Non-stick cooking spray

1 Preheat a flat grill or heavy skillet.

2 Arrange chicken strips on half the tortilla. Top with green onion, sliced Roma tomato, and cheeses. Fold tortilla in half. Spray the skillet with non-stick cooking spray. Pan-grill quesadillas until the tortilla is lightly browned on both sides and the cheese is melted. Serve immediately.

Per serving: 402 calories; 43 gm protein; 21 gm carbohydrates; 16 gm fat; 106 mg cholesterol; .46 gm fiber; 36% of calories from fat

Chicken Breast Olé

T hese filled breasts are delicious and quick to prepare. Use any variety of a low-fat cheese such as Monterey Jack or mozzarella.

Serves 1

1 skinless, boneless chicken breast, rinsed and dried, pounded 1/4-inch thick
2 tablespoons grated low-fat cheese (you can use 2 types of cheese)
1 tablespoon finely chopped poblano pepper
1 tablespoon finely chopped red onion
1 tablespoon chopped ripe olives
1 tablespoon light sour cream
   Parsley Plus or Mrs. Dash to taste
   Chili powder to taste
   Ground cumin to taste
1 teaspoon reduced-calorie butter or margarine

1 Preheat oven to 350°

2 In a bowl, blend the cheese, pepper, onion, olives, and sour cream. Spread each flattened breast with this mixture. Roll up breast and secure with a toothpick.

127

3 Place stuffed breasts in a baking dish. Sprinkle to taste with the parsley plus, chili powder, and cumin and top with butter. Bake in the preheated 350° oven for 20 minutes. Remove chicken from oven and baste with the pan drippings. Serve at once.

Per serving: *389 calories; 38 gm protein; 5.2 gm carbohydrates; 24 gm fat; 103 mg cholesterol; 1.05 gm fiber; 56% of calories from fat*

Chicken Breast Piccata

T his is a chicken breast variation of the classic Italian Veal Piccata. It's great served with your favorite pasta.

4 boneless chicken breasts
1/4 cup flour
1/4 teaspoon light salt
1/8 teaspoon black pepper
3 tablespoons reduced-calorie butter or margarine
1 tablespoon olive oil
1/4 cup sauterne or dry white wine
1/4 cup chicken broth or instant chicken bouillon
1 tablespoon lemon juice
4 to 8 ounces thickly sliced fresh mushrooms
2 tablespoons drained capers
4 thin lemon slices
4 thin lime slices

Serves 4

1/4 cup chopped fresh parsley

1 Rinse chicken breasts and pat dry. Using a metal mallet, pound out to 1/4-inch thick.

2 In a bowl, blend the flour, salt, and pepper. Coat both sides of each pounded chicken breast with the seasoned flour. Set chicken aside.

3 In a heavy skillet, over medium heat, heat butter or margarine and oil until foamy. Add the chicken. Cook about 2 minutes per

side. This is just enough to cook the meat. Do not cook any longer. Transfer to a warm plate and keep warm.

4 Pour off all but a light film of fat and drippings from the skillet.

5 Increase heat to medium high. Add wine, broth, lemon juice and mushrooms. Cook, stirring occasionally, until the liquid in the pan is reduced by half.

6 Pour the sauce evenly over the warm chicken breasts, and garnish with the capers, sliced lemon, lime, and parsley. Serve immediately.

Per serving: *314 calories; 31 gm protein; 8.76 gm carbohydrates; 15 gm fat; 83 mg cholesterol; .46 gm fiber; 43% of calories from fat*

Chicken Breast Diane

My interpretation of that culinary classic, steak Diane. To save time, pound boneless chicken breasts to 1/4-inch thickness ahead of time, wrap individually, and freeze until ready to use. Goes great with Garlic Pasta and Summer Stir-Fry.

Serves 4

4 boneless chicken breasts
   Lulu's Special Seasoning to taste
   Flour
2 tablespoons reduced-calorie margarine
2 tablespoons olive oil
3 tablespoons chopped green onions
3 tablespoons chopped fresh parsley
3 tablespoons brandy
1 teaspoon Dijon mustard
1/2 cup chicken broth

1 Place chicken breasts on cutting board and pound with a mallet to about 1/4 inch thick. Sprinkle both sides of the chicken lightly with special seasoning and flour.

2 Over medium heat, heat the margarine and oil in a skillet. Add the prepared chicken and cook 1 to 2 minutes per side. Do not

overcook or the meat will be tough and dry. Transfer to a warm serving platter.

3   To skillet add the green onion, parsley, brandy, and mustard. Cook sauce for 1 minute, whisking constantly. Whisk in the broth and stir until sauce is smooth.

4   Pour sauce over chicken and serve immediately.

Per serving: 287 calories; 30 gm protein; .37 gm carbohydrates; 17 gm fat; 83 mg cholesterol; .07 gm fiber; 53% of calories from fat

Umi's Spiced Chicken

A special "thanks" to my good friend Urmila Nagar for helping me develop this and the other Indian recipes in this book. I serve Umi's Spiced Chicken with Rice Pilau, Dahl Moong, and a salad. If I have any leftover chicken, I bone it and serve it stuffed inside a whole-wheat pita.

Serves 3 to 4

6 chicken thighs, skin and visible fat removed
1 tablespoon finely chopped fresh ginger
2 teaspoons finely chopped fresh garlic
1 teaspoon cayenne pepper
1/2 teaspoon turmeric
1/4 teaspoon light salt
3 tablespoons vegetable oil
2 pieces cinnamon (1 broken stick)
3 whole cloves
1 medium onion, chopped
1/2 teaspoon garam masala (optional)
Chopped fresh cilantro leaves

1   Sprinkle chicken with ginger, garlic, cayenne, turmeric, and salt. Place chicken in a baking dish and let stand for 30 minutes.

2   Heat the oil in a heavy pan over medium-high heat. Add the cinnamon, cloves, and onion. Cook, stirring occasionally, until onion is transparent, about 5 to 10 minutes.

3 Add the chicken. Reduce heat to low. Cover pan and cook, covered, turning as needed, for 30 to 45 minutes or until chicken is done. The meat will almost fall from the bone.

4 Stir in the garam masala. Garnish with the cilantro. Serve warm.

Per serving: *594 calories; 48 gm protein; 5.72 gm carbohydrates; 41 gm fat; 171 mg cholesterol; .39 gm fiber; 62% of calories from fat*

Stuffed Cornish Game Hens in Peach and Raisin Sauce

I f you prefer you can substitute a fryer for the Cornish hens. Just treat the fryer as you would the hen.

Serves 2 to 4

2 Cornish game hens (about 1 1/2 pounds each)
  Lulu's Special Seasoning
1 16-ounce box long grain and wild rice (I use Uncle Ben's)
1/2 cup chopped apples
1/2 cup chopped celery
1 tablespoon chopped shallots

1 Rinse and dry the Cornish hens and sprinkle them with the special seasoning.

2 Place rice, 2 cups water, apples, celery, and shallots in a 1 1/2-quart saucepan. Cook rice mixture for the length of time specified on the box. Cool slightly.

3 Heat oven to 350°. Stuff the hens with the rice mixture and place them in a baking dish. I make a layer of rice in the middle of the baking dish and place it so that I can cover just the rice with foil so it will not dry out, but allow the hens to cook uncovered.

4 Bake in the preheated 350° oven for approximately 45 minutes or until birds are done.

Peach and Raisin Sauce

1/2-ounce box of raisins, plumped
in 1/3 cup peach nectar
1 tablespoon reduced-calorie butter
or margarine
1 tablespoon honey
1 teaspoon brandy
1/2 teaspoon arrowroot, dissolved in 1
teaspoon hot water

In a small saucepan over medium heat, blend together all sauce
ingredients. Stir until hot and sauce thickens. Serve at once with or
over the rice-stuffed Cornish game hens.

*Per serving: 450 calories; 50 gm protein; 38 gm carbohydrates; 9.63 gm fat; 170 mg
cholesterol; 1.34 gm fiber; 19% of calories from fat*

Cornish Game Hens
with Red Currant Glaze

*I like to serve these
elegant glazed hens
during the holidays as a
change from stuffed
turkey.*

4 Cornish game hens
1 to 2 onions, coarsely chopped
1 apple, coarsely chopped
Light salt to taste
Black pepper to taste
White wine Worcestershire sauce
to taste
8 slices of your favorite bacon (2 slices
per hen)

Serves 4 to 6

Red currant glaze

1 Preheat grill to medium.

2 Wash hens. Drain, and pat dry with a paper towel.

3 Stuff each cavity with the coarsely chopped onions and apples.

4 Salt and pepper each hen to your taste and brush each hen with the Worcestershire sauce.

5 Wrap each hen with 2 slices of bacon, securing the bacon with several toothpicks. I wrap 1 slice of bacon one direction and the second slice in the other direction.

6 Using your outdoor grill, grill the hens (covered, for a smoked flavor) for 10 minutes per side turning several times so as not to burn the bacon.

7 Ten minutes before hens are finished cooking, preheat oven to 350°.

8 Remove hens from grill. Place on a shallow pan, brush with glaze, and place in the preheated 350° oven for 30 to 45 minutes or until done, basting with the glaze when you think about it.

Red Currant Glaze

1 tablespoon reduced-calorie butter
  or margarine
$1/2$ cup red currant jelly
2 tablespoons fresh lemon juice
$1/4$ cup cider vinegar
1 tablespoon cornstarch
$1/2$ teaspoon light salt
4 whole cloves

Preparing the Glaze:
Melt butter or margarine and jelly in a small saucepan. Add lemon juice, vinegar, cornstarch, salt, and cloves. Heat gently.

Per serving: *448 calories; 54 gm protein; 27 gm carbohydrates; 13 gm fat; 188 mg cholesterol; .51 gm fiber; 26% of calories from fat*

Turkey-Stuffed Jumbo Pasta Shells

Y ou can stuff these
shells with ground
chicken or turkey. I stuff
them with ground turkey
and fresh spinach. Serve
topped with Tomato
Oregano Sauce and
accompany with a
cucumber and onion
salad.

8 jumbo pasta shells
2 tablespoons olive oil
1/2 pound ground turkey
4 cups fresh spinach, cleaned and
   torn into bite-size pieces
1/3 cup chopped onion
1 tablespoon each chopped fresh
   parsley, basil, oregano, and mint
1 teaspoon minced fresh garlic
1 egg
1/2 cup skim-milk ricotta cheese
1/2 cup skim-milk mozzarella cheese
2 tablespoons freshly grated Romano
   cheese
1/4 cup low-sodium chicken broth or

Serves 4

water

1 Preheat oven to 350°.

2 Cook the pasta shells in boiling water for about 14 minutes or until tender, then drain and rinse in cold water until cool.

3 Heat oil in a skillet over medium heat. Add the turkey, spinach, onion, the 4 herbs, and the garlic. Sauté until the turkey is cooked, using a spoon to break up any clumps of turkey.

4 Remove from heat. Stir in the egg and the cheeses. Carefully stuff each cooked shell with about 1/4 cup of this mixture.

5 Pour the chicken broth or water in the bottom of a baking dish large enough to accommodate the stuffed shells. Bake in the preheated 350° oven for 20 to 30 minutes or until the shells are hot. The broth prevents the shells from sticking to the bottom of the pan.

Per serving: *522 calories; 41 gm protein; 50 gm carbohydrates; 18 gm fat; 135 mg cholesterol; 2.7 gm fiber; 31% of calories from fat*

Tender Turkey Cutlets in Lime-Wine Sauce

These sautéed turkey cutlets are served with a low-calorie lime-laced sauce that complements the turkey beautifully.

1 pound turkey tenderloin cut into 3 or 4 pieces and pounded 1/4-inch-thick with a meat mallet
1/3 cup all-purpose flour
1/2 teaspoon Lulu's Special Seasoning
1/2 teaspoon lemon pepper
1/2 teaspoon summer savory
1/4 teaspoon chervil
1/4 teaspoon cracked black pepper
1/4 teaspoon lemon zest
3 tablespoons reduced-calorie butter or margarine
1 cup homemade chicken broth or 1 package low-sodium instant chicken broth mixed with 1 cup hot water
2 tablespoons sauterne or dry white wine
2 tablespoons fresh lime juice
2 tablespoons reduced-calorie butter or margarine (additional)

Serves 3 to 4

1/2 teaspoon arrowroot

1 In a paper or plastic bag, place cutlets, flour, special seasoning, lemon pepper, summer savory, chervil, pepper, and lemon peel. Shake bag until the cutlets are lightly coated with the seasoned flour.

2 In a large skillet over medium-high heat, heat the butter or margarine until bubbly. Add the floured cutlets, and sauté until the first side is golden brown. Turn. Sauté until the second side is browned and the cutlet is cooked. Remove cutlets to a serving platter and keep warm.

3 Add the broth, wine, and lime juice to the skillet. Cook until the liquid is reduced to 1/2 cup. Whisk in the additional butter

and arrowroot and cook 2 minutes longer. Serve the sauce over
or alongside the cutlets.

Per serving: *314 calories; 35 gm protein; 8.98 gm carbohydrates; 14 gm fat; 87 mg
cholesterol; .16 gm fiber; 40% of calories from fat*

Sweet Sautéed Turkey Tenders

*I*ndividual, *low-calorie
marinated turkey
tenderloins are perfect for
pan sautéing or grilling
and the leftovers make
great turkey sandwiches.
Serve with Tangelo Honey
Sauce.*

Serves 4 to 6

2 **turkey tenderloins (about 1 to 1 1/4
pounds total weight)**

Marinade

1 **5 1/4-ounce can pear nectar**
1/4 **cup chopped fresh parsley**
2 **tablespoons molasses**
2 **tablespoons dry sherry**
2 **tablespoons light soy sauce**
2 **tablespoons olive oil**
2 **tablespoons finely chopped green
onion**
2 **teaspoons grated fresh ginger**
Non-stick cooking spray

1 Place turkey in a large glass dish or bowl. Blend all marinade
ingredients in a small bowl and pour over turkey. Cover.
Refrigerate for at least 30 minutes or up to 2 hours, depending
upon your schedule.

2 Spray a large skillet with non-stick cooking spray. Add 2
tablespoons of the marinade to the skillet. Add turkey. Sauté
over medium heat, cooking until turkey is golden brown and
cooked thoroughly, about 10 to 15 minutes. Add additional
marinade as needed and desired. Cut into medallions. Serve
immediately.

Per serving: *334 calories; 34 gm protein; 9.18 gm carbohydrates; 16 gm fat; 87 mg
cholesterol; .04 gm fiber; 43% of calories from fat*

SEAFOOD
EXTRAORDINAIRE

Pasta Santa Fe with Shrimp

Prepared with a Southwestern flair, the sautéed shrimp is served over a bed of cooked pasta.

Serves 2

2 tablespoons reduced-calorie butter or margarine
1 tablespoon olive oil
1/2 pound fresh peeled and deveined shrimp
1/2 deseeded, slivered poblano pepper
1/2 deseeded, slivered red bell pepper
1/4 thinly sliced red onion
1 finely chopped garlic clove
2 tablespoons chopped cilantro leaves
1 to 2 tablespoons tequila or gin
1/4 to 1/2 teaspoon each of Lulu's Special Seasoning, chili powder, cumin powder, and cracked black pepper
1/3 cup half and half
2 cups your favorite cooked pasta

1   In a large skillet over medium heat, heat the butter or margarine and oil. Add shrimp, and cook until done, about 10 minutes. Shrimp will be firm. Remove shrimp and set aside.

2   Add peppers, onion, garlic, and cilantro, and sauté until just tender. Remove vegetables and set aside.

3   To deglaze the skillet, add the tequila or gin, swirling it around in the pan. Add all the seasonings to taste. Stir in the seasoned cream and allow the sauce to thicken slightly. Return the shrimp and vegetables to the skillet and toss until everything is heated and coated with the cream.

4   Serve immediately over the cooked pasta. Grated Parmesan cheese is optional.

Per serving: *478 calories; 30 gm protein; 40 gm carbohydrates; 20 gm fat; 187 mg cholesterol; 1.81 gm fiber; 37% of calories from fat*

Shrimp Provençal

I like to use large shrimp because they butterfly nicely.

16 large shrimp (16 to 20 count or larger)
2 tablespoons reduced-calorie butter
1 tablespoon olive oil
1 tablespoon green peppercorns, soaked in water for 15 minutes and then drained
1/2 cup chopped green onion
1 tablespoon chopped shallots
1/2 cup dry vermouth
1/2 cup light cream
1/2 cup 2% milk
1/4 cup light sour cream
1/4 teaspoon Lulu's Special Seasoning
1/4 teaspoon light salt

Serves 4

1 Peel the shrimp but leave tail attached. Next, butterfly the shrimp by cutting lengthwise from the top almost through the shrimp to form a hinge. Rinse the shrimp and be sure the vein is removed and then flatten with your hand.

2 In a large skillet over medium-high heat, melt the butter and oil. Add the shrimp and sauté for 1 minute. Stir in the peppercorns, onion, and shallots and sauté for 1 minute longer, stirring constantly.

3 Add the vermouth and reduce the liquid by half. By this time the shrimp should be cooked just right. Remove shrimp. Using a wire whisk, whisk in the cream and milk, and reduce the sauce until it thickens nicely, about 5 to 7 minutes.

4 Remove from heat. Whisk in the sour cream and add the shrimp back to the pan. Stir in special seasoning and the salt and serve over cooked pasta or rice.

Per serving: 221 calories; 9.16 gm protein; 9.58 gm carbohydrates; 12 gm fat; 56 mg cholesterol; .29 gm fiber; 50% of calories from fat

Angel Hair Pasta
with Sautéed Scallops and Shrimp

Be gentle with this light and tender pasta, for it is fragile. It is very difficult to toss any type of sauce or seafood into this pasta, so I combine the seafood into the sauce and pour the combination over or alongside the angel hair pasta. Scallops and shrimp contain 30 calories per 1-ounce serving.

Serves 4

9-ounce package angel hair pasta
8 ounces unflavored low-fat yogurt
4 ounces skim-milk ricotta
1/4 cup half and half
1 egg
1/4 teaspoon light salt
1/8 teaspoon cayenne pepper
1 tablespoon reduced-calorie butter or margarine
2 tablespoons sauterne
1 tablespoon fresh lemon juice
1/2 pound rinsed medium scallops
1/2 pound medium fresh, rinsed, shelled and deveined shrimp
1/4 teaspoon Lulu's Special Seasoning
Garlic pepper to taste
1/4 cup freshly grated Parmesan cheese
1/4 chopped fresh parsley

1 Cook pasta according to package directions. Keep warm.

2 In a bowl using a wire whisk, or in an electric blender, blend or purée the yogurt, ricotta, half and half, egg, salt, and cayenne. This is your sauce. Set aside.

3 In a skillet over medium-high heat, melt the butter or margarine. Add sauterne and lemon juice. Add the scallops and shrimp, cooking until the seafood is done, about 10 minutes. Do not overcook or shellfish will toughen. Remove from the heat and add special seasoning and garlic pepper. Allowing the pan juices to remain in the skillet, transfer cooked seafood to a bowl. Keep warm.

4 Return the skillet to the heat, whisk in the reserved sauce. Cook 5 minutes, whisking constantly. Sauce will be bubbly.

140

5 To assemble, arrange pasta on a single, large serving platter or on individual plates. Spread the sauce over the pasta, and top with the sautéed scallops and shrimp. Garnish with the Parmesan and parsley. Serve hot. One hint: you may have to rinse the pasta in order to spread it nicely over the dish.

Per serving: 326 calories; 34 gm protein; 20 gm carbohydrates; 11 gm fat; 200 mg cholesterol; .28 gm fiber; 31% of calories from fat

Skewered Shrimp and Bacon Bundles

T*hese marinated shrimp are bundled in pieces of bacon and grilled to perfection. Be sure to buy lean bacon — preferably the no-added-sugar-or-salt bacon. To cut calories, grill the shrimp with the bacon, but do not eat the bacon. Just enjoy the flavor it has given the shrimp. Serve it with Trio of Grilled Bell Peppers and Robert's Favorite Salad. These bundles could be served as an appetizer.*

Serves 4

1 pound (16 to 20 count) fresh shrimp, peeled and deveined
1/3 cup light soy sauce
1/4 cup dry red wine
2 tablespoons chopped fresh parsley
1 tablespoon fresh lime juice
1 teaspoon sugar or 1 packet sugar substitute
1 teaspoon fresh garlic, chopped
1 teaspoon Lulu's Special Seasoning
1 teaspoon ground ginger
1/2 teaspoon lemon pepper
9 or fewer slices lean bacon

1 If using a grill, preheat.

2 In a tightly-lidded container combine and mix together the soy, wine, parsley, lime juice, sugar, garlic, special seasoning, ginger, and lemon pepper. Add the shrimp to this marinade and marinate for 1 hour or so.

3   Wrap each shrimp in a piece of bacon. Use as small a piece of bacon as you can, ½ to ⅓ of a slice, depending upon the length of the slices. Secure with a toothpick. Broil or grill, basting and turning the bundles, until bacon is crisp and the shrimp are bright pink and done.

Per serving: *193 calories; 28 gm protein; 3.02 gm carbohydrates; 7 gm fat; 182 mg cholesterol; .02 gm fiber; 33% of calories from fat*

Shrimp, Spinach, and Cashew Stir-Fry

A crunchy and colorful stir-fry chockfull of fresh vegetables and tender shrimp. Speedy cooking prevents nutrient loss. For best results when stir-frying, have everything ready to use before you begin.

3 tablespoons safflower or corn oil
1/2 cup low-sodium chicken broth
2 tablespoons light soy sauce
2 tablespoons sauterne
1 tablespoon cornstarch
1/2 teaspoon Lulu's Special Seasoning
1/4 teaspoon Tabasco sauce
1/4 cup cashews
1 cup slivered red bell pepper (about 1/2 medium bell pepper)
1/2 cup thinly sliced celery
6 to 8 ounces thickly sliced fresh mushrooms
20 snow peas (about 2 1/2 ounces)
1/3 cup coarsely diced green onion
1 teaspoon finely chopped fresh garlic
1 pound fresh peeled and deveined medium shrimp

Serves 4

2 cups coarsely torn fresh spinach

1   Place oil in a wok or a heavy-bottomed sauté pan and heat.

2   Meanwhile, in a measuring cup or small bowl, blend the broth, soy sauce, sauterne, cornstarch, special seasoning, and Tabasco, and set aside.

3 Add cashews to the hot oil, stirring constantly until they begin to brown and give off a nut-like aroma. Using a slotted spoon, quickly remove the cashews and set aside. They will be used as the garnish.

4 Add the red pepper, celery, mushrooms, snow peas, green onions, and garlic. Stirring frequently, cook uncovered for about 3 minutes. You want the vegetables to be slightly cooked but crisp.

5 Add shrimp, spinach, and reserved broth mixture. Cook uncovered, stirring frequently, for 5 minutes longer. Immediately remove from heat and transfer to a warm serving dish. Garnish with cashews. Serve over cooked rice.

Per serving: *317 calories; 28 gm protein; 13 gm carbohydrates; 17 gm fat; 172 mg cholesterol; .86 gm fiber; 47% of calories from fat*

Seafood Sauté

S erve this medley of seafood with Summer Stir-Fry and Potato Beet Salad with Mustardy Yogurt Dressing.

2 tablespoons reduced-calorie butter or margarine
1 tablespoon finely chopped shallots
1/2 pound peeled and deveined uncooked shrimp
1/2 pound scallops
3 squid, cleaned and sliced into circles (I use the body sac only) (optional)
3 tablespoons light cream or half and half
2 tablespoons white wine Worcestershire sauce
1/2 teaspoon Lulu's Special Seasoning
1/2 teaspoon fresh lemon juice
Cayenne pepper to taste
White pepper to taste

Serves 4

1 In a large skillet over medium heat, melt the butter or margarine and sauté the shallots, shrimp, scallops, and squid until they are cooked. Transfer to a medium bowl and keep warm.

2 Stir all remaining ingredients into the hot skillet. Cook over medium heat about 5 to 10 minutes or until sauce thickens slightly.

3 Pour sauce over hot sautéed seafood. Serve at once over cooked rice or pasta.

Per serving: 204 calories; 25 gm protein; 13 gm carbohydrates; 5.42 gm fat; 108 mg cholesterol; .35 gm fiber; 24% of calories from fat

Crabmeat Shrimp Casserole

T his elegant and easy delicious casserole is perfect for family dinners or entertaining. It can be prepared ahead of time and re-heated at the last moment. Smaller portions do double-duty as an appetizer. Lightly top the casserole with your favorite low-fat cheese.

1 tablespoon reduced-calorie butter or margarine
1 tablespoon olive oil
1 single serving boil-in-a-bag rice, cooked 10 minutes, drained well, and kept warm
1/2 pound (51–60 per pound) fresh shrimp, peeled, cleaned, and deveined (about 1 cup)
1/2 cup fresh crabmeat (I only use the real thing!)
2 tablespoons sauterne
1 tablespoon Dijon mustard
1 tablespoon fresh lemon juice
1/4 cup finely chopped green onions
1/4 cup half and half
1/2 teaspoon Lulu's Special Seasoning
Cayenne pepper to taste (I use 1/8 to 1/4 teaspoon)

Serves 3

3/4 cup grated low-fat skim milk cheese

1 Preheat broiler.

2 In a large skillet over medium heat, melt the butter and oil. Add all remaining ingredients except grated cheese. Sauté, stirring frequently, until the shrimp is cooked, about 5–8 minutes.

3 Sprinkle the top of the casserole with the grated cheese. Hold skillet under the broiler for 2 to 3 minutes or until the cheese melts. Serve at once over prepared rice.

Per serving: *530 calories; 42 gm protein; 40 gm carbohydrates; 21 gm fat; 172 mg cholesterol; .81 gm fiber; 35% of calories from fat*

Seafood Scampi

U se lobster, crab, mussels, or any combination seafood you desire. Serve as a hot appetizer over rice or pasta, or over angel hair pasta for a main course.

1/2 pound peeled and deveined uncooked shrimp
1/2 pound scallops
1/3 cup fresh bread crumbs
1/4 cup chopped green onions
1/4 cup dry white wine
2 tablespoons olive oil
2 tablespoons reduced-calorie butter or margarine
1 tablespoon fresh lime juice
1 tablespoon each chopped fresh parsley, oregano, and basil
1 medium-sized, fork-crushed clove garlic
1 teaspoon white wine Worcestershire sauce
1/2 teaspoon Lulu's Special Seasoning

Serves 4

Garlic pepper to taste

1 Place all ingredients in a large skillet and mix well.

2 Over medium heat, cook uncovered for approximately 8 to 10 minutes, stirring occasionally.

3 Remove from heat, cover, and let stand 10 minutes before serving.

Per serving: *257 calories; 19.8 gm protein; 6 gm carbohydrates; 10.7 gm fat; 103.5 mg cholesterol; .14 gm fiber; 38% of calories from fat*

Shrimp Marin

U se a good-sized
medium shrimp for
this dish.

2½ tablespoons reduced-calorie
butter or margarine
1 pound shrimp, peeled and
deveined
1 cup mushrooms, thickly sliced
2 tablespoons dry sherry
2 tablespoons chopped green bell
pepper
2 tablespoons chopped red bell
pepper
1 cup leeks, chopped (white part
only)
1 tablespoon tomato paste
¼ cup 2% milk
¼ cup half and half
¼ cup crème fraîche or light sour
cream
¼ teaspoon light salt
2 to 3 dashes Tabasco sauce

Serves 4

1 In a heavy skillet over medium heat, melt 1 tablespoon of the
butter. Add shrimp and cook until done, about 3 minutes. Do
not overcook. Remove shrimp and set aside.

2 Add another tablespoon of butter, reduce the heat to low and
sauté the mushrooms about 3 minutes. Add the sherry and
peppers and cook 3 minutes longer, stirring as needed.

3 Meanwhile in a separate pan, melt ½ tablespoon of butter and
sauté the leeks until tender; remove from heat and set aside.

4 To the large skillet, add the tomato paste, 2% milk, half and half,
and crème fraîche, whisking until all is well blended.

5 Add the salt, cooked leeks, cooked shrimp, and Tabasco and
cook using low heat for about 5 minutes or until sauce thickens
by reduction. Serve over cooked rice or pasta.

*Per serving: 242 calories; 26 gm protein; 10 gm carbohydrates; 9.04 gm fat; 179 mg
cholesterol; .83 gm fiber; 34% of calories from fat*

Asparagus Shrimp Fettuccine

If possible, use fresh tri-colored fettuccine or fresh green spinach-flavored fettuccine. If these are unavailable, you can always use regular dried fettuccine. However, the colored fettuccine contrast dramatically with the pink shrimp, the green asparagus, and the red bell pepper.

9 ounces fresh tri-colored or green fettuccine
2 tablespoons reduced-calorie butter or margarine
1 tablespoon olive oil
1 pound large, fresh, peeled and deveined shrimp
1/4 cup sauterne
1/4 cup finely chopped green onion
1 minced garlic clove
1 roasted, peeled, seeded red bell pepper, sliced into thin strips
2 cups fresh asparagus cut into 1 1/2-inch-long pieces
1 cup cleaned and sliced mushrooms
1 tablespoon chopped fresh basil
1/4 teaspoon each light salt, cracked black pepper, and lemon pepper (I use Lawry's)
Cayenne pepper to taste
1/4 cup freshly grated Parmesan

Serves 4

1 Drop the fresh fettuccine in boiling water and cook al dente (tender but firm). If you use fresh fettuccine, it needs only 2 to 4 minutes to cook. Rinse and drain.

2 In a large heavy skillet, melt the reduced-calorie butter and oil over medium-high heat. Sauté the shrimp, wine, green onions, and garlic until the shrimp are halfway done, about 5 minutes. Add red pepper and asparagus strips, mushrooms, and basil. Cook for 2 minutes longer or until shrimp are cooked. Do not overcook shrimp. Remove from heat and sprinkle shrimp with the salt and the 3 peppers. Mix well.

3 Toss the pasta with the cooked shrimp. Add the Parmesan and serve at once. Top with additional Parmesan if you like.

Per serving: *276 calories; 32 gm protein; 15 gm carbohydrates; 9.66 gm fat; 167 mg cholesterol; 1.04 gm fiber; 31% of calories from fat*

Sautéed Salmon Steaks with Lemon Thyme Butter

*T*art, tangy Lemon
Thyme butter is the
*crowning touch for these
nutritious and low-calorie
pan-sautéed salmon steaks
garnished with colorful
strips of red and green bell
pepper. Serve with
Sautéed New Potatoes in
Jackets and Lemoned
Squash Scramble.*

4 5-ounce center cut salmon steaks
¹/4 cup fresh lime juice
Non-stick cooking spray
Lulu's Special Seasoning
Lemon Thyme Butter
Red bell pepper strips (optional)
Green bell pepper strips (optional)
Mushroom slices (optional)
Fresh thyme (optional)

Serves 4

1   Rinse salmon steaks and pat dry with a paper towel. Sprinkle steaks with lime juice. Place in a baking dish or on a platter and let marinate in lime juice while you prepare the Lemon Thyme Butter.

2   Spray a large skillet with non-stick cooking spray. Over medium-high heat sauté steaks for approximately 3 minutes on the first side and 2 minutes on the second side. Turn over the first side for 1 minute longer. Salmon is done when the flesh in the center is barely opaque.

3   Remove steaks and keep slightly warm. Spoon sauce over fish.

4   Garnish with strips of red and green bell pepper and sliced fresh mushrooms, or a sprig of fresh thyme.

Lemon Thyme Butter

¹/4 cup reduced-calorie butter or
    margarine
1 tablespoon fresh lime juice
1 tablespoon fresh lemon juice
1 tablespoon chopped fresh parsley
1 teaspoon lemon thyme
1 teaspoon chervil

1 Melt reduced-calorie butter or margarine in saucepan and add all ingredients. Stir. Heat briefly. Keep warm while preparing salmon.

2 Spoon 1 tablespoon of flavored butter over each salmon steak.

Per serving: 289 calories; 35 gm protein; 2.05 gm carbohydrates; 13 gm fat; 100 mg cholesterol; .09 gm fiber; 40% of calories from fat

Sautéed Salmon Fillets with Minted Basil Butter

Quick, easy, and delicious! Serve with steamed yellow and green squash and new potatoes. There are five species of Pacific salmon in North American water: chinook or king, sockeye or red, pink or humpback, coho or silver, and chum or calico.

Serves 2 to 3

1 ³/4-pound fresh salmon fillet
  Lulu's Special Seasoning to taste
  Lemon pepper to taste
  Non-stick cooking spray
¹/4 cup reduced-calorie butter or margarine
2 tablespoons sauterne
1 tablespoon fresh lime or lemon juice
1 teaspoon chopped fresh basil
1 teaspoon chopped fresh mint

1 Sprinkle the salmon fillet with special seasoning and lemon pepper and let stand.

2 Spray a skillet with non-stick cooking spray. In the skillet blend the butter or margarine, sauterne, lime or lemon juice, basil, and mint. Cook over medium heat until sauce is hot. Add the prepared salmon and cook until salmon is flaky, about 3 minutes per side.

3 Serve at once, with sauce poured over, or to the side of the salmon. Garnish with sprigs of fresh basil and mint.

Per serving: 264 calories; 28 gm protein; 1.14 gm carbohydrates; 13 gm fat; 80 mg cholesterol; .12 gm fiber; 46% of calories from fat

Salmon Steaks with Lemon Dill Sauce

W ith today's bountiful world-wide supplies, you can now purchase excellent fresh salmon all year 'round. A cautionary note. All fish have bones, even the so-called "boneless" fillets. De-bone the fish by hand, but while you are eating, keep in mind that there are some bones you may have missed. For even cooking, select center-cut fillets, not from the tail end of the salmon.

4 5-ounce salmon steaks, center-cut preferred
1/4 cup fresh lime juice
    Non-stick cooking spray
    Lulu's Special Seasoning
    Summer savory
    Lemon Dill Sauce

Serves 4

1 Rinse salmon steaks and pat dry with paper towels. Place steaks in a dish. Sprinkle with lime juice and marinate while you prepare the Lemon Dill Sauce.

2 Preheat outdoor grill or broiler.

3 After you have prepared the sauce, and just before grilling, spray both sides of the marinated salmon steaks with the cooking spray. Lightly sprinkle both sides of steaks with special seasoning and summer savory.

4 Grill the steaks approximately 3 minutes per side or until the flesh is opaque. Keep the grill cover closed during cooking time.

5 Remove immediately. Spoon 1 tablespoon of Lemon Dill Sauce over each steak. For a beautiful garnish, use the airy fronds of the dill plant and a lemon twist.

Lemon Dill Sauce

1/4 cup olive oil
2 teaspoons corn syrup
1 teaspoon fresh lemon juice
1 teaspoon chopped fresh dill
1 teaspoon tarragon vinegar or any good white vinegar
1/8 teaspoon lemon
1/8 teaspoon onion powder
1/8 teaspoon paprika
1/8 teaspoon light salt

In a small saucepan over medium heat, combine and heat all the sauce ingredients. Keep warm until smoked salmon steaks are grilled and ready to be served.

Per serving: *365 calories; 26 gm protein; 2.84 gm carbohydrates; 27 gm fat; 75 mg cholesterol; .13 gm fiber; 67% of calories from fat*

Glazed Halibut

H alibut, a white, firm-fleshed fish is available from May through mid-July. If you cannot find Oriental sweet sauce, the closest substitute is Tiger Sauce, available in the Oriental foods section of some supermarkets.

2 6-ounce halibut steaks
2 tablespoons fresh lime juice
1 1/2 tablespoons light soy sauce
1 1/2 teaspoons Oriental sweet chili sauce
1 teaspoon fresh grated ginger
1 teaspoon chopped fresh garlic
1 teaspoon Oriental sesame oil
1/2 teaspoon sugar

Serves 2

1 Place halibut steaks in a shallow glass baking dish. In a small bowl, blend remaining ingredients. Pour marinade over fish. Marinate 1 hour turning fish several times.

151

2 About 10 minutes before you are ready to cook, preheat broiler. Broil the steaks, basting them with the marinade, until the flesh is cooked and flaky and the surface is slightly glossy and glazed. Allow 10 minutes total cooking time per inch thickness of fish.

Per serving: *312 calories; 41 gm protein; 2.5 gm carbohydrates; 14 gm fat; 124 mg cholesterol; .06 gm fiber; 40% of calories from fat*

Grilled Peppered Salmon Steaks with Cabernet Sauce

Deliciously different! The Cabernet sauce also goes well with chicken and beef.

5 tablespoons reduced-calorie butter or margarine, divided use
1/3 cup fresh peeled, deseeded, and chopped tomatoes
1 tablespoon finely chopped fresh shallot
1 teaspoon finely chopped fresh garlic
1 1/2 cups Cabernet Sauvignon
2 tablespoons Balsamic vinegar
1 cup low-sodium chicken or fish stock
3 tablespoons crushed black peppercorns
3 tablespoons grated fresh ginger

Serves 4

4 5-ounce salmon steaks

1 Preheat grill.

2 To make sauce, in a saucepan over medium heat, melt 2 tablespoons of reduced-calorie butter or margarine. Sauté the tomatoes, shallots, and garlic until tender, stirring occasionally. Add the wine and vinegar, and cook until only half the quantity of sauce remains. Add the stock and again reduce the volume by half. Remove the sauce from the heat and one tablespoon at a time, whisk in the remaining 3 tablespoons of reduced-calorie butter or margarine, whisking well between each addition. Keep the sauce warm until ready to serve. You may want to use a thermos.

3 In a bowl, mix together the crushed peppercorns and ginger, and use this to coat both sides of the salmon steaks.

4 Over medium heat, grill the coated steaks 8 to 10 minutes or until flesh is cooked and flaky.

5 To serve, pour the sauce around the steaks.

Per serving: *391 calories; 31 gm protein; 5 16 gm carbohydrates; 20 gm fat; 84 mg cholesterol; .17 gm fiber; 45% of calories from fat*

Grilled Orange Roughy

O*range roughy is delightfully mild, white-fleshed, low-calorie fish that comes from New Zealand. I buy the boneless fillets. Serve it with Trio of Grilled Bell Peppers, a steamed vegetable, and your choice of fresh fruit.*

Serves 2

2 5-to-6-ounce orange roughy fillets
2 tablespoons sauterne
1 tablespoon fresh lime juice
1 tablespoon very finely chopped onion
1/4 teaspoon white pepper
1/4 teaspoon Cavender's Greek Seasoning
2 tablespoons light mayonnaise
Chopped fresh parsley (optional)
Lemon slices (optional)
Orange slices (optional)

1 Preheat grill.

2 In a dish large enough to hold the fillets, combine the wine, lime juice, onion, pepper, and Cavender's; then whisk in the mayonnaise until well blended. Add the fillets and marinate one hour at room temperature, turning several times to coat the fillets well.

3 Grill the fillets about 10 minutes or until flesh flakes when probed with a fork. Garnish with chopped parsley and lemon and orange twists.

Per serving: *177 calories; 30 gm protein; 3.68 gm carbohydrates; 3.2 gm fat; 76 mg cholesterol; .05 gm fiber; 16% of calories from fat*

Trout in Cream

T his flavorful fish is simple to prepare. To remove the bones from the trout, slide a knife along the entire length of the backbone, cutting the trout in half. Starting from the tail, lift out the entire backbone. It should lift out in one piece.

Serves 2

2 whole fresh trout
1 tablespoon fresh lemon juice
1 teaspoon fresh chopped dill (¹/₄ teaspoon dried)
Light salt and white pepper to taste
Non-stick cooking spray
¹/₃ cup 2% milk
¹/₃ cup whipping cream
1 tablespoon fresh bread crumbs, seasoned with a pinch of freshly chopped parsley
Pinch of dried summer savory

1 Rinse trout and pat dry with paper towel.

2 Sprinkle the fish inside and out with the lemon juice, dill, salt, and pepper.

3 Spray a baking dish with non-stick cooking spray and place trout in a baking dish. Blend the milk with the cream and pour over the trout. Sprinkle with parsleyed bread crumbs. Bake in the preheated 400° oven for 15 minutes or until the flesh near the middle of the fish flakes easily when probed with a fork.

Per serving: *317 calories; 23 gm protein; 4.32 gm carbohydrates; 22 gm fat; 118 mg cholesterol; .08 gm fiber; 62% of calories from fat*

Orange Roughy Meunière

Fish cooked à la meunière is seasoned, lightly floured, and quickly sautéed in butter. Serve with an arugula and romaine salad and Glazed Carrots.

Serves 2

2 orange roughy fillets
1/4 cup flour
1/4 teaspoon Lulu's Special Seasoning
1/4 teaspoon dried summer savory
1/8 to 1/4 teaspoon cracked black pepper
1/8 teaspoon light salt
1/4 cup egg substitute in a small bowl
3 tablespoons reduced-calorie butter or margarine
1 tablespoon olive oil
1 whole, fork-pressed garlic clove
1 teaspoon each fresh lemon and lime juice

For Extra Sauce

2 tablespoons reduced-calorie butter or margarine
1 teaspoon fresh lime juice
1/4 teaspoon lemon thyme or a pinch of dried thyme

1 Place fish fillets on a plate.

2 On a double square of wax paper combine the flour, special seasoning, summer savory, pepper, and salt.

3 Dip fish in egg substitute then dredge each fillet in the seasoned flour.

4 In a skillet over medium heat, melt the butter or margarine. Add oil, garlic, and juices. Heat until bubbly; remove garlic.

5 Add the seasoned fish fillets and sauté 4 to 5 minutes per side, turning the fillets just once. The fish should be a golden brown. Transfer fish to a warm serving plate, pouring any pan juices over the fish.

6 For the extra sauce, place the reduced-calorie butter or margarine, lime juice, and thyme in a glass measuring cup and microwave on high for 30 seconds. Whisk. Serve hot.

Per serving: 371 calories; 30 gm protein; 13 gm carbohydrates; 20 gm fat; 0.0 mg cholesterol; .19 gm fiber; 49% of calories from fat

Bass Au Gratin

For variety you can substitute trout, flounder, haddock, red snapper—virtually any 2¹/₂-to-3-pound whole, pan-dressed boned fish for the bass. A pan-dressed fish has been scaled, boned, and gutted. Its head, tail, and fins have been removed. Au gratin indicates the presence of bread crumbs.

Serves 2

2 12-ounce whole, pan-dressed bass, rinsed and patted dry with paper towels
Light salt and black pepper to taste
Non-stick cooking spray
¹/₄ pound thickly sliced mushrooms
4 tablespoons reduced-calorie butter or margarine (divided)
1 tablespoon flour
¹/₃ cup dry white wine
¹/₃ cup water
2 tablespoons tomato purée
¹/₂ cup fresh bread crumbs (for fresh bread crumbs, crumble 2 slices of white or whole wheat bread and process in a blender or food processor)
Chopped fresh parsley to taste (I use 1 tablespoon per fish)

1 Preheat oven to 400°.

2 Season fish with salt and pepper to taste and place fish in an oblong baking dish sprayed with non-stick cooking spray. Set aside.

3 Sauté the mushrooms in 3 tablespoons of the butter until soft, 4 to 5 minutes. Blend in flour.

4 Stir in the wine, water, and tomato purée and season, if needed, with salt and pepper. Pour mixture over fish.

5 Sprinkle with bread crumbs and dot fish with remaining tablespoon butter. Bake in the 400° oven for 20 minutes or until the fish flesh is flaky and the bread crumbs are brown.

6 Garnish with chopped parsley.

Per serving: *673 calories; 91 gm protein; 11 gm carbohydrates; 23 gm fat; 0 mg cholesterol; .68 gm fiber; 31% of calories from fat*

Mesquite-Grilled Truite de Herbes

T *rout is 42 calories per edible ounce. I prefer to use "dressed" trout, which means scaled and eviscerated.*

Serves 2

2 12-ounce, ready-to-cook trout, smaller if desired
Lemon pepper to taste
Lulu's Special Seasoning to taste or any low-sodium herb and spice combination
3 tablespoons olive oil
1 1/2 tablespoons Balsamic vinegar
1 tablespoon light soy sauce
1 teaspoon minced fresh garlic
Cracked black pepper to taste
2 3-inch-long sprigs fresh rosemary
2 3-inch-long sprigs fresh thyme
2 3-inch-long sprigs fresh mint
2 3-inch-long fresh oregano
2 slices bacon

1 Preheat grill, adding mesquite or hickory chips.

2 Rinse trout and pat dry. Place in a dish and sprinkle to taste with lemon pepper and special seasoning.

THE 30-MINUTE LIGHT GOURMET

3   In a small bowl or container combine the oil, vinegar, soy sauce, garlic, and pepper. Brush both sides of the trout with the oil and vinegar mixture until most of the mixture is used. Stuff each trout with half the herbs and one slice of bacon.

4   Grill covered over preheated mesquite and/or hickory and charcoal fire for about 10 minutes on the first side and about 7 minutes on the second side or until desired degree of doneness is reached. Watch trout (or for that matter any grilled fish) to prevent overcooking.

5   Pour remaining oil/vinegar mixture over the trout and serve at once. To debone trout, slide your boning knife along the backbone, stopping just behind the head, then lift out the entire backbone. Serve at once.

Per serving: *585 calories; 45 gm protein; 2.41 gm carbohydrates; 42 gm fat; 147 mg cholesterol; .05 gm fiber; 65% of calories from fat*

Herb-Baked Red Fish
with Brown Scallop Sauce

P lain baked red fish is delicious, but the added brown sauce is so elegant. For the garnish I sprinkle the red fish with sautéed scallops and serve the brown sauce along side. Always make sure that the fish is very fresh.

Baked Red Fish

1   **(1½ pound) whole dressed red fish, rinsed and drained**
1   **thinly sliced onion**
1   **thinly sliced lemon**
1   **tablespoon instant vegetable bouillon dissolved in 1 cup hot water**
1   **cup sauterne or dry white wine Lulu's Special Seasoning to taste Lemon Pepper to taste**
2   **to 3 sprigs each of fresh parsley, oregano, basil, rosemary, and mint**
2   **tablespoons reduced-calorie butter or margarine**

158

Brown Scallop Sauce

2 tablespoons reduced-calorie butter
   or margarine
1/4 cup chopped shallots
1/2 pound bay scallops
2 tablespoons sauterne or dry white
   wine
1 teaspoon fresh lime or lemon juice
   Lulu's Special Seasoning to taste
   Lemon pepper to taste

Serves 3 to 4   1/4 cup half and half

1 Preheat oven to 400°.

2 In a large ovenproof baking dish, layer sliced onion and then sliced lemon. Lay the red fish on top. Pour the broth and wine over the fish, sprinkle the fish with special seasoning and lemon pepper to taste, and then cover the entire fish with the fresh herbs. Dot with the reduced-calorie butter or margarine and bake in the preheated 400° oven for 30 minutes.

3 Meanwhile, to prepare sauce, melt the butter in a skillet over medium heat. Add the shallots, and cook until tender. Add the scallops, wine, lemon or lime juice, special seasoning, and the lemon pepper. Cook until scallops are opaque, about 8–10 minutes. Remove scallops and set aside for garnish. Cook sauce until you have about 1/4 cup sauce, then whisk in the half and half. Let sauce simmer for several minutes longer or until the sauce thickens slightly. Set aside and keep warm.

4 When fish is done, discard herbs. Transfer fish to a warm serving platter. Sprinkle with the cooked scallops, and serve with the brown sauce.

Per serving: *407 calories; 44 gm protein; 12 gm carbohydrates; 8.43 gm fat; 26 mg cholesterol; .22 gm fiber; 19% of calories from fat*

Saffroned Sea Scallops

I like to use the 10 to 20 count per pound sea scallops. Serve the scallops over cooked rice or angel hair pasta. I sometimes top each serving with a dab of microwave Hollandaise Sauce and broil until the sauce bubbles. Telma soup base is available in the Kosher or Jewish food section of many supermarkets.

Serves 2 or 3

2 tablespoons reduced-calorie butter or margarine
2 tablespoons sauterne
1 tablespoon chopped shallots
1/2 teaspoon chopped garlic
1/2 cube Telma brand mushroom soup base dissolved in 1/4 cup hot water
1/2 pound (10 to 20 count) rinsed and drained sea scallops
8 ounces thickly sliced mushrooms
1/4 cup 2% milk
1/4 cup half and half
1/8 teaspoon crushed saffron threads soaked in 1 tablespoon water
1 teaspoon lemon juice
1/4 to 1/2 teaspoon sugar
1/4 teaspoon Parsley Plus
1/4 teaspoon Lulu's Special Seasoning
1/4 teaspoon light salt
1/4 teaspoon freshly ground black pepper
1/4 teaspoon summer savory

1 In a large heavy skillet over medium heat, melt the butter. Add the wine, shallots, and garlic. Sauté about 3 minutes, stirring as needed.

2 Stir in the mushroom soup base dissolved in water.

3 Add the scallops and mushrooms, and cook until scallops are done, turning frequently. Remove scallops and mushrooms, but keep warm.

4 Stir in all the remaining ingredients. Cook, stirring occasionally, until the sauce's volume has been reduced by half and the sauce

thickens. Return the scallops and mushrooms to the sauce and reheat briefly. Serve with or without the Hollandaise Sauce.

Per serving: *155 calories; 13 gm protein; 6.35 gm carbohydrates; 6.99 gm fat; 36 mg cholesterol; .08 gm fiber; 41% of calories from fat*

Grilled Halibut
with Rosemary Lime Butter

J ust try it! Halibut is a white-fleshed fish. One ounce contains only 55 calories.

Serves 2 to 4

4 4-ounce halibut steaks (1 per serving)
Olive oil
Light salt and black pepper to taste
1/4 cup of Red Bell Pepper Butter, softened
2 tablespoons fresh lime juice
1 teaspoon finely chopped fresh garlic
1 tablespoon fresh minced rosemary
1/2 teaspoon dried summer savory

1 Preheat or fire up your grill.

2 Rub the halibut steaks with olive oil and sprinkle lightly with light salt and pepper. Let stand at room temperature for 30 minutes, if possible.

3 To prepare butter, in a small bowl blend Red Bell Pepper Butter with lime juice, garlic, rosemary, and summer savory and set aside. Rosemary lime butter can be prepared ahead of time.

4 Grill the steaks about 4 minutes per side, turning once. Allow 10 minutes total cooking time per inch thickness of fish. Fish is done when the flesh is flaky.

5 Serve with the Rosemary Lime Butter at once.

Per serving: *242 calories; 25 gm protein; .69 gm carbohydrates; 15 gm fat; 78 mg cholesterol; .03 gm fiber; 56% of calories from fat*

Blackened Fillet of Fish

U*se your favorite fish fillet. I have used red fish, pompano, red snapper, catfish, and others with excellent results. And, yes, every time I prepare this dish indoors, it sets off my fire alarm system.*

Serves 3

3 teaspoons paprika
1 teaspoon garlic powder
1 teaspoon onion powder
2 teaspoons light salt
1 teaspoon crushed red pepper
1 teaspoon white pepper
1 teaspoon black pepper
1/2 teaspoon thyme
1/2 teaspoon oregano
3 3/4-inch-thick fish fillets
1/2 cup melted reduced-calorie butter or margarine

1 On a square of waxed paper, mix together the paprika, garlic and onion powder, salt, the 3 peppers, thyme, and oregano. This is your blackening mixture.

2 Brush the fish fillets with the melted butter or margarine, coating both sides.

3 Generously sprinkle both sides of the fish with the blackened mixture, coating both sides well.

4 Heat a large cast-iron skillet over very high heat until it is beyond the smoking stage, about 10 minutes. The skillet cannot be too hot for this dish.

5 Place the blackened fillets in the heated skillet, add 1 teaspoon melted reduced-calorie butter or margarine on top of each fillet. Cook fish 2 minutes per side. Serve immediately.

Per serving: *236 calories; 18 gm protein; 0 gm carbohydrates; 16 gm fat; 0 mg cholesterol; 0 gm fiber; 61% of calories from fat*

BEEF
&
VEAL:
THE LIGHT TOUCH

Veal Chops with Sautéed Vegetables and Avocado Sauce

This dish is great for everyday or for entertaining cuisine. It is elegant, easy, and pretty.

2 veal loin chops, about 3/4 to 1 pound total weight
Lulu's Special Seasoning to taste
Lemon pepper to taste
Flour to taste (I keep it in a shaker, like salt)
2 tablespoons reduced-calorie butter or margarine
1 fresh garlic clove, pressed with a fork
1/2 cup coarsely diced tomato
4 ounces thickly sliced mushrooms
1/4 medium slivered red bell pepper
1/4 medium slivered green bell pepper
1 small onion, sliced into rings, separated
1 tablespoon olive oil
1/4 cup 2% milk
1/4 cup half and half
1/4 cup low-sodium beef broth
1/4 cup diced avocado
2 tablespoons sauterne
1 teaspoon reduced-calorie butter or margarine, melted
1/4 teaspoon light salt
1/8 teaspoon cracked black pepper

Serves 2 to 3

1 Sprinkle the veal with special seasoning, lemon pepper, and flour. In a large skillet over medium heat, sauté the first side of the chops in the butter and pressed garlic until a medium golden brown.

2 Move the chops to one side of the skillet. Discard the garlic and turn the chops over to sauté the second side. Add the vegetables and sprinkle with 1 tablespoon olive oil. Sauté vegetables until they are tender but still retain some texture. Transfer chops and vegetables to a warm serving platter and keep warm.

3 Meanwhile, in a blender, combine the milk, half and half, broth, avocado, sauterne, butter, salt, and pepper, and process until smooth. Pour sauce into the empty skillet. Stirring constantly, cook sauce about 5 minutes, or until it thickens slightly. Serve the sauce alongside the veal chops and vegetables.

Per serving: *731 calories; 85 gm protein; 13 gm carbohydrates; 34 gm fat; 13 mg cholesterol; 1.5 gm fiber; 42% of calories from fat*

Bourbon Marinated Steaks

U*se a fillet steak, T-bone, porterhouse, or any well-trimmed strip steak. I like to use a 1 1/2-inch-thick fillet steak. The beef is marinated prior to pan sautéing, broiling, or grilling.*

Serves 2 to 4

1/4 cup bourbon
2 tablespoons olive or corn oil
1 tablespoon Worcestershire sauce
3 garlic cloves, finely chopped or pressed
1 tablespoon finely chopped onion
1/4 teaspoon lemon pepper
1/4 teaspoon garlic pepper
2 to 4 small fillets of beef, 1 1/2 inches thick, about 6 uncooked ounces per person

1 Blend the bourbon, oil, Worcestershire, garlic, onion, and peppers in a baking dish or casserole. Add the steaks, coating both sides with the marinade, and refrigerate. Marinate several hours if possible, turning several times. Remove from refrigerator 30 minutes before cooking.

2 Preheat a heavy-bottom skillet, broiler, or grill.

3 Cook to desired degree of doneness. To grill, cook the steaks about 5 minutes per side in a covered grill.

Per serving: *183 calories; 16 gm protein; 1.89 gm carbohydrates; 8.9 gm fat; 0 mg cholesterol; .01 gm fiber; 44% of calories from fat*

Standing Rib Roast
with Horseradish Cream

This is what I mean by "treat yourself." Since a rib roast is a high-fat meat, eat a small portion and trim away all the visible fat. Rib roast is expensive, so make sure that your butcher trims it well. The Horseradish Cream is also grand served over sliced, ripe tomatoes.

Serves 4

1 3 1/2-pound rib roast, well trimmed (3 ribs)
1 teaspoon Lulu's Special Seasoning
1 teaspoon ground black pepper
1/4 cup liquid cane syrup, or 1/4 cup packed dark brown sugar moistened with 1 to 2 tablespoons water
Horseradish Cream

1 Preheat oven to 375°.

2 Rub the roast with special seasoning, pepper, and the liquid cane syrup.

3 Roast in the preheated 375° oven for 40 minutes. Reduce heat to 325°, and cook for 20 minutes longer, or until desired degree of doneness.

4 Place on a serving platter and garnish as desired (try parsley, julienned carrots and yellow squash, and cherry tomatoes). Carve and serve with the Horseradish Cream.

Horseradish Cream

1/4 cup light mayonnaise
1/4 cup light sour cream
3 tablespoons prepared horseradish
1/4 teaspoon light salt
Makes 1/2 cup cream 1/4 teaspoon Worcestershire sauce

166

Blend all ingredients. Chill several hours if possible.

Per serving with cream: *802 calories; 111 gm protein; 17 gm carbohydrates; 35 gm fat; 271 mg cholesterol; .1 gm fiber; 39% of calories from fat*

Per tablespoon cream: *24 calories; .58 gm protein; 1.92 gm carbohydrates; 1.75 gm fat; 1 mg cholesterol; .08 gm fiber; 65% of calories from fat*

Veal Tenderloin in Honey Cream

O*ut of this world! If you cannot find a veal tender, use a veal steak, turkey tenderloin, or boneless chicken breast. Serve with cooked pasta or rice and Lemoned Squash Scramble.*

Serves 3 to 4

3/4 to 1 pound veal tenderloin
1 tablespoon vegetable oil
   Lulu's Special Seasoning
   Parsley Plus
   Garlic pepper
3 tablespoons reduced-calorie butter
   or margarine
1 tablespoon finely chopped shallot
2 tablespoons fresh orange juice
1 tablespoon honey
1/3 cup half and half

1 Fire up your grill.

2 Meanwhile, rub the veal with oil so the herbs will stick. Sprinkle to taste with special seasoning, parsley plus, and garlic pepper. Let stand at room temperature for 30 minutes before grilling. Over medium heat, cook the veal about 5 to 7 minutes per side, basting it with the following as needed.

3 In a saucepan, melt the butter, add the shallot, and over medium heat, sauté until tender. Stir in the juice and honey. Use half of this mixture to baste the veal. Add the ⅓ cup of cream to the other half and over medium heat, reduce the sauce until it thickens slightly, whisking as needed.

4 Slice the grilled tender into medallion-shaped pieces and dribble the sauce over them. Serve at once.

Per serving: *348 calories; 41 gm protein; 7.9 gm carbohydrates; 16 gm fat; 7.34 mg cholesterol; .1 gm fiber; 41% of calories from fat*

Veal Piccata

Y ou can substitute two 6-ounce boneless chicken breasts for the veal in this recipe. Just pound the breasts to ¼-inch thickness.

Serves 2

3 tablespoons flour
¼ teaspoon light salt
⅛ teaspoon black pepper
½ pound veal scallops
1 tablespoon reduced-calorie butter or margarine
1 cup sliced mushrooms
1 minced garlic clove
¼ cup sauterne or dry white wine
2 tablespoons chopped fresh parsley
1 tablespoon fresh lemon juice

1 In a small bowl blend the flour, salt, and pepper. Dredge the veal in the seasoned flour, coating both sides lightly. Reserve seasoned flour.

2 In a skillet large enough to hold the veal, melt the butter or margarine over medium-high heat. Add the veal and brown it quickly on both sides. Transfer to a warm platter and keep warm.

3 In the same skillet, sauté the mushrooms and garlic over medium-high heat, stirring constantly. Cook until mushrooms are lightly browned.

4 Sprinkle the mushrooms with the remaining seasoned flour and stir quickly to combine. Gradually add the wine, parsley, and lemon juice, bring to a boil, then reduce the heat and simmer until the sauce thickens slightly. Pour sauce over the veal. Sprinkle with additional chopped parsley. Serve at once.

Per serving: 341 calories; 43 gm protein; 15 gm carbohydrates; 9.09 gm fat; 0 mg cholesterol; 85 gm fiber; 24% of calories from fat

Glazed Blue Cheese Veal Balls

T his recipe is for those who love the combination of blue cheese and veal. Serve these flavorful veal balls as an entree over your favorite cooked pasta or in a chafing dish as a hot appetizer.

Makes 12 meatballs

1 pound ground veal
1/3 cup crumbled blue cheese
1/4 cup chopped onion
2 teaspoons Worcestershire sauce
1/2 teaspoon Lulu's Special Seasoning
1/4 cup reduced-caloric butter or margarine
1/2 cup evaporated skim milk
Chopped fresh parsley (optional)

1 Blend the veal, blue cheese, onion, Worcestershire, and special seasoning, and shape into equal-size meatballs.

2 Melt the butter in a large skillet. Add the meatballs and brown on all sides. Cover skillet, reduce heat to low and cook 5 minutes longer.

3 Transfer meatballs to a warm serving dish. Add milk to skillet drippings. Cook glaze over medium-high heat, stirring occasionally, for about 2 minutes or until satiny.

4 Spoon glaze over meatballs and sprinkle with parsley.

Per meatball: 97 calories; 12 gm protein; 1.46 gm carbohydrates; 4.2 gm fat; 3.56 mg cholesterol; .01 gm fiber; 39% of calories from fat

Green Chiles Flank
with Tomatoes and Squash

This dish features an unusual combination of colors, flavors, and textures. It is delicious and different. I make it in my wok, but you can make it in a large skillet. Do not overcook. Serve over cooked rice.

Serves 4

1 pound tomatoes, peeled, deseeded, and cut into large chunks
1/2 teaspoon light salt
1/2 large avocado, peeled and diced
1 tablespoon fresh lime juice
2 tablespoons olive oil, divided use
3/4 to 1 pound flank steak, cut against the grain into 2 1/2-inch-long strips
1 1/2 cups peeled, seeded, and diced acorn squash
1/2 small onion, thinly sliced
2 tablespoons minced fresh green Anaheim pepper
1 teaspoon chopped garlic
1 teaspoon ground cumin
1/2 teaspoon ground coriander
1/8 to 1/4 teaspoon cayenne pepper
1/3 cup low-sodium chicken stock mixed with 1 teaspoon arrowroot
3 tablespoons white wine
2 tablespoons chopped fresh cilantro

1 In a bowl, toss tomatoes with the salt. Set aside.

2 In a separate bowl, combine the avocado and lime juice.

3 Heat 1 tablespoon of the oil over high heat in a wok or skillet. Add beef and brown on all sides, about 2 minutes. Transfer beef to a warm bowl and keep warm. To skillet add and heat remaining 1 tablespoon oil. Stir in the squash, onion, pepper, garlic, cumin, coriander, and cayenne, and stir about 20 seconds. Stir in the stock with arrowroot, add wine, and cook 1 minute longer. Cover and cook until the squash is almost tender, 2 to 4 minutes.

4   Add the tomatoes, beef, and any exuded meat juices and cook
    about 1½ minutes for medium-rare meat.

5   Stir in the avocado and cilantro and toss well. Serve at once.

*Per serving: 403 calories; 38 gm protein; 18 gm carbohydrates; 18 gm fat; 128 mg
cholesterol; 2.6 gm fiber; 40% of calories from fat*

Gingered Tenderloin of Beef

*If you only like well-
done steaks, I suggest
that you choose another
recipe. Tenderloin is too
delicious to be cooked
more than medium. I
always trim off any excess
fat from the meat's
surface. Garnish with a
sprig of fresh herbs.*

Serves 4

1 ¼ pounds beef tenderloin
    Lulu's Special Seasoning to taste
    Garlic pepper to taste
    Lemon pepper to taste
1   tablespoon olive oil
1   tablespoon Worcestershire sauce
    A large knob fresh ginger, peeled
    and thinly sliced into rounds,
    about ⅓ cup
¼ cup dry sherry

1   Preheat oven to 500°.

2   Lightly sprinkle the beef with special seasoning and peppers.
    Place oil and Worcestershire in the bottom of the baking dish,
    then roll the beef in it.

3   Cover surface of the beef with thin slices of ginger, baste with
    the sherry. Place in the preheated 500° oven and immediately
    reduce the heat to 350°. Cook 15 to 30 minutes in all, or until a
    meat thermometer inserted into the meat registers 125° for rare
    or 140° for medium. Let stand 10 minutes before carving.

*Per serving: 315 calories; 42 gm protein; 1.8 gm carbohydrates; 13 gm fat; 100 mg
cholesterol; 0 gm fiber; 37% of calories from fat*

Peppered Steak Flambé

I n this recipe I use green peppercorns, which are merely immature black peppercorns. To flambé meat, pour 1 ounce of hot (not boiling) brandy over each cooked steak and ignite. Let the liqueur burn out on its own. Serve immediately either plain or with a sauce. Filet mignons (cut from the tenderloin) are one of the few steaks that I serve my family because they are virtually free from fat.

2 tablespoons rinsed drained green peppercorns (*poivre vert*)
1 tablespoon reduced-calorie butter or margarine
1 teaspoon Dijon mustard
4 1-inch-thick filet mignons
1 tablespoon olive or peanut oil
8 tablespoons hot brandy (2 tablespoons per steak)
Light salt to taste (optional)
1 tablespoon finely chopped shallots
1 teaspoon tomato paste
1/4 cup whipping cream
1/4 cup 2% milk
1/4 cup sauterne

Serves 4

1 Using a rolling pin or a mortar and pestle, crush the peppercorns and blend to a paste with the butter and mustard. Coat both sides of each steak with this paste. Cover steaks and refrigerate for 2 hours if possible. Otherwise, cover and let stand at room temperature for 1 hour before cooking.

2 Heat oil in a large heavy skillet over medium-high heat. Add steaks, and sauté 3 to 4 minutes per side for a rare steak, 5 minutes per side for a medium steak, turning only once so each side of the steak browns well.

3 Remove skillet from the heat. Sprinkle the brandy over the steaks and very carefully ignite from the side of the skillet (so you don't ignite your hand). While flames diminish, baste steaks with the pan juices.

4 Transfer steaks to a warm serving platter, and sprinkle with salt. Keep steaks warm.

5 Return the skillet to the heat. Add all remaining ingredients. Stirring frequently, cook quickly until the sauce is slightly thickened and reduced by about one-fourth.

6 Pour the sauce evenly over the warm steaks and serve at once.

Per serving: *445 calories; 33 gm protein; 3.8 gm carbohydrates; 21 gm fat; 113 mg cholesterol; .04 gm fiber; 42% of calories from fat*

Wiener Schnitzel

A Viennese treat, Wiener Schnitzel are thin, boneless, veal scallops that are breaded then quickly sautéed (usually in butter) and garnished with lemon and lime slices and capers.

Serves 3

3 5-ounce boneless veal scallops, pounded thin with a flat metal meat mallet
Light salt and black pepper to taste
1/4 cup egg substitute
1/3 cup dry bread crumbs mixed with 2 tablespoons flour
3 tablespoons reduced-calorie margarine
Lemon slices
Lime slices

1 Lightly sprinkle the scallops with the salt and pepper.

2 Dip scallops into the egg substitute, then into the bread crumbs and flour.

3 In a large skillet over medium-high heat, melt the margarine and quickly sauté the scallops, turning once (this helps the breading adhere to the veal), until both sides are golden brown.

4 Garnish and serve hot.

Per serving: *302 calories; 36 gm protein; 8.25 gm carbohydrates; 12 gm fat; 100 mg cholesterol; .44 gm fiber; 36% of calories from fat*

Tournedos with Filled Artichoke Bottoms and Béarnaise Sauce

T ournedos are thick, 3½- to 4-ounce, tender slices of meat cut from the narrow end of a fillet of beef (tenderloin). The tenderloin is my favorite cut of beef because it is both lean and tender. Béarnaise is a most suitable sauce. Serve with a robust red wine.

Serves 4

4 freshly cooked, warm artichoke bottoms or 4 canned artichoke bottoms, rinsed, drained, and gently warmed in liquid from can
1 10-ounce box frozen green peas, cooked according to package directions and drained
2 tablespoons reduced-calorie butter or margarine
4 1-inch thick tournedos, about 12 ounces of meat
Cracked black pepper to taste
Light salt to taste
Microwave Béarnaise Sauce

1 Fill artichoke bottoms with peas and keep warm. Refrigerate any leftover peas.

2 Melt the butter in a large skillet and sauté tournedos over medium-high heat until brown on both sides. Beef will be rare. Continue cooking until beef has achieved degree of doneness desired. Sprinkle with salt and pepper.

3 Slip one tournedo under each filled artichoke bottom. Drizzle with warm béarnaise.

Per serving: *314 calories; 32 gm protein; 19 gm carbohydrates; 12 gm fat; 85 mg cholesterol; 2.17 gm fiber; 34% of calories from fat*

Cheese- and Herb-Stuffed Flank Steak

W hat's nice about flank steak is that you pay for the meat and not fat or bone.

1 1/4 pounds flank steak
2 teaspoons Oriental chili oil
  Dijon mustard to taste
  Lemon Pepper to taste
  Garlic Pepper to taste
2 ounces softened light cream cheese
1 ounce softened blue cheese
1/4 cup chopped fresh parsley
2 tablespoons crumbled cooked bacon
1 tablespoon fresh tarragon, or 1 teaspoon dried
1 tablespoon fresh thyme, or 1 teaspoon dried
1 teaspoon chopped shallot
1/2 cup beef broth

Serves 4

1 Preheat oven to 350°.

2 Rub both sides of flank with the chili oil and mustard, then sprinkle to taste with the lemon and garlic peppers.

3 Blend all ingredients except beef broth in a small bowl.

4 Spread one side of the flank with the cheese-herb mixture. Then roll the steak up and secure it with toothpicks.

5 Seam side down, place rolled flank steak in an oven-proof baking dish. Add the broth (to prevent sticking).

6 Bake in the preheated 350° oven for 45 minutes, basting once or twice.

Per serving: *399 calories; 48 gm protein; 1.5 gm carbohydrates; 21 gm fat; 151 mg cholesterol; .01 gm fiber; 47% of calories from fat*

Marinated Eye-of-Round Roast

E ssentially fat-free, the eye-of-round (cut from the hindquarter) is especially suitable for long, moist cooking. Marinating tenderizes and flavors the meat. Serve with Tarragon Horseradish Cream. Use leftovers for Beef Salad with Sweet Pepper Dressing.

Serves 4

1 2-pound eye-of-round roast
4 cloves garlic, sliced in half
Garlic pepper to taste
Lemon pepper to taste
1/4 cup chopped fresh parsley
2 tablespoons chopped fresh basil
2 tablespoons chopped fresh oregano

Marinade

1/4 cup dry red wine
2 tablespoons olive oil
2 tablespoons light soy sauce
2 tablespoons Worcestershire sauce

1 Make 8 slits 1/2-inch deep in the meat and fill each slit with a garlic clove half. Place roast in a medium bowl.

2 Combine marinade ingredients. Pour over meat and marinate the roast at room temperature for 1 hour. Drain off marinade and discard.

3 Preheat oven to 450°.

4 Sprinkle meat to taste with the garlic pepper and lemon pepper. Roll the roast in the parsley, basil, and oregano. Transfer meat to a roasting pan. Cover pan.

5 Roast in the preheated 450° oven for 20 minutes. Uncover and cook 10 minutes longer or until an internal temperature of 140° is reached. Serve with Tarragon Horseradish Cream.

Per serving: *293 calories; 36 gm protein; 2 gm carbohydrates; 15 gm fat; 107 mg cholesterol; 0 gm fiber; 46% of calories from fat*

Veal Steak with Mushroom Herb Cream

If you have a hard time finding a veal steak, you can substitute a veal chop or veal scallops. With this steak serve Warm Asparagus Pasta Salad with Balsamic Lemon Vinaigrette and fresh sliced Roma tomatoes. If need be, substitute dried herbs for fresh but remember when substituting to use 1/3 teaspoon powdered and 1/2 teaspoon crushed for every tablespoon of fresh chopped herbs.

1 tablespoon reduced-calorie butter or margarine
1 pound veal sirloin steak, cut from the leg
1/4 pound cleaned and thickly sliced mushrooms (if you want to get fancy, use quartered shiitake or oyster mushrooms)
1/2 cup sauterne
1/2 cup beef or veal stock, or instant beef bouillon (I prefer homemade)
2 tablespoons half and half
Cracked black pepper to taste
1 teaspoon each chopped fresh parsley, thyme, and tarragon

Serves 2

1 Melt the butter in a large skillet over medium heat. Add the steak, and sauté it about 5 minutes per side turning only once. Add mushrooms and toss them about the skillet for several minutes coating them with the pan juices.

2 Add the wine and stock. Cook uncovered for 10 minutes. Transfer steak to a warm plate. Add the half and half, pepper, and herbs to the skillet. Cook gently until 1/3 cup sauce remains in the skillet. Pour sauce over steak. Serve at once.

Per serving: 546 calories; 82 gm protein; 4.75 gm carbohydrates; 17 gm fat; 6 mg cholesterol; .34 gm fiber; 28% of calories from fat

177

Beef Patties Chasseur

C hasseur, a French term, indicates that the food is being served "hunter's style"—with a multitude of mushrooms. Veal and chicken chasseur are classic French fare, but my ground beef variation is delicious.

Serves 4

1 pound lean ground beef
2 tablespoons reduced-calorie butter or margarine
1/2 pound thickly sliced mushrooms
1 tablespoon finely chopped shallot
1 cup dry white wine
1 cup low-sodium beef broth
1 teaspoon each dried chervil and tarragon
2 tablespoons chopped fresh parsley

1 Shape the beef into 3 or 4 1-inch-thick oval patties. In a skillet over medium heat, sauté the patties in the butter for about 3 1/2 minutes per side or until meat is medium rare. Transfer to a warm platter.

2 Add mushrooms and shallot to pan coating them with the pan drippings. Sauté for 3 minutes, stirring constantly. Increase heat to medium-high and add wine, broth, chervil, and tarragon, and cook the sauce until it is reduced by half and slightly thickened. Stir in parsley.

3 Pour the sauce over the patties and serve at once.

Per serving: 240 calories; 16 gm protein; 3.1 gm carbohydrates; 14 gm fat; 49 mg cholesterol; .36 gm fiber; 52% of calories from fat

GREAT
GRILLING

Southwestern Roast Corn in Cumin Butter

C orn on the cob never tasted so good! You can also drizzle the seasoned butter over steamed vegetables.

Serves 2

2 ears corn, with husks
1 tablespoon reduced-calorie butter
1/4 teaspoon ground cumin
1/4 teaspoon ground coriander
1/4 teaspoon chili powder
1/8 teaspoon cayenne pepper
1/8 teaspoon cracked black pepper

For Gas Grill:
2 cups mesquite chips soaked in water for 30 minutes

1 Remove racks from grill then fire it up.

2 Carefully pull back corn husks (without detaching) and remove corn silk.

3 Blend butter with the spices. Brush the corn with the seasoned butter, then replace husk, tying it in place with a thin strip of the husk.

4 When coals are red-hot and no longer flaming, bury the corn deep in the coals. Cover grill and cook for 20 minutes, turning 2 to 3 times.
  If you are using a gas grill, add the water-soaked mesquite chips, return grilling racks to proper position, and once the chips no longer flame, place the corn on the grill. Cover and cook 20 minutes or until kernels are tender, turning 2 to 3 times.

5 At the end of 20 minutes, check the kernels for doneness.

Per serving: 113 calories; 3.08 gm protein; 19 gm carbohydrates; 3.6 gm fat; 0 mg cholesterol; .64 gm fiber; 29% of calories from fat

Turkey Tenderloin in Cumin and Cayenne

T he virtually fat-free turkey tenderloin is steeped in a citrus-flavored marinade, then grilled to perfection over a mesquite fire. This is a wonderfully simple dish and the leftovers make great sandwiches.

1 1/4 pounds turkey tenderloin (in 3 pieces)

Marinade

3 tablespoons olive oil
1 tablespoon fresh lemon juice
1 tablespoon fresh lime juice
1 tablespoon chopped fresh parsley
1 1/2 teaspoons ground cumin
1 teaspoon grated onion
1 teaspoon finely chopped fresh lemon thyme
1/4 teaspoon cayenne pepper
1/4 teaspoon light salt
1/4 teaspoon dry mustard

2 to 4 cups mesquite chips soaked in water for 30 minutes

Microwave Sauce Moutarde

Serves 4

1 Place turkey and all marinade ingredients in a baking dish and marinate for 1 hour at room temperature, turning once or twice.

2 Fifteen minutes prior to grilling, remove grates from grill. Fire up your grill using the hottest temperature for 10 minutes and add 2 to 4 cups of the pre-soaked mesquite wood. Replace grates and grill turkey for about 5 minutes per side or until nicely grilled on the surface and desired degree of doneness is reached.

3 Roll the cooked turkey in the marinade and serve at once with Microwave Sauce Moutarde.

Per serving: *322 calories; 42 gm protein; .92 gm carbohydrates; 16 gm fat; 98 mg cholesterol; .06 gm fiber; 45% of calories*

Cherry Lime Glaze

T his is a great and
easy glaze for
chicken, Cornish hens,
quail, or any bird, and for
ribs, chops, and even pork
roast.

Makes ¹/₂ cup

¹/₄ cup cherry preserves
¹/₄ cup lime marmalade
2 tablespoons reduced-calorie
margarine
1 tablespoon cornstarch dissolved in
1 tablespoon water
¹/₄ teaspoon light salt
¹/₄ teaspoon white pepper

Place all glaze ingredients in a small saucepan and heat gently until
melted and thickened, about 3 minutes. Stir once or twice.

Per tablespoon: *57 calories; .1 gm protein; 11.75 gm carbohydrates; 1.25 gm fat; 0 mg cholesterol; .05 gm fiber; 20% of calories from fat*

Flank Steak in Dijon Marinade

S erve the flank steak
as an entree, then use
any leftovers to garnish a
tossed salad made from
lettuces, watercress,
tomato wedges, shredded
carrots, and your favorite
dressing.

Serves 4 to 6

1 to 1¹/₄ pounds flank steak

Marinade

¹/₃ cup Dijon mustard
2 tablespoons light soy sauce
1 tablespoon whipping cream
1 teaspoon fresh ginger, peeled and
minced
¹/₂ teaspoon lemon pepper
¹/₂ teaspoon Parsley Plus
¹/₂ teaspoon fresh ground black
pepper, or cracked black pepper

1 Place all ingredients in a baking dish. Stir to blend. Cover dish,
and refrigerate for at least 6 hours or overnight.

2 Fifteen minutes before you are ready to cook, fire up your grill to medium-high heat. Add steak and cook about 6 to 8 minutes per side or until the desired degree of doneness is reached, frequently basting steak with the marinade.

3 Diagonally slice the steak against the grain of the meat.

Per serving: *206 calories; 30 gm protein; .49 gm carbohydrates; 7.16 gm fat; 110 mg cholesterol; .02 gm fiber; 31% of calories from fat*

Country-Style Pork Ribs

S elect the ribs that are nice and lean; that way you are paying for meat, not fat and bone. For ribs to double as an appetizer —just cut them into bite-size pieces.

1 pound boneless country-style pork ribs

Marinade

¹/4 cup bottled Tiger sauce
2 tablespoons brown sugar
1 tablespoon A-1 Steak Sauce
1 tablespoon finely chopped shallot or onion

Serves 2 to 3

1 teaspoon prepared horseradish

1 In a baking dish combine the Tiger sauce with sugar, steak sauce, shallots, and horseradish. Add ribs and marinate at room temperature for 30 minutes.

2 Fifteen minutes before you are ready to cook, fire up your grill. Over medium-low heat, cook for 20 minutes, basting and turning every 5 minutes.

Per serving: *382 calories; 41 gm protein; 7.51 gm carbohydrates; 20 gm fat; 112 mg cholesterol; .03 gm fiber; 47% of calories from fat*

Kay's Smokie Mustard Sauce

T his mustard sauce is delicious on chicken, pork, or ribs. You can use your charcoal smoker with or without using the drip pan. If you do not want to mess with your smoker at all, use your electric grill, but grill the chicken very slowly, basting the pieces frequently.

Makes 1 1/2 cups

1 cup reduced-calorie butter
1/2 cup prepared mustard
1/2 cup white vinegar
1/2 cup sugar
1/2 teaspoon Tabasco sauce
1/8 to 1/4 teaspoon ground black pepper

Melt the butter in a small saucepan. Whisk in all the remaining ingredients and let sauce simmer over low heat for 15 minutes.

Per tablespoon: *47 calories; 0 gm protein; 4.48 gm carbohydrates; 2.5 gm fat; 0 mg cholesterol; .03 gm fiber; 48% of calories from fat*

Bacon-Wrapped Quail with Basil

T hese little birds are very tasty; however, they do not have much meat. For the hearty appetite I suggest 2 quail and for the light appetite just one.

Serves 4

4 quail, washed and dried
White wine Worcestershire sauce
Light salt to taste
Black pepper to taste
Lemon pepper to taste
12 fresh basil leaves
4 large parsley sprigs
4 slices smoked peppered bacon

1 Preheat grill to low.

2 Take a sharp paring knife and flatten the quail by splitting the breast bone on the cavity side.

3   Sprinkle each quail with Worcestershire, salt, pepper, and lemon pepper to taste.

4   Place 3 basil leaves and one parsley sprig on each quail's breast and wrap with a bacon slice, securing the bacon with a toothpick.

5   Grill quail (covered) to the degree of doneness you desire, approximately 20 minutes.

Per serving: 436 calories; 60 gm protein; 2.38 gm carbohydrates; 19 gm fat; 5.2 mg cholesterol; .09 gm fiber; 39% of calories from fat

Trio of Grilled Bell Peppers

T his trio of bell peppers is very striking, tasty, and low in calories. Serve with grilled meat, fish, or poultry.

Serves 3

1 **green bell pepper**
1 **red bell pepper**
1 **golden yellow bell pepper**
1/4 **cup olive oil**
    Lulu's Special Seasoning to taste
    Lemon pepper to taste

1   Rinse peppers. Remove stem and blossom ends. Halve peppers, remove ribs and seeds, and cut each half into 4 or 5 chunks.

2   Place pepper pieces in a medium bowl and toss with oil, special seasoning, and lemon pepper. Marinate for about 20 minutes.

3   About 15 minutes before cooking fire up your grill.

4   Thread peppers onto skewers, alternating the colors. Grill, uncovered, approximately 20 to 25 minutes turning once. Do not overcook the peppers or they will be soggy.

Per serving: 46 calories; 0 gm protein; 3 gm carbohydrates; 3.5 gm fat; 0 mg cholesterol; .64 gm fiber; 67% of calories from fat

Barbecued Jumbo Prawns
in Their Shell

*P*rawn and shrimp are given counts per pound. The "count" tells you how many prawns or shrimp are in one pound. The smaller the number, the larger the size of the shrimp or prawn. For this recipe, I used a 10- to 15-count shrimp. Though they are expensive, you get shrimp instead of shell and 3 per person is ample. Prawns are large shrimp.

Serves 4

1 pound (10 to 15 count) prawns, deveined, shells left intact

Marinade

1/4 cup reduced-calorie Italian-style salad dressing
1/4 cup chopped fresh parsley
2 tablespoons extra virgin olive oil
2 tablespoons fresh lime juice
2 tablespoons sauterne
1 tablespoon chopped shallot
2 teaspoons chopped fresh garlic
1 teaspoon chopped fresh basil
1 teaspoon fresh grated ginger
1/2 teaspoon cracked black pepper
1/4 teaspoon liquid smoke

1 Rinse prawns, pat dry, and place in a baking dish.

2 Blend all marinade ingredients together in a jar with a tight-fitting lid and pour over prawns. Cover dish lightly. Refrigerate and let marinate several hours or overnight.

3 About 15 minutes before cooking, preheat grill to hot. Grill the prawns, covered, about 5 minutes per side. Serve at once.

Per serving: *195 calories; 23 gm protein; 2.75 gm carbohydrates; 9 gm fat; 172 mg cholesterol; .06 gm fiber; 42% of calories from fat*

Grilled Lamb Loin Chops
with Fresh Rosemary

For light fare I serve 1 chop per person; but for entertaining plan on 1 1/2 to 2 chops per person. Trim all excess fat and marinate the chops for at least 1 or, preferably, several hours, turning frequently. I use fresh rosemary because it is more effective compared to the dried.

Serves 3

3 lamb loin chops, each at least 1-inch thick

Marinade

1/4 cup sauterne
1 tablespoon water
1 tablespoon fresh rosemary (discard stalk) or 1 teaspoon dried rosemary
1 tablespoon fresh lime or lemon juice (I prefer lime)
1 tablespoon minced onion
1 tablespoon Worcestershire sauce
2 teaspoons Dijon mustard
1 teaspoon minced garlic
1/4 teaspoon liquid smoke
Non-stick cooking spray

1 Combine all marinade ingredients in a large baking dish. Rub the chops with the marinade and place them in the baking dish. Cover and refrigerate. Marinate several hours refrigerated or one hour at room temperature.

2 About 15 minutes before you are ready to cook, fire up your grill (sprayed with non-stick cooking spray) and cook the chops, turning and basting frequently, about 20 minutes or until desired degree of doneness.

Per serving: *174 calories; 18 gm protein; 4.3 gm carbohydrates; 7.8 gm fat; 59 mg cholesterol; .4 gm fiber; 40% of calories from fat*

Peppered Butterflies of Pork

"Butterfly" pork chops are chops cut from the loin. You can use a regular chop, but be sure to trim all visible fat. Garam masala is a curious curry-like blend of black pepper, cinnamon, cloves, cardamom, fenugreek, aniseed, coriander, cumin, red chiles, and other spices. It is generally ground to order and used to flavor Indian and Pakistani vegetable and meat dishes. You can find it at Indian markets.

Serves 2

2 butterfly pork chops
Olive oil to taste
Garam masala to taste
1 tablespoon crushed black peppercorns
1 tablespoon grated fresh ginger
Szechuan seasoning to taste (I prefer Spice Island)

1 Fire up your grill to medium.

2 Rub the chops with olive oil and the garam masala. Mix the crushed peppercorns and ginger together and coat both sides of the chops with this mixture, then sprinkle the chops with the Szechuan seasoning.

3 Grill one side of the chop about 8 to 10 minutes. Turn and grill the second side about 5 minutes or until degree of doneness is reached (internal temperature of 170°). Serve at once.

Per serving: *202 calories; 23 gm protein; 1.15 gm carbohydrates; 12 gm fat; 71 mg cholesterol; .2 gm fiber; 53% of calories from fat*

Javanese Pork Kabobs

I cube the boneless pork loin into kabob-size pieces (1 1/2-inch chunks) and marinate with well-seasoned olive oil, bell peppers, and onion. Red Pepper Sauce complements this wonderful kabob as either a dip or as a sauce to be poured directly over the kabob. Or serve with Brown Rice Bake and Robert's Favorite Salad.

Serves 4

2 pounds boneless pork loin roast
3/4 cup chopped onion
1/4 cup beer
1/4 cup light soy sauce
1/4 cup olive oil
3 tablespoons finely chopped walnuts
2 tablespoons orange juice
2 tablespoons lemon juice
2 tablespoons ground coriander
2 tablespoons brown sugar
2 minced garlic cloves
1/4 teaspoon crushed red pepper
1 medium green bell pepper, cubed
1 medium red bell pepper, cubed
1 medium yellow bell pepper, cubed
1 large onion, cut into wedge-shaped quarters, each quarter halved

1 Trim all visible fat from roast and cut into 1 1/2-inch kabobs.

2 In a 2-quart bowl with a tight-fitting lid place pork kabobs and all remaining ingredients, stirring so that meat is well coated with the marinade. Refrigerate. Marinate for at least 30 minutes. Several hours is even better. When I think about it I shake the bowl to recoat the meat.

3 Preheat grill 10 minutes before you are ready to cook.

4 To assemble kabobs, alternately thread chunks of yellow, red, and green bell peppers, onion, and pork on each of 4 skewers.

5 Grill covered over medium heat until the desired degree of doneness, turning kabobs at least once. This usually takes 20 to 25 minutes. You want the pork to be evenly browned and the vegetables to be cooked but crunchy.

Per serving: *494 calories; 64 gm protein; 15 gm carbohydrates; 18 gm fat; 198 mg cholesterol; 1.43 gm fiber; 33% of calories from fat*

Chutney Grilled Pork Ribs

T hese wonderful boneless country-style pork ribs are perfect finger foods for picnics or family-style meals. You can also use any of my glazes for pork or chicken on the backbones.

Makes 3

1 pound (6 count) package boneless country-style pork ribs
Lulu's Special Seasoning to taste
1/2 cup bottled chutney
1/4 cup chopped pineapple, fresh or canned
2 tablespoons apple juice or cider
2 tablespoons finely chopped onion
1 tablespoon brown sugar
1 teaspoon light soy sauce
1/2 teaspoon ground ginger
1/2 teaspoon garlic pepper

1 Fire up your grill to medium-low heat, or preheat oven to 350°.

2 Place the ribs on a tray and sprinkle with my seasoning.

3 Blend all the remaining ingredients in a small bowl, and brush the boneless ribs with this mixture.

4 Grill the ribs covered, turning as needed (so as not to burn the ribs or glaze) for 20 to 30 minutes, or bake in the preheated 350° oven for 30 minutes.

Per serving: 281 calories; 19 gm protein; 11 gm carbohydrates; 18 gm fat; 61 mg cholesterol; .06 gm fiber; 58% of calories from fat

Grilled Herbed Chicken Breasts

G reat for a picnic,
these grilled boneless
chicken breasts are low in
calories and very tasty.
Cold leftovers are good
alone, stuffed into a pita
bread, or with a mixed
lettuce salad. Mango
chutney is an ideal
accompaniment.

4 boneless chicken breasts, rinsed and dried

Marinade

1 6-ounce can pineapple juice
$1/4$ cup olive oil
2 tablespoons fresh lime juice
2 tablespoons chopped fresh parsley or cilantro
2 tablespoons chopped fresh basil
1 tablespoon finely chopped onion
1 tablespoon brown sugar
1 teaspoon light soy sauce
1 teaspoon white wine Worcestershire
$1/2$ teaspoon chopped fresh garlic
$1/2$ teaspoon summer savory

Serves 4

1 In a bowl, combine and mix all the marinade ingredients and add the chicken breasts. Refrigerate and marinate for at least 30 minutes or for several hours.

2 Fire up your grill about 20 minutes before you want to cook and grill about 7 minutes per side over medium heat. Serve at once. Do not overcook or the meat will be tough and stringy.

Per serving: *341 calories; 48 gm protein; 9.07 gm carbohydrates; 12 gm fat; 128 mg cholesterol; .1 gm fiber; 32% of calories from fat*

PORK
&
LAMB:
THE LIGHT TOUCH

Fruited Pork Paupiettes

To create paupiettes, pork tenderloin medallions (rounds) are pounded thin, stuffed with a plump prune, rolled up, then finished with a light cream sauce. I serve them with small sweet potatoes baked in their jackets and a sautéed green leafy vegetable such as spinach or Swiss chard.

Serves 8

1 pound boneless pork tenderloin, trimmed of any visible fat and cut into 8 equal pieces
Light salt, white pepper, and ground nutmeg to taste
8 pitted prunes
1 tablespoon reduced-calorie butter or margarine
1 large Granny Smith apple, peeled, cored, and cut into 1/2-inch thick slices
1/2 cup dry Marsala
1/4 cup low-sodium chicken broth
1/4 cup whipping cream

1 Pound the pork medallions 1/4-inch-thick and sprinkle to taste with the light salt, pepper, and nutmeg.

2 Place a prune at one end of each slice and roll up, tucking in the sides of the pork paupiettes. Secure each little roll with a wooden toothpick.

3 In a large skillet over medium heat, melt the margarine, add the pork rolls, and brown them on all sides, removing the rolls as they brown.

4 Brown the apple slices slightly in the same pan. Return the pork rolls to the skillet, pour in the Marsala and broth, and bring to a boil. Reduce heat to simmer. Cover and continue to cook for about 20 minutes.

5 Remove the pork rolls and apples and keep warm. Skim off any excess fat, add the cream, and bring the sauce to a boil. Stirring frequently, cook and reduce the sauce until it thickens. Pour sauce over the pork and apples and serve at once.

Per serving: 226 calories; 19 gm protein; 12 gm carbohydrates; 9.76 gm fat; 72 mg cholesterol; .46 gm fiber; 39% of calories from fat

Mesquite-Grilled Red Chili Pork Kabobs

*T*he kabob is low in calories, spunky in flavor, but not hot. The colors, flavors, and textures create a beautiful presentation. Serve with white, brown, wild, or pecan rice, or a combination of several. Cold leftovers make a wonderful submarine sandwich. The sweet chili sauce is available at Oriental markets.

Serves 4

1 pound well-trimmed pork loin, cut into 1-inch cubes

Marinade

3 tablespoons light soy sauce
3 tablespoons peanut oil
2 tablespoons fresh lemon juice
2 tablespoons minced onion
1 tablespoon brown sugar
1 tablespoon finely chopped walnuts
1 tablespoon chopped fresh parsley
2 teaspoons sweet chili sauce
1 teaspoon chopped fresh garlic
1 large peeled onion, cut into 6 wedges
1 large, seeded, cored red bell pepper, cut into 8 to 10 pieces
1 large, seeded, cored green bell pepper, cut into 8 to 10 pieces
8 ounces halved fresh mushrooms
2 cups mesquite chips soaked in water for 30 minutes

1 Place cubed pork and all remaining ingredients except mesquite chips in a large bowl. Cover and marinate at least 1 hour (20 minutes minimum) at room temperature or several hours in the refrigerator. When you think of it, shake the bowl to recoat the meat with the marinade.

2 Fifteen minutes before you are ready to cook, add wet mesquite chips and fire up your grill.

3 Thread the pork and vegetables onto 4 skewers in this order: pork, red pepper, onion, green pepper, and mushroom. Repeat until all is skewered.

4 Grill the kabobs about 10 minutes per side or until desired degree of doneness. Serve at once on the skewers.

Per serving: 445 calories; 40 gm protein; 12 gm carbohydrates; 26 gm fat; 127 mg cholesterol; 1 gm fiber; 53% of calories from fat

Cranberry Glazed Baby Back Ribs

I bake the cranberry glazed ribs in the oven and then finish them off in my outdoor grill to give the ribs a smoked flavor. I order 3 to 4 racks at a time and just freeze what I don't use. Baby back ribs are cut from the pork loin. Each rack weighs about 1 pound and has 12 3½-inch-long ribs.

Serves 3

1 pound rack baby back ribs
White wine Worcestershire sauce to taste
Lulu's Special Seasoning to taste
1 8-ounce can cranberry sauce
1 tablespoon brown sugar
1 tablespoon lemon juice
1 teaspoon white wine Worcestershire sauce
¼ teaspoon garlic powder
¼ teaspoon lemon pepper

1 Preheat oven to 350°.

2 Place ribs on a low-sided baking sheet and sprinkle with the Worcestershire sauce and special seasoning. In a small bowl blend the remaining ingredients. This is your cranberry glaze. Using all the glaze, coat both sides of the ribs.

3 In the preheated oven cook the ribs for 30 minutes. After 15 minutes cooking time, preheat an outdoor grill to medium-low heat. Transfer ribs to the preheated grill and, over medium-low heat, grill the ribs covered about 20 minutes longer or until done. Turn the ribs several times so the glaze will not burn.

Per serving: 163 calories; 15 gm protein; 10 gm carbohydrates; 6.67 gm fat; 0 mg cholesterol; .07 gm fiber; 37% of calories from fat

Apple-Pepper Pork Kabobs

I use a pork tenderloin. If a tenderloin is unavailable, substitute a boneless pork loin roast. You can also thread zucchini slices, cherry tomatoes, and whole mushrooms on skewers and grill along with the pork kabobs.

3/4 pound pork tenderloin (may come in 2 pieces)

Marinade

1/2 cup applesauce
1/4 cup chopped fresh parsley
3 tablespoons olive oil
2 tablespoons light soy sauce
2 tablespoons Grand Marnier, bourbon, or dark rum
2 tablespoons brown sugar
1 tablespoon chopped fresh lemon zest
1 tablespoon fresh lime juice
2 teaspoons chopped fresh garlic
1 teaspoon Balsamic vinegar
1/2 teaspoon ground allspice
1/2 teaspoon black pepper
1 large seeded red bell pepper, cut into 2-inch chunks
1 large seeded poblano pepper, cut into 2-inch chunks (use green bell pepper if poblano is not available)

Serves 4

1 medium onion, cut into 6 wedges

1 Remove fat and membrane from pork, and cut into 10 to 12 chunks.

2 In a container with a tight-fitting lid, blend the applesauce, parsley, oil, soy, Grand Marnier, brown sugar, lemon zest, lime juice, garlic, vinegar, allspice, and black pepper. This is your marinade. Add pepper chunks and onion wedges.

3 Add the pork cubes and blend well. Cover and refrigerate. Marinate for several hours or, if possible, overnight. Be sure the lid fits tightly so you can shake the container to recoat the pork with the marinade occasionally.

4 Fifteen minutes before you are ready to cook, preheat grill to medium.

5 Arrange the pork on 4 or 5 skewers alternately with the onion and red and poblano pepper chunks.

6 Cook the kabobs, covered, over medium heat, for about 10 minutes per side until desired degree of doneness. Turn once during cooking. Serve kabobs at once.

Per serving: *255 calories; 21 gm protein; 17 gm carbohydrates; 9.5 gm fat; 63 mg cholesterol; .68 gm fiber; 34% of calories from fat*

Stuffed Knackwurst

K nackwurst are plump German garlic sausages. They can be stuffed in advance and baked as needed. By slicing the knackwurst and covering it with the other ingredients as you would a casserole, this dish could double as an appetizer.

Serves 4

4 knackwurst
Non-stick cooking spray
8 ounces cleaned and finely chopped fresh mushrooms
1/3 cup finely chopped onion
2 tablespoons reduced-calorie butter or margarine
1 tablespoon Dijon mustard
1/4 cup half and half
1 to 2 Roma tomatoes, thinly sliced
3/4 cup skim-milk farmer's cheese

1 Preheat oven to 450°.

2 Split the sausages and place them in a baking dish sprayed with non-stick cooking spray.

3 In a skillet over medium heat, sauté the mushrooms and onion in the butter until lightly browned. Add the mustard and half and half and blend well. Cook until the liquid in the skillet is reduced and slightly thickened.

4 Stuff each sausage with one quarter of this mixture, top with tomatoes and cheese, and bake in the preheated oven 15 minutes or until sausage is hot and cheese melts.

Per serving: *410 calories; 23 gm protein; 22 gm carbohydrates; 32 gm fat; 89 mg cholesterol; .7 gm fiber; 70% of calories from fat*

Mediterranean Lamb Stew

T*he lamb, eggplant, tomato, and zucchini flavors blend well to create a savory stew.*

Serves 4

2 tablespoons reduced-calorie butter or margarine
3/4 pound lamb cubes
1 small onion, cut into thin rings
1/2 cup water
1 small unpeeled eggplant, cubed (about 4 cups)
1 zucchini, sliced
1/2 green bell pepper, sliced
1 14 1/2-ounce can Italian-style stewed tomatoes
2 tablespoons fresh lemon juice
1 teaspoon minced garlic
1/2 teaspoon Lulu's Special Seasoning
1/4 to 1/2 teaspoon Tabasco sauce
Black pepper to taste

1 Melt the margarine in a large, heavy saucepan. Add the lamb and onion and cook until lamb is browned and the onion is tender.

2 Add the water. Cover and cook for 15 minutes. Stir in the eggplant, zucchini, bell pepper, tomatoes, lemon juice, garlic, special seasoning, Tabasco, and pepper.

3 Cover and cook 30 minutes longer over low heat or until the lamb is tender. Do not overcook or the vegetables will be mushy.

Per serving: *336 calories; 36 gm protein; 15 gm carbohydrates; 13 gm fat; 104 mg cholesterol; 1.85 gm fiber; 36% of calories from fat*

Grilled Lamb Loin
with Balsamic Vinegar Sauce

I am very picky about my lamb, but this is definitely my best lamb recipe. Even non-lamb lovers love it.

12 ounces well-trimmed, boneless lamb loin

Marinade

1/4 cup melted red currant jelly (I microwave the jelly)
2 tablespoons dry red wine
1 tablespoon chopped fresh parsley
1 teaspoon minced fresh rosemary
1 teaspoon minced fresh garlic
1/2 teaspoon cracked black pepper
1/2 teaspoon summer savory

Sauce

1/2 cup sauterne
3 sprigs rosemary
1 tablespoon chopped shallot
1 1/2 teaspoon Balsamic vinegar
1/4 teaspoon cracked black pepper
2 cups homemade beef stock, or low-sodium instant beef broth (homemade stock really makes a better sauce)
1 tablespoon marinade
1/4 teaspoon arrowroot
2 tablespoons reduced-calorie butter or margarine
Light salt to taste
Ground black pepper to taste

Serves 2 to 3

1 In a baking dish, blend the jelly, wine, parsley, rosemary, garlic, pepper, and summer savory. Add the lamb and marinate for at least 15 minutes or longer if possible. The lamb should be at room temperature. Reserve marinade.

200

2 About 15 minutes before you are ready to cook, preheat grill to medium.

3 Grill the lamb over medium heat, about 5 to 7 minutes per side, turning as needed. Transfer lamb to serving platter and keep warm.

4 Meanwhile, make sauce. In a saucepan over medium-high heat, boil the wine, rosemary, shallot, vinegar, and pepper for 6 minutes or until about 1/4 cup sauce remains in the pan. Discard the rosemary. Add the broth and the 1 tablespoon of marinade. Cook for about 5 minutes or until 1/2 cup sauce remains in the pan.

5 In a small bowl, whisk together 2 tablespoons of the hot sauce with 1/4 teaspoon of arrowroot. Return this to the hot sauce. Reduce the heat to low, and whisk in the butter, 1 tablespoon at a time. Season the sauce, if necessary, with light salt and pepper.

6 To serve, slice lamb and serve napped with the sauce.

Per serving: 359 calories; 35 gm protein; 11 gm carbohydrates; 14 gm fat; 104 mg cholesterol; 0 gm fiber; 35% of calories from fat

Jezebel Baby Back Ribs

One of the ingredients I use in this recipe is my Jezebel Sauce. These ribs are delicious, easy to prepare, and a fun entree for entertaining.

Serves 3

1 pound rack baby back ribs
Non-stick cooking spray
White wine Worcestershire sauce to taste
Bottled Tiger sauce to taste
Jezebel Sauce to taste

1 Preheat oven to 350°.

2 Place ribs on a low-sided baking sheet sprayed with non-stick cooking spray and sprinkle to taste with the Worcestershire,

Tiger, and Jezebel sauces. Coat both sides of the rack with the sauce blend.

3   In the preheated 350° oven, cook the ribs for 30 minutes. After 15 minutes of cooking time has elapsed, preheat your outdoor grill to medium-low. Then transfer the ribs to the preheated, medium-low grill and grill for about 20 minutes longer or until done. Turn the ribs several times so the glaze will not burn.

Per serving: *124 calories; 15 gm protein; .23 gm carbohydrates; 6.67 gm fat; 0 mg cholesterol; 0 gm fiber; 48% of calories from fat*

Lamb in Wine Sauce

Y ou'll want to use a rack of lamb. Have your butcher debone it and cut it into steaks. Pound the steaks to ¼-inch thickness. If a rack of lamb is not available, use lamb chops, deboned, fat removed, and sliced in half. Pound to ¼-inch thickness.

Serves 4

1¾ to 2 pounds rack of lamb, or 4 lamb chops
Lulu's Special Seasoning to taste
Flour
1 tablespoon reduced-calorie butter or margarine
1 tablespoon olive or corn oil
2 tablespoons minced shallot
1 teaspoon finely chopped garlic
1 tablespoon tomato paste
½ cup dry red wine
½ cup Madeira
8 ounces mushroom caps
Chopped fresh parsley (optional)

1   Lightly sprinkle the lamb with special seasoning and dust with flour.

2   Heat the butter and oil in a large skillet over medium heat. Add the lamb and sauté about 3 to 4 minutes per side or until brown. Transfer lamb to a warm platter and keep warm.

3 Add the shallot and garlic to the skillet and sauté for 2 minutes. Whisk in the tomato paste and wines; add the mushrooms and simmer for 5 minutes or until sauce has thickened slightly.

4 Surround lamb with wine sauce. Garnish with mushroom caps and chopped parsley.

Per serving: 740 calories; 81 gm protein; 6.14 gm carbohydrates; 38 gm fat; 277 mg cholesterol; 46% of calories from fat

Cajun Pork Tenderloin

A*subtle blend of ten spices flavors this lean pork tenderloin that, thinly sliced, can double as an appetizer. For a speedy cleanup, I blend the spices on waxed paper.*

2 tablespoons paprika
2 teaspoons garlic powder
1 teaspoon oregano
1 teaspoon thyme
1/4 teaspoon cayenne pepper
1/4 teaspoon black pepper
1/4 teaspoon white pepper
1/4 teaspoon cumin
1/4 teaspoon light salt
1/8 teaspoon nutmeg
1 teaspoon olive oil

Serves 4

1 pound whole pork tenderloin

1 Preheat oven to 350°.

2 Blend the spices on a doubled square of waxed paper. Rub the pork with the olive oil and roll the pork in the spice blend.

3 Bake in the preheated oven for 30 minutes or until the internal temperature is 170°. Remove from oven and let it rest for 10 minutes.

Per serving: 302 calories; 37 gm protein; 3.23 gm carbohydrates; 15 gm fat; 127 mg cholesterol; .82 gm fiber; 45% of calories from fat

Marinated Lamb Kabobs

erfect for parties, the savory lamb cubes are grilled with pineapple, prunes, bell pepper, and onion. As a side dish, I serve ripe papaya wedges.

12 to 16 ounces boneless lamb loin, cut into 1 1/2-inch cubes
1/2 pound fresh cubed pineapple, or 1 small can pineapple cubes
8 pitted prunes
4 to 8 ounces medium-size fresh mushrooms
1 medium onion, cut into large chunks
1 to 2 bell peppers, cubed (use one color or a mixture of colors)

Marinade

1/3 cup fresh or canned pineapple juice
1/4 cup light or dark beer
3 tablespoons olive oil
2 tablespoons fresh cilantro
2 tablespoons finely chopped walnuts
2 teaspoons soy sauce
2 teaspoons finely chopped fresh garlic
1 teaspoon Balsamic vinegar
1 teaspoon Worcestershire sauce
1/2 teaspoon ground ginger
1/2 teaspoon lemon pepper
1/2 teaspoon crushed red pepper
1/2 teaspoon chopped fresh mint

Serves 4

1 Place lamb, fruit, vegetables, and all marinade ingredients in a large bowl. Stir well to blend. Cover bowl, and refrigerate for several hours.

2 Preheat grill to medium 15 minutes before you are ready to cook.

3 Arrange lamb on 4 or 5 skewers, alternating with the pineapple, prunes, mushrooms, onion, and bell pepper.

4 Grill kabobs to desired degree of doneness, basting occasionally with the reserved marinade.

Per serving: *503 calories; 37 gm protein; 30 gm carbohydrates; 25 gm fat; 104 mg cholesterol; 1.93 gm fiber; 45% of calories from fat*

Apple- and Prune-Stuffed Pork Chops

T hese fruit-stuffed chops are pretty as well as delicious. Trim all visible fat from the pork chops. Do not overcook or they will be tough.

Serves 4

4 center-cut pork chops, at least 1-inch thick
1 apple, cored and coarsely chopped
4 prunes, chopped
1 tablespoon brown sugar
1/8 teaspoon allspice
1/8 teaspoon light salt
2 tablespoons olive oil
1/2 cup sauterne
1 4-gram package low-sodium beef broth dissolved in 1/4 cup hot water
2 tablespoons fresh lemon juice
1/4 cup 2% milk
1/4 cup whipping cream
Sliced Roma tomatoes
Watercress

1 To form a pocket, slit each chop, slicing from the fat edge of the chop towards the bone.

2 In a small bowl, blend the apple, prunes, brown sugar, allspice, and salt. Stuff each chop with one quarter of the fruit mixture. Skewer shut with a toothpick.

3 In a heavy skillet over medium heat, heat the oil and sauté each side of the chops for about 5 minutes or until nicely browned. Add the sauterne, the broth dissolved in hot water, and the lemon juice. Simmer for 20 minutes.

4 Remove the chops to a warm platter and keep warm. Heat the pan juices to boiling and reduce the quantity of sauce to ⅓ cup. Then add the milk and whipping cream. Cook, stirring constantly, until your sauce is caramel-colored. Return the chops to the pan long enough to reheat thoroughly.

5 Serve immediately, garnished with tomatoes and watercress.

Per serving: *378 calories; 24 gm protein; 22 gm carbohydrates; 20 gm fat; 89 mg cholesterol; .7 gm fiber; 48% of calories from fat*

Lime Pork Roast

S erve this roast with *Sautéed New Potatoes in Jackets.*

Serves 3 to 4

1½ to 2 pounds pork loin roast
6 garlic buds cut into 14 slivers
Lulu's Special Seasoning to taste
¼ cup water
⅓ cup fresh lime juice
¼ coarsely chopped fresh parsley
1 teaspoon chopped fresh rosemary

1 Preheat oven to 325°.

2 Using a small, sharp paring knife, make 14 evenly spaced ½-inch-deep slits on the roast's surface. Insert a garlic sliver into each slit. Rub roast with special seasoning and place in a roasting pan.

3 Pour water and lime juice over roast so juices do not dry up. Sprinkle roast with parsley and rosemary.

4 Roast in the preheated 325° oven for 45 minutes per pound or until a meat thermometer inserted into the meat registers 185°.

Per serving: *560 calories; 74 gm protein; 3.16 gm carbohydrates; 27 gm fat; 253 mg cholesterol; .08 gm fiber; 43% of calories from fat*

Fruit-Stuffed Pork Tenderloin

G rill or oven-roast this succulent fruit-stuffed pork tenderloin. I circle the medallions with Pineapple Sauce.

Serves 3 to 4

3/4 to 1 pound well-trimmed pork tenderloin
3/4 cup dried mixed fruit, chopped (I use 2 pieces each)
1/4 cup raisins
1/3 cup brandy or your favorite liqueur
Olive oil to rub pork
Lulu's Special Seasoning
Lemon Pepper

1 To plump, steep the dried chopped fruit and the raisins in the brandy or liqueur until soft, about 2 hours. Drain fruit and reserve liqueur.

2 Insert a knife-sharpening steel lengthwise through the pork to create a tunnel.

3 Fifteen minutes before cooking, preheat grill to medium.

4 Rub the outside of the pork with oil and sprinkle it lightly with special seasoning and lemon pepper.

5 Stuff the pork with the plumped fruit. Secure the ends of the tenderloin with toothpicks.

6 Grill until the interior of the pork is 170°, turning occasionally.

Note: You can oven-roast pork in a preheated 350° oven for 30 to 45 minutes.

Per serving: *294 calories; 26 gm protein; 24 gm carbohydrates; 5.5 gm fat; 79 mg cholesterol; .94 gm fiber; 17% of calories from fat*

Yogurt Marinated Leg of Lamb with Grilled Peppers

A sk your butcher to debone a leg of lamb. If possible, marinate it overnight for at least 8 hours. Serve the grilled lamb and peppers with mint jelly, Cheesy Rice Soufflé, Eggplant Stacks, and Watercress Salad with Creamy Garlic Dressing. For dessert, Mount Fuji makes a splendid finale.

Serves 4

1 1/2 pounds boneless leg of lamb

Marinade

1 cup unflavored non-fat yogurt
1/2 cup chopped onion
1 tablespoon fresh garlic
1 tablespoon fresh ginger
1/4 teaspoon ground cumin
1/4 teaspoon coriander
2 seeded red bell peppers
2 seeded poblano peppers (wear gloves or your fingers will burn for several minutes)
2 cups mesquite chips soaked in water for 30 minutes

1 In a bowl or baking dish blend the yogurt, onion, garlic, ginger, cumin, and coriander. Add lamb. Stir to coat the lamb with the yogurt marinade. Cover bowl or dish and marinate lamb overnight if possible.

2 Fifteen minutes prior to cooking, add mesquite chips to grill and preheat grill to hot.

3 Grill lamb covered for about 10 to 15 minutes per side, or until desired degree of doneness. Grill the peppers along with the lamb for about 7 minutes per side, turning once. Remove peppers when done. (Peppers will still have some crunch without being mushy.) Peel the poblano peppers before eating.

4 Remove the lamb from the grill and let stand 15 minutes before carving.

Per serving: *468 calories; 61 gm protein; 10 gm carbohydrates; 18 gm fat; 190 mg cholesterol; .73 gm fiber; 35% of calories from fat*

Pork Tenderloin Diane

Quick to prepare, this is a nice variation to a pork roast. At the beginning of the recipe I say to sprinkle the medallions with seasoned flour. I keep a large-holed shaker filled with ½ cup all-purpose flour touched with ¼ teaspoon each light salt and black pepper so that I don't have to mix a batch every time I need it. I cover the top with a piece of foil.

Serves 4

1 pound pork tenderloin, cut into equal rounds
Seasoned flour to taste
Lemon pepper to taste
2 tablespoons reduced-calorie margarine
¼ cup brandy
1 tablespoon Dijon mustard
1 tablespoon fresh lemon juice
1 tablespoon fresh lime juice
1 tablespoon Worcestershire sauce
2 tablespoons whipping cream
¼ cup chopped fresh parsley (optional)

1 Using your hands or a flat metal meat mallet, press or pound each pork slice to 1-inch thickness, and lightly sprinkle both sides of the pork with seasoned flour and lemon pepper.

2 Meanwhile, melt the margarine in a large skillet over medium-high heat. Sauté the pork medallions 3 to 4 minutes per side. Transfer to a serving platter and keep warm.

3 To the skillet add brandy, mustard, lemon and lime juices, and Worcestershire. Cook, stirring, until the sauce is hot. Stir in cream and cook several minutes longer or until sauce thickens slightly.

4 Pour sauce over the pork. Garnish with parsley. Serve at once.

Per serving: *349 calories; 37 gm protein; 1.27 gm carbohydrates; 18 gm fat; 122 mg cholesterol; .04 gm fiber; 47% of calories from fat*

ELEGANT
ACCOMPANIMENTS

Cauliflower Cheese Casserole

T his casserole can be prepared one day ahead of when you need to serve it. Let it sit at room temperature for 30 to 45 minutes prior to baking.

Serves 4

4 cups 1 1/2-inch-long cauliflower florets (from a 1-pound head)
1/4 cup water
4 ounces frozen petite green beans, thawed
3 tablespoons reduced-calorie butter, divided use
1/4 cup coarsely chopped green bell pepper
1/4 cup coarsely chopped red bell pepper
1 tablespoon chopped shallot
1 cup 2% milk
2 tablespoons all-purpose flour
1/4 teaspoon Lulu's Special Seasoning
1/4 teaspoon light salt
    White pepper to taste
    Cayenne pepper to taste
3/4 cup shredded mozzarella
2 tablespoons fresh bread crumbs (optional)

1 Preheat oven to 350°.

2 Place the cauliflower florets in a 2-quart glass dish. Add 1/4 cup water, cover, and microwave on high power for 6 minutes, stirring after 3 minutes of cooking time has elapsed. Drain, then toss cauliflower with green beans.

3 Melt 1 tablespoon of butter in a small pan over medium heat. Add the bell peppers and shallots and sauté until tender. Stir into the cauliflower and green beans.

4 Meanwhile, in a 4-cup glass measure whisk together the milk, 2 tablespoons butter, flour, special seasoning, salt, and peppers. Microwave sauce on high power for 2 minutes. Remove from microwave and whisk again. Return sauce to microwave and cook on high power for 1 minute longer. Remove and stir well. Stir in mozzarella and melt. Stir again.

5 Pour the cheese sauce over the vegetables. Sprinkle with the bread crumbs and bake in the preheated 350° oven for 20 minutes or until the casserole is bubbly.

Per serving: 162 calories; 13 gm protein; 15 gm carbohydrates; 6.29 gm fat; 20 mg cholesterol; 1.35 gm fiber; 35% of calories from fat

Spinach Madeleine

E*ven people who don't like spinach will adore this savory side dish. Serve with Glazed Cornish Game Hens or Grilled Herbed Chicken Breast.*

Serves 4

16	**ounces frozen leaf spinach**
1/4	**cup chopped onion**
2	**cups water**
1 1/2	**tablespoon reduced-calorie margarine**
1/2	**teaspoon Lulu's Special Seasoning**
1/4	**teaspoon garlic powder**
1/4	**teaspoon light salt**
1/4	**teaspoon fresh cracked black pepper**
1/8	**teaspoon ground nutmeg**
1/8	**teaspoon cayenne pepper**
1/2	**cup low-fat cottage cheese**
1/2	**cup grated cheddar cheese**
1/2	**cup grated Monterey Jack cheese**
1/2	**cup grated Parmesan cheese, plus additional to garnish**
1/4	**cup bread crumbs**

1 Place spinach, onion, and 2 cups water in a small saucepan. Cook uncovered over medium-high heat until spinach is done and onion is transparent, about 5 minutes. Drain in a collander. Using a large spoon, press as much of the water as you can from the spinach.

2 Stir in the margarine and spices.

3 In a small bowl blend the 3 cheeses.

4 Preheat oven to 350°, and spray a 6-inch, oven-proof casserole dish with non-stick cooking spray.

5 Place half the spinach in the baking dish in an even layer. Top with all the mixed cheeses, followed by a second layer of spinach. Sprinkle with grated Parmesan and dust lightly with bread crumbs. Bake in the preheated 350° oven until bubbly, about 20 minutes.

Per serving: 318 calories; 23 gm protein; 17 gm carbohydrates; 18 gm fat; 28 mg cholesterol; 1.59 gm fiber; 51% of calories from fat

Brussels Sprouts in Sesame Cream

W*ith few exceptions, I prefer fresh vegetables to frozen; Brussels sprouts are one of the exceptions. I find the frozen variety more consistent in texture and flavor than the fresh.*

Serves 2 to 4

1 10-ounce package frozen Brussels sprouts
¼ cup water
1 tablespoon reduced-calorie margarine
1 tablespoon chopped shallot
1 teaspoon sesame seeds
2 tablespoons light sour cream
1 tablespoon 2% milk

1 Microwave Brussels sprouts with ¼ cup water on high power for 5 minutes. Cool slightly.

2 Melt the margarine in a small skillet. Add the shallot and sesame seeds and sauté until the sesame seeds are golden brown.

3 Stir in the sour cream and milk. Add the Brussels sprouts and toss until they are covered with the sesame cream. Serve immediately.

Per serving: 55 calories; 2.8 gm protein; 5.7 gm carbohydrates; 2.7 gm fat; .28 mg cholesterol; .77 gm fiber; 45% of calories from fat

Two-Cheese Spinach and Mushroom Casserole

Made with well-seasoned fresh spinach, fresh, sautéed mushrooms, and a creamy layer of cheese this make-ahead casserole can be served as either an entree or a side-dish. For speed you can use the 16-ounce bag of frozen, no-added salt, cut spinach. Garnish with fresh tomato slices.

Serves 4 to 6

12 ounces fresh well-washed, stemless, torn spinach leaves
1 cup water
1/2 teaspoon Lulu's Special Seasoning
1/4 teaspoon garlic powder
1/4 teaspoon light salt
1/4 teaspoon cracked black pepper
1/8 teaspoon cayenne pepper
1/8 teaspoon ground nutmeg
3 tablespoons reduced-calorie butter or margarine
8 ounces sliced fresh mushrooms
1/2 cup chopped onion
2 to 3 ounces cubed light cream cheese
1 1/2 cup grated cheddar cheese
Tomato slices (optional)

1 Preheat oven to 325°. Spray an oven-proof casserole with non-stick coating.

2 Place spinach and water in a small saucepan. Bring to a boil. Cook 5 minutes. Transfer spinach to a sieve and press out excess liquid with the back of a long-handled mixing spoon. Return to pan. Stir in special seasoning, garlic powder, salt, pepper, cayenne, and nutmeg into the drained spinach. Mix well.

3 In a skillet, melt the butter over medium heat, and sauté mushrooms and onion until tender.

4 Place the cream cheese and mushroom mixture in an even layer over the bottom of prepared casserole. Top with an even layer of seasoned spinach and sprinkle with the grated cheese. Bake in the preheated 325° oven for 20 minutes or until thoroughly heated.

Per serving: 190 calories; 8.92 gm protein; 5.42 gm carbohydrates; 15 gm fat; 40 mg cholesterol; .70 gm fiber; 71% of calories from fat

Cottage-Stuffed Squash

T his dish is an easy and nutritious way to serve flavorful yellow summer squash.

1 whole 1 1/2-inch-diameter yellow summer squash, washed, ends removed
2 tablespoons low-fat cottage cheese
1 teaspoon freshly-grated Parmesan cheese
1 teaspoon freshly-grated Romano cheese
1/8 teaspoon onion powder
Pinch summer savory
Cayenne pepper to taste
Cracked black pepper to taste
Serves 1
Paprika to taste

1 Preheat oven to 350°.

2 Place squash on paper towel in the microwave oven and cook on high power for 5 minutes. If you are cooking 2 squash, increase the cooking time to 8 to 10 minutes.

3 Allow squash to cool slightly. Slice off a lengthwise strip of skin just deep enough so you can reach the pulp. (You want to leave as much of the squash whole as possible.)

4 Carefully scoop out all the squash pulp and seeds and transfer to a small bowl. Add the remaining ingredients. Mix well and stuff the mixture back into squash, mounding it high for effect. Sprinkle to taste with paprika.

5 Bake in the preheated 350° oven for 15 to 20 minutes or until well heated.

Per serving: *88 calories; 7.4 gm protein; 8.9 gm carbohydrates; 4.1 gm fat; 10 mg cholesterol; 1.08 gm fiber; 42% of calories from fat*

Apple-Stuffed Butternut Squash

T he butternut is a
hard-shelled mature
winter squash.

1 medium butternut squash, washed
   and dried
1/2 cup water
1 cup peeled, diced, fresh apple
1/4 cup chopped onion
1 1/2 tablespoon reduced-calorie
   margarine
1 tablespoon fresh orange juice
1/2 cup 2% fat cottage cheese
1/2 cup grated cheddar cheese
1/4 teaspoon Lulu's Special Seasoning
1/4 teaspoon white pepper
1/8 teaspoon ground cinnamon

Serves 4

1/8 teaspoon ground ginger

1 Preheat oven to 350°.

2 Slice squash lengthwise in half. Using a spoon, scrape the seeds and strand from the squash cavity. Place squash, cavity side down, on a low-sided baking sheet. Add the water and bake in the preheated 350° oven for 30 to 40 minutes or until squash is tender-firm. Let squash cool. When cool, carefully remove the squash leaving the shell intact. Place squash in a mixing bowl.

3 Meanwhile, melt margarine in a small skillet over medium heat. Sauté the apple and onion in the melted margarine until onion is tender, about 5 to 7 minutes.

4 Add apple mixture and all remaining ingredients to squash and mix well. Stuff each squash half with filling mixture. Bake in the preheated 350° oven for 15 minutes or until hot. Serve at once.

Per serving: 206 calories; 9.5 gm protein; 28 gm carbohydrates; 7.2 gm fat; 17 mg cholesterol; 2.79 gm fiber; 31% of calories from fat

Savory Spinach

C reamed spinach goes with any variety of meat whether it be baked, broiled, or grilled. It is easy to prepare, nutritious, and light.

Makes 2 cups

2 10-ounce boxes frozen chopped spinach
1 cup chopped onion
1 tablespoon reduced-calorie margarine
1/2 teaspoon Lulu's Special Seasoning or light salt
1/4 teaspoon black pepper
1/8 teaspoon cayenne pepper
1/4 cup whipping cream

1 Put the packages of frozen spinach in your microwave and cook on high for 8 minutes. Put the microwaved spinach in a saucepan large enough to hold it, add onion, and cover with hot water. Cook until spinach and onion are tender. Drain and, using a large spoon, press all the fluid out of the spinach.

2 Return the spinach to the saucepan, add and blend all the remaining ingredients, heat, and serve hot.

Per cup: *211 calories; 9.13 gm protein; 20 gm carbohydrates; 12 gm fat; 33 mg cholesterol; 3.04 gm fiber; 50% of calories from fat*

Broccoli Florets in Oyster Sauce

A light and unusual way to serve broccoli. When you entertain, garnish the broccoli with Candied Lemon Peel. Broccoli comes from the Italian word brocco, which means "branch."

Serves 4

4 cups 2 1/2-inch broccoli florets (from a 1-pound bunch)
Lemon pepper to taste
Light salt to taste
2 tablespoons reduced-calorie butter
1 teaspoon Chinese-style oyster sauce
1 teaspoon light soy sauce

218

1 Place broccoli in a vegetable steamer with 1 inch of water. Steam 5 minutes or until broccoli is cooked but firm. Drain broccoli and arrange in an attractive serving dish. Sprinkle to taste with lemon pepper and salt.

2 Meanwhile, melt the butter (I use my microwave) and stir in the oyster and soy sauces.

3 Pour sauce over broccoli. Serve while warm.

Per serving: 72 calories; 5.26 gm protein; 9.25 gm carbohydrates; 2.5 gm fat; 0 mg cholesterol; 1.88 gm fiber; 31% of calories from fat

Summer Squash in Cream

If you can, use homegrown, tender, new yellow squash. Otherwise, select small, smooth, 4- to 5-inch yellow squash.

Makes 3 cups

4 small yellow squash (about ³/4 pound), ends removed, cut into ¹/2-inch-thick rounds
1 cup coarsely chopped onion
¹/4 cup water
¹/4 teaspoon Lulu's Special Seasoning
Cracked black pepper to taste
2 teaspoons reduced-calorie butter
2 ounces light cream cheese

1 Place squash, onion, and water in a 1-quart saucepan. Cover. Cook over medium heat about 5 minutes, stirring occasionally.

2 Uncover, increase the heat to medium-high. Cook until water evaporates and squash is slightly browned. Stir several times during cooking.

3 Remove from heat. Add special seasoning, pepper, butter, and cream cheese and stir gently until well-mixed. Serve at once. The squash should be chunky but creamy.

Per serving: 114 calories; 4.33 gm protein; 12 gm carbohydrates; 6.6 gm fat; 17 mg cholesterol; 1.19 gm fiber; 52% of calories from fat

Glazed Carrots

E *veryone needs a special recipe for glazed carrots, the perfect complement to any gourmet entree.*

Makes 2 cups

4 to 5 peeled medium carrots, cut diagonally into 1/4-inch-wide rounds (about 2 cups)
1 tablespoon reduced-calorie butter or margarine
2 tablespoons brown sugar
1/8 teaspoon lemon zest
1/8 teaspoon orange zest
1/2 teaspoon Lulu's Special Seasoning
1/8 to 1/4 teaspoon lemon pepper
1/8 to 1/4 teaspoon cracked black pepper

1   Place the carrots in a small saucepan and cover with water. Bring water to a boil and cook carrots until tender yet firm. Drain at once.

2   Add all remaining ingredients. Stir and reheat.

Per 1/2 cup: *73 calories; 1 gm protein; 15 gm carbohydrates; 1.25 gm fat; 0 mg cholesterol; 1.15 gm fiber; 15% of calories from fat*

Lemoned Squash Scramble

I *n order to get the correct julienne cut, I use the #3 blade of a Mouli Julienne machine, an inexpensive, easy-to-clean piece of equipment that you'll enjoy owning.*

Serves 2 to 3

1 medium yellow summer squash
1 medium zucchini squash
1 1/2 tablespoons reduced-calorie butter
1 tablespoon chopped parsley
1/2 teaspoon Lulu's Special Seasoning
1/2 teaspoon lemon zest
1/8 teaspoon white pepper to taste

1   Clean squash, discard ends, and cut into pieces small enough to fit into the Mouli Julienne machine. Cut into juliennes. Otherwise, cut into matchstick julienne strips.

2 In a small skillet melt the butter. Add squashes and seasonings and cook, stirring occasionally until squash is barely tender. Do not overcook or the squash will become mushy.

Per serving: *71 calories; 2.8 gm protein; 10 gm carbohydrates; 3.3 gm fat; 0 mg cholesterol; 1.49 gm fiber; 42% of calories from fat*

Spinach Pudding

T his simple vegetable pudding tastes like it took hours instead of minutes to prepare. It can also be made ahead of time and reheated just before serving.

Serves 4

1 16-ounce bag frozen leaf spinach, thawed and well-drained
1/2 cup low-fat cottage cheese
1/3 cup finely chopped onion
1/4 cup grated Romano cheese
1/4 cup fresh bread crumbs
1/2 cup evaporated skim milk
1 egg
1 tablespoon Worcestershire sauce
1/2 teaspoon Lulu's Special Seasoning
Non-stick cooking spray
Grated Parmesan cheese to taste

1 Preheat oven to 350°.

2 Combine the spinach, cottage cheese, onion, Romano cheese, and bread crumbs in a large bowl.

3 Add evaporated skim milk, egg, Worcestershire, and special seasoning. Blend well. Spray a 1-quart baking dish with non-stick cooking spray. Pour spinach mixture into prepared pan.

4 Bake in the preheated 350° oven for 30 minutes or until top is light brown and slightly crusty. Sprinkle top with Parmesan cheese.

Per serving: *227 calories; 20 gm protein; 14 gm carbohydrates; 11 gm fat; 103 mg cholesterol; 1.16 gm fiber; 44% of calories from fat*

Eggplant Stuffing

T his meatless dish is almost a meal in itself. Serve it with several of your favorite fresh vegetables.

5 cups diced eggplant (1 medium eggplant)
2 tablespoons water
1 1/2 tablespoons olive oil
1/2 cup chopped onion
1/2 cup chopped green bell pepper
1 teaspoon chopped fresh garlic
1/2 cup sliced fresh mushrooms
1/2 cup diced fresh tomatoes
2 slices cubed reduced-calorie wheat bread (40 calories per slice)
2 egg whites and 1 egg yolk, slightly beaten
1/2 teaspoon light salt
1/2 teaspoon ground black pepper
1/2 teaspoon thyme
1/2 teaspoon summer savory
1 cup grated Monterey Jack cheese
Grated Parmesan and Romano cheeses to taste

Serves 4

1 Preheat oven to 350°.

2 Place diced eggplant and 2 tablespoons water in a microwave-safe dish and cook on high power for 5 minutes.

3 Meanwhile, in a small skillet over medium-high heat, cook the onion, peppers, and garlic in the olive oil until onion is transparent. Remove from heat.

4 Spray a 1-quart baking dish with non-stick cooking spray. Combine and gently toss together until well-blended the cooked onion, pepper, and garlic with the eggplant and tomatoes, mushrooms, bread cubes, eggs, seasonings, and Monterey Jack. Sprinkle with grated Parmesan and Romano.

5 Bake in the preheated 350° oven for 20 to 25 minutes or until lightly browned.

Per serving: 288 calories; 14 gm protein; 18 gm carbohydrates; 18 gm fat; 69 mg cholesterol; 1.79 gm fiber; 57% of calories from fat

Eggplant Stacks

T hese stacks can be prepared ahead of time and finished off at the last minute. They are a good accompaniment to lamb and could double as an appetizer by using the small Japanese eggplant and Roma tomatoes.

Serves 4 to 6

Non-stick cooking spray
1 small eggplant, about 1 pound
2 teaspoons reduced-calorie butter
1 or 2 tomatoes (about the same diameter as the eggplant), cut into 6 1/2-inch slices
8 ounces thickly sliced fresh mushrooms
Lulu's Special Seasoning to taste
Oregano to taste
Garlic Pepper to taste
1/3 cup grated cheddar cheese
1/3 cup grated skim-milk mozzarella cheese
Grated Parmesan and Romano cheese (optional)

1 Preheat broiler.

2 Coat a skillet with non-stick cooking spray. Add mushrooms and sauté until tender. Set aside.

3 Cut the eggplant into 6 slices 1/2-inch thick. Rub both sides of the slices with the margarine. Arrange the eggplant on a cookie sheet and place about 5 inches from the preheated broiler. Broil until golden brown, about 3 minutes per side.

4 Top each eggplant round with a tomato slice and some cooked mushrooms. Season to taste with special seasoning, oregano, and garlic pepper. Top with the grated cheddar and mozzarella and sprinkle to taste with the Parmesan and Romano.

5 Just before serving, broil the eggplant stacks long enough to melt the cheese. Transfer to a serving platter or individual plates and serve at once.

Per serving: *112 calories; 7.7 gm protein; 7.8 gm carbohydrates; 5.96 gm fat; 16 mg cholesterol; 1.06 gm fiber; 48% of calories from fat*

Caribbean Plantains

P lantains are 9- to 12-inch long less-sweet cousins of traditional bananas. They require cooking to be edible. A staple of tropical cuisines, they are hard when ripe and never get as soft as a banana. Plantains are generally available year 'round throughout North America.

Non-stick cooking spray
1 medium plantain (about 12 ounces), peeled, cut into 1/3-inch-thick rounds
1/4 cup evaporated skim milk
2 tablespoons dry sherry or vermouth
1/4 teaspoon hot curry powder
1/4 teaspoon ground ginger
1/8 teaspoon ground cinnamon

Serves 3

1 Preheat oven to 350°.

2 Spray a 1-quart baking dish with non-stick cooking spray and arrange sliced plantain in the prepared dish.

3 Blend milk and all remaining ingredients in a measuring cup and pour mixture over plantain slices.

4 Cover baking pan with foil and bake in the preheated 350° oven for 15 minutes. Uncover and bake 5 minutes longer. Serve hot.

Per serving: *94 calories; 1.37 gm protein; 21 gm carbohydrates; .33 gm fat; .33 mg cholesterol; .3 gm fiber; 3% of calories from fat*

Taos Tators

Filled with sautéed onions, tomatoes, and poblano peppers or green chiles, these julienned potatoes are then topped with baby Chihuahua cheese, then garnished with Seabury Pickled Peppers, avocados, and light sour cream. For those who like it hot, serve with a side dish of picante sauce. To peel the pepper, cut it in half, remove seeds, and place on a baking sheet, skin side up, under a hot broiler until the skin pops up, about 3 to 5 minutes.

Serves 3

Non-stick cooking spray
1 large potato, julienned (I use the #3 blade of my Mouli Julienne machine)
1 to 2 tablespoons olive oil
1/2 medium onion, thinly sliced
1/2 poblano pepper, peeled and coarsely diced, or 2 to 4 ounces canned whole green chiles, coarsely chopped
1/4 cup diced fresh tomato
Lulu's Special Seasoning to taste
Paprika to taste
Cracked black pepper to taste
1 cup grated Chihuahua cheese or your favorite white stringy cheese
Seabury Pickled Peppers (optional)
Diced avocado (optional)
Light sour cream (optional)

1 Spray a large oven-proof skillet with non-stick cooking spray and, over medium-high heat, heat the oil, add the onion, pepper, and tomato, and sauté until tender. Add the potato and seasonings and cook until potato is done and browned, turning as needed. You want to turn them as few times as possible.

2 Turn on your oven broiler.

THE 30-MINUTE LIGHT GOURMET

3 Sprinkle with the grated cheese and run under the broiler until the cheese is melted. Garnish with all the goodies and serve hot.

Per serving: *238 calories; 15 gm protein; 16 gm carbohydrates; 13 gm fat; 25 mg cholesterol; .52 gm fiber; 49% of calories from fat*

Herbed Mushroom-Potato Bake

G*reat for entertaining because it can be made in advance and just heated at the last minute. Serve with grilled or barbecued fish or poultry.*

Serves 4

Non-stick cooking spray
1 1/2 pounds cleaned, peeled potatoes, sliced about 1/4-inch thick
1 medium onion, peeled and thinly sliced
8 ounces fresh mushrooms, cleaned and sliced
1/2 teaspoon light salt
Cracked black pepper to taste
1 tablespoon parsley
1 teaspoon tarragon
1 cup half and half

1 Spray a 1-quart baking dish with non-stick cooking spray.

2 Preheat oven to 350°.

3 Layer the potatoes, onions, and mushrooms in the prepared baking dish.

4 Sprinkle with the salt, pepper, parsley, and tarragon. Pour in the cream and cover dish with foil.

5 Bake in the preheated 350° oven for 30 minutes or until the potatoes are fork-tender. Serve at once.

Per serving: *296 calories; 7.13 gm protein; 53 gm carbohydrates; 7.25 gm fat; 22 mg cholesterol; 1.46 gm fiber; 22% of calories from fat*

Fluffy Spuds

L ight and luscious, my potatoes are hard to resist. You would never guess they were made with 2% milk, reduced-calorie margarine, and light sour cream.

Makes 6 cups

3 medium potatoes, peel
¹/8 cup reduced-calorie margari.
¹/4 cup 2% milk
¹/4 cup light sour cream
1 teaspoon light salt
¹/2 teaspoon Lulu's Special Seasoning
¹/4 teaspoon ground black pepper

1 Place the potatoes in a pot and just cover them with water. Bring to a boil and cook until tender, testing tenderness with a fork. Drain off water.

2 Add all the remaining ingredients to the pot, and using your electric hand mixer, beat until light and luscious. Serve while hot.

Per cup: 109 calories; 2.67 gm protein; 15 gm carbohydrates; 3.88 gm fat; .75 mg cholesterol; .25 gm fiber; 32% of calories from fat

Sautéed New Potatoes in Jackets

T hese new potatoes accompany red meats nicely, especially Tournedos with Artichoke Bottoms with Microwave Béarnaise Sauce.

Serves 3

6 medium well-scrubbed new potatoes (each the size of a large egg)
1 tablespoon reduced-calorie margarine
1 tablespoon olive oil
Lulu's Special Seasoning
Fresh cracked black pepper to taste
¹/4 cup chopped fresh parsley (optional)

1 Using a paring knife, peel a 1-inch-wide strip of peel from the center of the potato, leaving the peel on the end of the potato.

Place potatoes in a saucepan and cover with water. Bring water to a boil and cook until potatoes are firm but tender when pierced with a fork. Drain.

3   In a skillet over medium-high heat, heat the margarine and oil until hot. Add the potatoes, season them with the special seasoning and pepper to taste and sauté until the peeled part of the potato is golden brown.

4   Sprinkle with chopped parsley. (Sometimes I garnish the potatoes with grated Parmesan cheese.) Serve hot.

Per serving: *178 calories; 3 gm protein; 27 gm carbohydrates; 6.33 gm fat; 0 mg cholesterol; .43 gm fiber; 32% of calories from fat*

New Potatoes Sautéed in Rosemary and Blue Cheese

S *imply a wonderful blend of flavors.*

Serves 4

6 2-inch-diameter new potatoes, halved, skins intact
1 tablespoon reduced-calorie margarine
1 tablespoon olive oil
1/3 cup blue cheese
1 tablespoon fresh rosemary
Light salt to taste
Cracked black pepper to taste
Garlic pepper to taste

1   Place potato halves in a vegetable steamer and steam until fork-tender, about 8 to 10 minutes. Drain. (Or, cook potatoes in boiling water until tender.)

2   Heat the margarine and oil until hot in a heavy skillet over medium-high heat. Add the potatoes, blue cheese, and rosemary. Sauté quickly until potatoes are golden brown and cheese melts, forming a light coating on the potatoes.

3 Season to taste with the salt and peppers. Discard the rosemary. Serve hot.

Per serving: *356 calories; 12 gm protein; 42 gm carbohydrates; 15 gm fat; 28 mg cholesterol; .64 gm fiber; 38% of calories from fat*

Fiesta Red Rice

F iesta red rice goes with just about anything. Serve it with broiled or grilled meats of any kind.

3 slices lean bacon (optional)
1/2 cup chopped red or green bell pepper
1/2 cup chopped celery
1/2 cup chopped green onions
2 tablespoons olive oil
1 cup brown rice
1 14 1/2-ounce can stewed tomatoes
1 cup hot water
1 teaspoon curry powder
1 teaspoon Worcestershire sauce
1/2 teaspoon Lulu's Special Seasoning
1/2 teaspoon Tabasco sauce
1/4 teaspoon cayenne pepper

Serves 4

1 Microwave the bacon on high for 4 1/2 minutes; drain, and blot with paper towel.

2 In a skillet, using medium heat, sauté the peppers, celery, and green onions in the olive oil until they are tender; stir in the rice and cook several minutes longer, stirring the rice. Place in your food processor or blender the tomatoes, water, and all the remaining ingredients. Purée.

3 Pour the puréed mixture into the skillet with the rice mixture, reduce the heat to low, and cook 10 minutes longer.

4 Spoon into a 1 1/2 quart casserole and bake covered in a preheated 350° oven for 30 minutes.

5   Serve hot. Top with bacon slices if you wish.

Per serving: *158 calories; 2.56 gm protein; 21 gm carbohydrates; 7.74 gm fat; 0 mg cholesterol; 1.41 gm fiber; 44% of calories from fat*

Brown Rice Medley

A nother versatile dish. Serve with grilled meats or incorporate leftovers into chicken salad. Brown rice supplies more protein, calcium, phosphorus, potassium, niacin, and vitamin E and is lower in sodium than enriched white rice.

Serves 3 to 4

1/4 cup slivered almonds
2 tablespoons reduced-calorie margarine
1 cup brown rice
1 cup cleaned, sliced fresh mushrooms
1/2 cup thinly sliced carrots
1 3/4 cups low-sodium chicken broth
1 cup water
1 tablespoon light soy sauce
1/4 cup chopped green onion

1   In a skillet, sauté the almonds in 1 tablespoon of margarine until golden brown. Remove from skillet to a small plate. Set aside.

2   Using the same skillet, melt the remaining 1 tablespoon margarine. Stir in the rice and sauté until lightly browned, stirring frequently.

3   Add the mushrooms, carrots, broth, water, and soy sauce. Bring to a boil, cover, and lower the heat to simmer.

4   Cook 45 minutes or until rice is tender. Garnish with almonds and green onions.

Per serving: *167 calories; 5.34 gm protein; 19 gm carbohydrates; 8.04 gm fat; 0 mg cholesterol; 1.37 gm fiber; 43% of calories from fat*

Bell Peppers with Cheesy Rice

A colorful vegetarian dish, serve these low-fat, rice-stuffed bell peppers with either winter or summer fruits and a frosty glass of iced tea.

Serves 2

2 large bell peppers (use red, yellow, green, or a combination)
Non-stick cooking spray
1 tablespoon reduced-calorie margarine
1/3 cup chopped onions
1 cup thickly sliced fresh mushrooms
1 single-serving bag of rice
1/4 cup cubed white skim-milk cheese
1/4 cup low-fat cottage cheese
2 tablespoons chopped fresh tomatoes
1 tablespoon chopped fresh parsley
1/4 teaspoon Lulu's Special Seasoning
Cracked black pepper to taste

1 Preheat oven to 400°.

2 Cook rice 10 minutes. Drain rice, and set aside.

3 Wash the peppers, cut off tops and remove seeds. Put peppers in a lidded steamer, tops included, and steam until barely tender. Immediately drain and spray the inside and outside of the peppers with non-stick cooking spray.

4 Meanwhile, in a skillet, melt the margarine and sauté the onions and mushrooms until soft. Stir in all the remaining ingredients and spoon this mixture into the peppers.

5 Bake in a preheated 400° oven for 15 minutes.

Per serving: *276 calories; 16 gm protein; 34 gm carbohydrates; 8.5 gm fat; 17 mg cholesterol; 1.4 gm fiber; 28% of calories from fat*

Dahl Moong

D*ahl is an East Indian term for puréed lentils, chick peas, or beans. This dish is made with split yellow lentils. Once the lentils are cooked, I beat them briefly with my electric mixer to create a creamy purée. Do not overbeat. Serve dahl with or over Pilau.*

Makes 3 cups

1 cup yellow lentils, soaked in cold water to cover for 30 minutes then drained
3 cups water
1 tablespoon finely chopped jalapeño pepper
1/2 teaspoon finely chopped fresh garlic
1/2 teaspoon peeled and finely chopped fresh ginger
1/2 teaspoon turmeric
1 teaspoon light salt
1/2 teaspoon garam masala
2 tablespoons vegetable oil
1/4 teaspoon whole mustard seed
Chopped fresh cilantro leaves

1 Place lentils in a heavy pot. Cover with 3 cups water. Bring to a boil and cook, uncovered, until the lentils are soft, about 30 minutes.

2 Add the jalapeño, garlic, ginger, turmeric, salt, and garam masala and mix well. Beat the dahl until smooth, but not totally puréed.

3 Meanwhile, heat the oil in a separate pan. Add the mustard seeds. Pour in the dahl. Stir, then cook, covered, 5 minutes longer. Turn off the heat and let stand until ready to serve.

4 Serve with chopped cilantro.

Per cup: *160 calories; 5.53 gm protein; 14 gm carbohydrates; 9.8 gm fat; 0 mg cholesterol; 1.83 gm fiber; 55% of calories from fat*

Pilau

F or an Eastern feast,
  serve the Pilau with
*Dahl Moong and Umi's
Spiced Chicken. I always
rinse my rice in cold
water.*

Makes 5 cups

¹/₄ cup corn oil
1 cinnamon stick
2 whole cloves
1 cup chopped onion
1 cup frozen mixed vegetables
1 tablespoon finely chopped
  jalapeños
¹/₂ teaspoon finely chopped garlic
¹/₂ teaspoon peeled, finely chopped
  ginger
2 teaspoons light salt
¹/₄ teaspoon turmeric
1 cup long-grain rice, rinsed in cold
  water
4 cups boiling water

1   Heat the oil in a heavy saucepan. Add the cinnamon stick,
    cloves, and onion and sauté over medium-low heat until onion is
    transparent, about 5 to 10 minutes.

2   Add frozen vegetables, jalapeños, garlic, ginger, salt, and
    turmeric and cook for 5 minutes, stirring once or twice. Add the
    rice and cook for 5 minutes, stirring occasionally.

3   Stir in the boiling water, reduce the heat to medium-low, and
    cook covered for 30 to 45 minutes longer, or until the rice is
    tender and the water has been absorbed. Do not overcook.

Per cup: *274 calories; 4.67 gm protein; 39 gm carbohydrates; 12 gm fat; 0 mg
cholesterol; 2.13 gm fiber; 39% of calories from fat*

Pasta Twists with Sautéed Vegetables

T his vegetarian entree is a complete and colorful meal. If you must add a meat, serve it with Tender Turkey Cutlets in Lime-Wine Sauce and Robert's Favorite Salad.

Serves 4

6 ounces garden-style twist noodles
Non-stick cooking spray
1 tablespoon reduced-calorie butter or margarine
2 tablespoons chopped shallots or onions
1 teaspoon chopped fresh garlic
1 peeled and thinly sliced carrot
1 thinly sliced medium summer yellow squash
1 thinly sliced medium zucchini squash
corn kernels cut from 1 ear of corn or 1/2 cup frozen corn
1/2 cup coarsely chopped tomato
1 tablespoon chopped fresh parsley
1 teaspoon chopped fresh basil or 1/4 teaspoon dried basil
1 teaspoon chopped fresh oregano or 1/4 teaspoon dried oregano
1/2 to 1 teaspoon Lulu's Special Seasoning
1/4 to 1/2 teaspoon cracked black pepper
2 tablespoons light cream cheese

1 Cook noodles according to package directions, but do not salt cooking water. Drain, rinse with warm water, and drain again. Transfer to a vegetable dish and keep warm.

2 Spray a large skillet with non-stick cooking spray and over medium heat, gently cook shallots or onions, garlic, and carrots in butter or margarine 2 to 3 minutes or until shallots are tender.

3 Add the squash, zucchini, corn, tomato, parsley, basil, oregano, special seasoning, and pepper. Sauté for 3 to 4 minutes or until

vegetables are tender but still have some texture. Blend in cream cheese. Spoon the vegetables over the noodles and serve at once.

Per serving: *274 calories; 5.26 gm protein; 44 gm carbohydrates; 4.73 gm fat; 7.75 mg cholesterol; .74 gm fiber; 16% of calories from fat*

Pasta with Five Cheeses

Microwave the cheese sauce at the same time you cook the fresh pasta. I use fresh angel hair pasta, but linguine or fettuccine would work equally well. Serve with Curly Endive and Red Cabbage Salad lightly laced with Garlic Vinaigrette.

Makes 1 1/3 cups of sauce
Serves 4

1 10 1/2-ounce package fresh angel hair pasta
2 tablespoons reduced-calorie butter or margarine
1 tablespoon shallots
1 teaspoon finely chopped garlic
1/2 cup low-sodium chicken broth
1/2 cup half and half
2 tablespoons flour
1/4 teaspoon Lulu's Special Seasoning
1/4 teaspoon Parsley Plus
1/4 teaspoon fresh ground or cracked black pepper
1/8 teaspoon cayenne
1/4 cup each of grated cheddar, Swedish farmer's, Chihuahua cheese, and gorgonzola cheese
2 tablespoons shredded or grated Romano cheese

1 Cook pasta al dente according to package directions.

2 Meanwhile, to make sauce, place butter or margarine, shallots, and garlic in a 1-quart glass measure and microwave on high for 4 minutes. Whisk in stock, half and half, flour, special

seasoning, parsley plus, black pepper and cayenne. Microwave on high for 2 minutes, then whisk again. Microwave on high for 1 minute longer. All at once, whisk in the cheeses. Let stand for 5 minutes. If cheeses have not fully melted, return sauce to the microwave and cook on high for 1 minute longer.

3 Drain pasta, and place on a large serving plate.

4 Dribble sauce over cooked pasta and serve at once.

Per serving: 331 calories; 18 gm protein; 23 gm carbohydrates; 19 gm fat; 38 mg cholesterol; .51 gm fiber; 52% of calories from fat

Summer Stir-Fry

T his is both pretty and healthful. Remember to leave some crunch to your vegetables. Over-cooked vegetables lose nutrients rapidly.

Serves 3

1 tablespoon olive oil
1 tablespoon reduced-calorie butter
1 1/4-inch-thick slice red onion, separated into rings
1 zucchini, diagonally sliced
1 yellow summer squash, diagonally sliced
1/2 red bell pepper, cut into strips
1 cup thickly sliced mushrooms (leave whole if small)
1/2 teaspoon summer savory
1/4 teaspoon light salt
White pepper to taste

In a skillet over medium heat, heat the oil and butter. Add all remaining ingredients. Stir-fry vegetables until tender yet crisp, about 4 minutes. Serve hot.

Per serving: 136 calories; 4.73 gm protein; 17 gm carbohydrates; 7.85 gm fat; 0 mg cholesterol; 2.49 gm fiber; 52% of calories from fat

Sautéed Vegetables in a Shell with Mustard Cream

A colorful medley of sautéed garden-fresh vegetables in a delicately flavored mustard sauce fill a freshly baked pastry shell. Use my vegetable mixture or your own favorite. Instead of the mustard cream, simply add 2 or 3 tablespoons of light cream cheese to the sautéed vegetables; then fill the cooked pastry shell and serve hot.
I use The Mouli Julienne Machine to cut the carrots, it makes the perfect julienne.

Serves 2

2 frozen pastry shells (I prefer Pepperidge Farm)
2 tablespoons reduced-calorie butter or margarine
1/2 cup 2-inch-long fresh broccoli florets
12 thin slivers green bell pepper (scant 1/4 cup)
12 thin slivers red bell pepper (scant 1/4 cup)
1/4 cup julienned yellow summer squash
1/2 thinly sliced large shallot
1/4 cup julienned carrots
1/4 cup half and half
1 tablespoon Dijon mustard
Lulu's Special Seasoning
Fresh cracked black pepper
Light salt

1 Preheat the oven to 400°. Place the shells on an ungreased cookie sheet and bake for about 15 minutes or until golden brown. (If you have baked the shells in advance, microwave the baked shells at full power for 45 seconds just prior to filling, or reheat in a 350° oven for 8 to 10 minutes.

2 In a skillet, over medium heat, melt the butter or margarine. Add all of the vegetables, stirring to coat them with the fat. Cover pan and cook for 3 minutes.

3 Uncover pan and stir in the half and half and mustard. Cook 2 minutes longer, stirring 3 or 4 times. Season lightly with special seasoning, salt, and pepper. Fill warm baked pastry shells with equal amounts of the vegetable mixture. Serve at once. Some of the vegetables may cascade over the sides, but it looks pretty that way.

Per serving: *363 calories; 6.16 gm protein; 53 gm carbohydrates; 15 gm fat; 11 mg cholesterol; 2.15 gm fiber; 37% of calories from fat*

Garlic Pasta

T his side-dish goes
with anything. Use
your favorite pasta. I
prefer any thin spaghetti
or angel hair. Fresh-
cooked pasta is best, but
reheated leftover pasta is
acceptable.

Serves 1 to 2

1 tablespoon reduced-calorie butter
or margarine
1 tablespoon olive oil
1 teaspoon minced fresh garlic
2 cups cooked pasta
2 tablespoons shredded Parmesan or
Romano cheese
Lulu's Special Seasoning to taste
Fresh ground black pepper to taste
Fresh chopped parsley (optional)

Heat the butter and oil in a skillet over medium heat. Add garlic and
sauté for 1 minute. Add the pasta and cheese, and season to taste with
special seasoning and black pepper. Garnish with fresh chopped
parsley.

Per serving: *273 calories; 7 gm protein; 33 gm carbohydrates; 13 gm fat; 4 mg
cholesterol; 1.05 gm fiber; 43% of calories from fat*

Sky-High Biscuits

I t's nice to know there is
a reduced calorie
biscuit and here it is.
Serve hot from the oven.

Makes 12 biscuits

2 cups sifted all-purpose flour
1 tablespoon baking powder
1/2 teaspoon baking soda
1/2 teaspoon light salt
1/4 teaspoon sugar
1/3 cup reduced-calorie margarine
3/4 cup buttermilk

1 Preheat oven to 450°.

2 In a mixing bowl, using a wire whisk, mix together well the
flour, baking powder and soda, salt, and sugar.

3 Cut in the margarine until the mixture resembles coarse cornmeal.

4 Add the buttermilk and mix to a smooth dough. Knead lightly on floured board. Roll or pat out to ½ inch thick. Cut with a 2½-inch diameter biscuit cutter.

5 Place biscuits on an ungreased cookie sheet, 1 inch apart, and bake in a preheated 450° oven for approximately 10 minutes.

Per biscuit: *94 calories; 2.5 gm protein; 16 gm carbohydrates; 1.96 gm fat; .56 mg cholesterol; .25 gm fiber; 19% of calories from fat*

Sweet Potato Biscuits

T *hese biscuits are as delicious as they are beautiful. Two to three medium sweet potatoes, or a 29-ounce can of drained sweet potatoes yields 1½ cups mashed. To microwave, pierce skins and microwave on high power for about 12 minutes.*

Makes 15 biscuits

1½ cups unbleached, all-purpose flour
1 tablespoon baking powder
1 teaspoon baking soda
½ teaspoon ground nutmeg
½ teaspoon light salt
⅓ cup reduced-calorie margarine
1½ cups cooked, mashed sweet potatoes
⅓ cup low-fat buttermilk

1 Preheat oven to 450°.

2 In a mixing bowl, stir flour, baking powder, baking soda, nutmeg, and salt.

3 Cut in margarine until the mixture resembles coarse cornmeal.

4 Stir potatoes and buttermilk into dry ingredients, blending to make a soft dough.

5 Turn dough onto a lightly floured surface and knead until dough forms a ball. (This is a very light dough so work quickly.) Adding flour as needed, pat dough to a 1/2-inch-thick circle. Cut straight down with a 2 1/2-inch diameter biscuit cutter. (Twisting the biscuit cutter causes low biscuits.)

6 Place biscuits 1 inch apart on an ungreased cookie sheet. Bake in the preheated oven for approximately 10 minutes or until puffy and lightly browned.

Per biscuit: *90 calories; 1.9 gm protein; 15 gm carbohydrates; 2.05 gm fat; 0 mg cholesterol; .3 gm fiber; 20% of calories from fat*

Blue Cornmeal Sticks

D ue to its *refined texture and subtle flavor, New Mexican blue cornmeal has attained tremendous popularity in our marketplace.*

Makes 14 sticks

1 cup low-fat buttermilk
1 egg, separated
2 tablespoons melted reduced-calorie margarine
1/2 cup all-purpose flour
1/2 cup blue cornmeal
1 tablespoon sugar
1 1/2 teaspoon baking powder
1/4 teaspoon light salt

1 Preheat oven to 425°.

2 In a bowl or 4-cup measuring container, combine and mix together the buttermilk, egg yolk, and melted margarine.

3 In another small bowl, using a wire whisk, whisk until well blended the flour, cornmeal, sugar, baking powder, and salt.

4   Add the dry ingredients to the wet ingredients just until the dry ingredients are moistened. Do not over-mix. In a small bowl, beat the egg white (at room temperature) until stiff peaks form, then gently fold into cornmeal mixture.

5   Place 2 (7 count) cast-iron corn stick pans sprayed well with non-stick cooking spray in preheated 425° oven for about 3 minutes or until hot. Remove pans from oven and pour batter into the molds, filling about ³/₄ full. Return filled pans to the hot oven and bake for about 12 to 15 minutes or until sticks are set and lightly browned. Serve immediately.

Per stick: *57 calories; 1.89 gm protein; 8.96 gm carbohydrates; 1.39 gm fat; 20 mg cholesterol; .41 gm fiber; 22% of calories from fat*

MICROWAVE
MAGIC

Microwave Magic

Microwaving means to cook, heat, or defrost foods using microwave energy. Like other types of cooking, it has its own characteristics. Microwaves are very short, high frequency radio waves. Think of your microwave as a self-contained broadcasting system similar to your radio. When the door is closed and the oven is turned on, a transmitter, called a magnetron, sends a signal to a receiver within the oven. Open the door and the broadcasting stops.

Microwaves penetrate foods to a depth of ¾ to 1¼ inches, where they are absorbed by water, sugar, or fat molecules. The energy agitates the molecules to produce heat within the food itself, and the food begins to cook.

Not all foods microwave well. Large meat items such as turkeys, eggs in shell, food items with a crust such as pancakes, and food items which require lots of water such as pastas and some cakes just don't work well in the microwave.

To clean your microwave, place ½ cup water in oven, microwave on high power, then just wipe clean. Always use microwave-safe utensils such as heat-proof glass or plastic. No metal or foil please.

Microwave cooking takes some getting used to, but it is a clean, time-saving cooking method. For consistent results, I recommend that you write down the length of time it takes to microwave your favorite foods. Since the microwave cooks on the basis of mass, remember to double the time you cook an item when you double the quantity.

Although I've included the microwave in recipes throughout the book, this chapter shows the versatility of the microwave. I've included recipes for all types of dishes, from salads and sauces to meats and desserts. I've based these recipes on my 1.5 cubic-foot Toshiba oven with a 720 wattage and with 9 power levels: level 1 is 72 watts and level 9 is 720 watts. You may have to adjust the cooking time slightly for your own model.

Melting and Clarifying Butter

To melt, place 1 stick (about 4 ounces) butter in a 2-cup glass measure and microwave on high power for 1 minute. To make clarified butter, microwave butter on high power for 2 minutes or until butter boils. Skim and discard the foam on the surface. Pour off the clear layer, the clarified butter. Discard the layer of milk solids that remains on the bottom.

Toasting Nuts and Seeds

Place 1/4 cup nuts or seeds and 1 teaspoon reduced-calorie butter or margarine in a 9-inch glass pie pan. Microwave on high power for 5 to 6 minutes, stirring every 2 minutes until toasted.

Tangelo Honey Sauce

This microwaves quickly and is delicious served with grilled poultry, pork, and fish. If tangelos are not in season, use orange juice.

Makes 1/2 cup sauce

2 tablespoons all-purpose flour
2 tablespoons reduced-calorie butter
1/2 cup low-sodium chicken broth
3 tablespoons fresh tangelo juice
3 tablespoons half and half
2 tablespoons pineapple juice
2 teaspoons sauterne
2 teaspoons honey
1/2 teaspoon lemon juice
1/4 teaspoon light salt

In a 1-quart glass measure whisk all listed ingredients and microwave on high power for 2 minutes. Whisk briskly. Microwave on high power for 1 minute longer. (If the sauce tastes starchy, microwave on high power for another minute.) Briskly whisk the sauce again. Sauce should be creamy.

Per tablespoon: 39 calories; .38 gm protein; 4.3 gm carbohydrates; 2.11 gm fat; 2.25 mg cholesterol; .04 gm fiber; 49% of calories from fat

Hollandaise Sauce

Microwaving this luscious hollandaise is easy. And it is just as good as any stove-top hollandaise sauce. The sauce made with fresh egg yolks has a bit more flavor than the sauce made with the egg substitute. If you use egg substitute, you may want to add an additional teaspoon of fresh lemon juice to the cooked sauce, but taste it first.

1/4 cup reduced-calorie butter
2 well-beaten egg yolks, or the equivalent well-beaten egg substitute
1 tablespoon fresh lemon juice
1/4 cup half and half (or 2 tablespoons each cream and 2% milk)
1/2 teaspoon dry English mustard
1/8 teaspoon light salt
Dash of cayenne

Makes 2/3 cup

1 Melt the butter on high power for 45 seconds to 1 minute in a 1-quart glass measure.

2 Whisk in all remaining ingredients in the order listed.

3 Microwave on high power for 1½ to 2 minutes or until sauce is thick, whisking every 15 seconds. Serve at once.

Note: The cooked sauce can be refrigerated. Reheat on medium-low power (30%) until hot, whisking every 15 seconds.

Per tablespoon: 39 calories; .76 gm protein; .36 gm carbohydrates; 3.86 gm fat; 53 mg cholesterol; .01 gm fiber; 89% of calories from fat

The Perfect Potato

F or perfect potatoes, never microwave more than 4 medium potatoes at one time. If you need 8 potatoes, microwave them in 2 batches. The secret to the perfect potato is the foil-wrapped standing time.

1 Scrub, pierce potato's skin, and place on a paper towel.

2 Microwave potatoes on high power as follows:

1 average-sized potato:	5 minutes
2 average-sized potatoes:	9 minutes
3 average-sized potatoes:	13 minutes
4 average-sized potatoes:	17 minutes
More than 4 potatoes:	microwave in 2 batches

3 Immediately wrap each potato in aluminum foil and let stand for 5 minutes. Foil-wrapped potatoes will stay hot for up to 45 minutes.

Zesty Croutons

T hese croutons stay fresh for weeks stored in an air-tight container.

Makes 5 cups

10 slices 40-calorie wheat bread
1/2 cup reduced-calorie butter or margarine
2 tablespoons grated Parmesan cheese
1/2 teaspoon Parsley Plus or parsley flakes
1/2 teaspoon garlic powder

1 Dice bread.

2 In a small bowl, melt butter or margarine in the microwave on high power for 1 minute.

3 Stir in cheese, parsley plus, and garlic powder.

4 Place the bread cubes in an 11 × 7-inch glass pan. Microwave on high power for 6 minutes.

5 Drizzle seasoned butter over bread, tossing to coat. Microwave on high power for 4 to 6 minutes longer, stirring every minute. Croutons will be crisp and dry.

Per tablespoon: *14 calories; .43 gm protein; 1.63 gm carbohydrates; .73 gm fat; .1 mg cholesterol; .05 gm fiber; 47% of calories from fat*

Cheese Broccoli Soup

T his flavorful, easy-to-prepare soup is made in a 2-quart glass measure. It's almost as fast as opening a can, but so much better. Quick clean-up, too.

1 10-ounce box frozen chopped broccoli
2 tablespoons reduced-calorie butter or margarine
2 tablespoons finely chopped shallot or onion
1/4 cup all-purpose flour
1 12-ounce can evaporated skim milk
2 cups low-sodium chicken broth
2 tablespoons dry sherry
1/2 teaspoon light salt
1/4 teaspoon black pepper
1/8 teaspoon cayenne pepper
1/8 teaspoon summer savory

Serves 4 to 6

1 cup cubed Velveeta cheese

1 Microwave broccoli (in box) on high power for 6 minutes. Transfer broccoli to a chopping board and chop fine.

2 Place butter and shallots in the 2-quart glass measure and microwave 4 minutes on high power.

3 Whisk in the flour, milk, broth, sherry, salt, and seasonings. Microwave on high power for 6 minutes, briskly whisking the mixture after 3 minutes of cooking time have elapsed.

4 Whisk in the cheese and let soup stand 5 minute

5 Just before serving, microwave the soup on high power ⅃ minutes. Stir well and serve.

Per cup serving: *222 calories; 18 gm protein; 16 gm carbohydrates; 9.13 gm fat; 22 mg cholesterol; .55 gm fiber; 37% of calories from fat*

Stuffed Bell Peppers

Microwave-made stuffed peppers save you the time and trouble it takes to precook the peppers. For fun, I use half red and half green bell peppers.

Serves 4

1 pound lean ground beef
2 cups cooked rice
1/4 cup light mayonnaise
1/4 cup chopped fresh parsley
2 tablespoons chopped fresh tomato
1 tablespoon chopped cilantro leaves
1 tablespoon Worcestershire sauce
1 tablespoon chopped fresh thyme or 1/2 teaspoon dried thyme
1 teaspoon Lulu's Special Seasoning
1/4 teaspoon garlic pepper
4 medium bell peppers (any color you prefer)
1 slice mozzarella or Monterey Jack cheese (or a combination of low-fat cheeses), cut into 8 strips

1 In a bowl blend all ingredients except the bell peppers and cheese strips. Fill the peppers with this mixture.

2 If necessary, place a few wooden toothpicks around the bottom of the peppers to prop them up. Insert a microwave-safe roasting rack in a microwave-safe casserole dish.

3 Place peppers on rack, cover with wax paper, and microwave on high power for 6 to 7 minutes. Rearrange. Cook on high power

for 6 to 7 minutes more or until meat is cooked and the peppers are tender.

4 Top each pepper with 2 cheese strips and microwave for 1 to 2 minutes or until cheese melts. Let stand 5 minutes before serving.

Per serving: 482 calories; 33 gm protein; 32 gm carbohydrates; 25 gm fat; 104 mg cholesterol; 1.44 gm fiber; 47% of calories from fat

Creamy Broccoli and Artichoke Bake

T op this tasty casserole with grated Parmesan and Romano cheeses.

Serves 4 to 6

4 cups chopped fresh broccoli or 2 10-ounce packages frozen chopped broccoli
1 10-ounce box frozen artichoke hearts
¹/₄ cup reduced-calorie butter or margarine
¹/₄ cup chopped onion
8 ounces light cream cheese, softened
¹/₂ cup 2% milk
2 teaspoons fresh lemon juice
¹/₂ teaspoon Lulu's Special Seasoning
¹/₂ teaspoon garlic pepper
¹/₂ teaspoon Szechuan seasoning (I use Spice Island)
Grated Parmesan and Romano cheeses

1 Microwave the frozen broccoli for 7 minutes per package on high power.

2 Microwave artichoke hearts for 5 to 6 minutes on high power. Drain.

3 In a microwave-safe dish, microwave butter 45 seconds on high power. Add the onion and microwave on half power for 5 minutes, or until onions are soft.

4 Place the artichoke hearts on the bottom of a 1 1/2-quart microwave-safe casserole dish.

5 Blend the cream cheese, milk, melted butter, lemon juice, and seasonings. Add broccoli and onion, mix well, and spread evenly over artichokes.

6 Sprinkle with grated cheeses. Microwave uncovered for 7 to 10 minutes on 3/4 power (power level 7 on my microwave).

Per serving: *232 calories; 9.28 gm protein; 13 gm carbohydrates; 17 gm fat; 35 mg cholesterol; 1.74 gm fiber; 66% of calories from fat*

Fresh Vegetable Medley

U*se a variety of your favorite garden vegetables, but remember to place the denser vegetables (such as potatoes) on the outside and the more tender ones (such as summer squash) toward the inside. Here is my favorite medley.*

Serves 2 to 4

1 small zucchini, sliced into 1/4-inch-thick rounds
1 small yellow summer squash, sliced into 1/4-inch-thick rounds
6 fresh 2- to 3-inch-long broccoli florets
6 fresh 2- to 3-inch-long cauliflower florets
1/2 red bell pepper, slivered
4 to 8 mushroom caps, cleaned and thickly sliced
Lulu's Special Seasoning
Garlic and/or lemon pepper to taste
1 to 2 tablespoons melted reduced-calorie butter or margarine (microwave on high power 30 seconds)

1 Arrange the vegetables on a large microwave-safe platter, turning the stalks outward and placing the squashes toward the inside. Sprinkle with mushrooms. Lightly sprinkle with seasoning mixture and peppers. Drizzle with the melted butter.

2 Cover with plastic wrap and microwave on high power for 6 minutes. Let stand covered 2 minutes. For softer vegetables cover and microwave on high power 2 minutes longer. Let stand 2 minutes and test for tenderness. Follow this procedure until desired degree of doneness is reached.

Per serving: *117 calories; 8.05 gm protein; 20 gm carbohydrates; 3.55 gm fat; 0 mg cholesterol; 3.77 gm fiber; 27% of calories from fat*

Savory Corn Muffins

Great with soups and stews, and only about 80 calories per muffin.

Makes 10 to 12 muffins

1/2 cup unbleached all-purpose flour
1/2 cup whole wheat flour
Egg substitute to equal 2 eggs
1/2 cup fresh or frozen thawed whole kernel corn
1/2 cup grated cheddar cheese
1/3 cup 2% milk
1/4 cup chopped onion
2 tablespoons chopped red bell pepper
2 tablespoons chopped green bell pepper
1 tablespoon corn or olive oil
1 tablespoon granulated sugar
1 tablespoon baking powder
1 tablespoon chopped fresh parsley
1/2 teaspoon light salt
1/2 teaspoon summer savory
1/8 teaspoon garlic powder

1 In a bowl, blend all the listed ingredients well.

2 Line each microwave-safe muffin or custard cup with 2 paper liners and fill 2/3 full.

3 Microwave on high power as follows or until the top springs back when touched. Bake a maximum of 6 muffins at one time.

1 muffin: ¼ to ¾ minute   4 muffins: 1 to 2½ minutes
2 muffins: ½ to 2 minutes   6 muffins: 2 to 4½ minutes

Per muffin: *80 calories; 3.13 gm protein; 10 gm carbohydrates; 3.04 gm fat; 5.45 mg cholesterol; .45 gm fiber; 34% of calories from fat*

Creamy Brussels Sprouts

O*nly 12 minutes to prepare these delectable sprouts.*

Serves 3

1 10-ounce package frozen Brussels sprouts
1 tablespoon reduced-calorie butter
2 tablespoons light cream cheese
Lulu's Special Seasoning to taste
Cracked black pepper to taste

1 Microwave the package of frozen Brussels sprouts (wrapper and all) for 5 minutes on high power. Let stand 5 minutes.

2 Transfer to an 8-inch square (or similar size) microwave-safe dish. Add the butter, cream cheese, special seasoning, and pepper. Microwave for 2 minutes on high power. Stir well. Serve hot.

Per serving: *97 calories; 4.5 gm protein; 6.08 gm carbohydrates; 6.75 gm fat; 17 mg cholesterol; .93 gm fiber; 63% of calories from fat*

Sautéing Frozen Vegetables

Place 1 cup vegetables and 1 teaspoon reduced-calorie butter or margarine in a 1-quart casserole. Cover. Microwave on high power 3 to 4 minutes, or until crisp yet tender.

Cauliflower by the Head

Microwaving is the *hassle-free way to cook perfect cauliflower.*

Serves 4

1 medium head cauliflower
3 tablespoons light mayonnaise
1 teaspoon prepared mustard
1 tablespoon minced onion
1/4 teaspoon Lulu's Special Seasoning
1/4 teaspoon white pepper
1/2 to 1 cup grated cheddar cheese

1 Rinse cauliflower, remove stalk, and place upside down on a paper plate. Microwave on high power for 3 1/2 minutes. Turn upright and microwave on high power 3 1/2 minutes longer. Cool slightly.

2 Blend the mayonnaise, coat cauliflower with this mixture, then sprinkle with cheese. Just before serving, microwave cauliflower on medium-high power for 2 minutes.

Per serving: *133 calories; 7.28 gm protein; 7.89 gm carbohydrates; 8.44 gm fat; 24 mg cholesterol; 1.04 gm fiber; 57% of calories from fat*

Chicken with Apple

Microwaving is a fast *and easy way to cook a perfect fryer. See if you don't agree. The herbs and spices help the chicken look "brown."*

Serves 4

1 2 1/2- to 3-pound fryer
1/2 medium onion, diced
1/2 medium apple, diced
1 carrot, cut into 1-inch long pieces
   Olive oil
   Parsley Plus
   Paprika
   Lulu's Special Seasoning
   Garlic powder
   Cracked black pepper

1 Wash, drain, and place fryer in a glass pan or a microwave-safe casserole dish. Stuff with onion, apple, and carrot. Rub the skin with olive oil and sprinkle to taste with remaining seasonings.

2 Microwave on high power for 17 minutes. Let stand in microwave for 10 minutes.

3 Check thigh meat for doneness. Joint should move easily and juices should run clear. If more cooking time is needed, microwave on high power for 2 minutes. Let stand for 5 minutes. Recheck for doneness.

Per serving: *256 calories; 32 gm protein; 4.63 gm carbohydrates; 11 gm fat; 96 mg cholesterol; .33 gm fiber; 39% of calories from fat*

Clay Pot Chicken

T his chicken comes out scrumptious and very moist. It is great just as it is, or you can use the drained off-drippings in the following conventionally-cooked sauce recipe.

Serves 3 to 4

1 2 ³/4-pound fryer
1 onion, coarsely chopped
    Olive oil
    Lulu's Special Seasoning to taste
    Parsley Plus
4 carrots, peeled, diced, and cut into 2-inch-long pieces

Sauce

³/4 cup chicken drippings
¹/4 cup port wine
1 tablespoon light sour cream
¹/4 teaspoon arrowroot
¹/4 teaspoon light salt
¹/8 teaspoon white pepper

1 Fill clay pot with water and let sit for 10 to 15 minutes.

2 Wash chicken and pat dry. Stuff body cavity with the chopped onion. Rub chicken with olive oil, then sprinkle to taste with special seasoning and parsley plus.

3 Place chicken and carrots in pot. Cover. Microwave on high power for 30 minutes (power level 7 on my microwave).

4 For sauce, pour the broth into a saucepan. Add port. Cook until ½ cup sauce remains in pan. Whisk in sour cream, arrowroot, salt, and pepper. Cook gently until sauce thickens, about 2 minutes.

Per serving: *338 calories; 36 gm protein; 13 gm carbohydrates; 13 gm fat; 109 mg cholesterol; 1.19 gm fiber; 35% of calories from fat*

Chicken and Broccoli Stir-Fry

T*he microwave does the work for you. The cashews are delicious but add calories.*

3 tablespoons water
1 tablespoon light soy sauce
1 tablespoon cornstarch
1 tablespoon sherry
1 teaspoon sugar
1 teaspoon low-sodium instant chicken broth or water
1 teaspoon finely chopped fresh garlic
½ teaspoon Lulu's Special Seasoning
¼ teaspoon Tabasco sauce
1 tablespoon olive oil
¼ cup chopped green onion
2 skinless, boneless, julienned chicken breasts (about ½ to ¾ pound)
3 cups fresh broccoli florets
1 cup thickly sliced fresh mushrooms
2 tablespoons chopped cashew nuts

Serves 4
(optional)

1 In a small bowl combine the water, soy sauce, cornstarch, sherry, sugar, chicken broth, garlic, special seasoning, and the Tabasco sauce and set aside.

2 Preheat a 10-inch browning dish on high power for 5 minutes. Pour in oil, and add onion, chicken strips, and broccoli. Stir until sizzling stops. Transfer to a 1-quart casserole.

3 Cover casserole and microwave on high power for 5 minutes or until chicken is no longer pink and broccoli is tender-crisp.

4 Add mushrooms and reserved soy sauce mixture, stirring to coat the chicken. Cover and microwave on high power for about 3 minutes or until sauce thickens and the mushrooms are tender. Stir well. Sprinkle with cashews.

Per serving: 204 calories; 25 gm protein; 13 gm carbohydrates; 6.01 gm fat; 55 mg cholesterol; 1.8 gm fiber; 27% of calories from fat

Smoked Fillet of Catfish with Garden-Fresh Vegetables

T*his is a colorful, low-calorie, and delicious one-dish meal. Use any fresh, white-fleshed fish fillets.*

2 tablespoons reduced-calorie butter
2 tablespoons fresh lemon juice
1/2 teaspoon liquid smoke
2 catfish fillets (about 1/2 pound)
1/2 cup red or green bell pepper strips
1 small yellow squash, julienned
1 small, ripe tomato, coarsely chopped
Lemon pepper to taste
Lulu's Special Seasoning to taste
Paprika

Serves 2

1 Place the butter, lemon juice, and liquid smoke in a 1-cup glass measure and microwave on high power for 1 minute.

2 Place fish in the bottom of a microwave-safe dish. Cover fish with bell pepper, squash, onion, and tomato. Lightly sprinkle to taste with lemon pepper and special seasoning. Cover and microwave on medium power for 5 minutes. Give dish a half turn and microwave on medium power for 3 minutes longer. Sprinkle with paprika and serve at once with cooked brown or white rice.

Per serving: 178 calories; 12 gm protein; 17 gm carbohydrates; 7.7 gm fat; 0 mg cholesterol; 2.14 gm fiber; 39% of calories from fat

Crab-Stuffed Fillet of Fish

U *se your favorite fresh fish fillets. Sole, orange roughy, or cod are delicious prepared this way. You can use canned crab meat, but I prefer to buy a whole Dungeness crab and pick out the crab meat myself.*

Serves 2

2 6-ounce fish fillets (sole, orange roughy, or cod)
2 tablespoons reduced-calorie butter or margarine
1/2 cup chopped onion
1/4 cup chopped red bell pepper
1/4 cup chopped green bell pepper
2/3 cup crab meat
1/4 cup plus 2 tablespoons fresh bread crumbs
2 tablespoons light mayonnaise
2 tablespoons light sour cream
8 thin strips tomato
2 teaspoons lemon juice
Lulu's Special Seasoning
1 teaspoon reduced-calorie butter or margarine

1   Rinse fish and pat dry. Set aside.

2   Place the butter, onion, and chopped peppers in a small microwave-safe bowl and microwave on high power for 5 minutes.

3   Stir in crab meat, bread crumbs, mayonnaise, and sour cream. This is your stuffing.

4   Lightly coat the outside of the fillets with mayonnaise. Place stuffing in center of the fish and roll up. Place fish, seam side down, in a microwave-safe dish.

5   Top each roll with 4 slices of thinly sliced tomato, 1 teaspoon of lemon juice, and a dab of butter. Lightly sprinkle the top with special seasoning, garlic pepper, paprika, and cayenne pepper.

6   Microwave on 50% power for 9 minutes, then 2 minutes longer on high power.

Per serving: *457 calories; 54 gm protein; 22 gm carbohydrates; 15 gm fat; 161 mg cholesterol; 1.37 gm fiber; 30% of calories from fat*

Browning Ground Meat

O nce you have
browned ground
meat in your microwave,
you will always cook it this
way because microwaving
is a quick, clean way to
brown meat. You can also
brown ground pork,
sausage, veal, and chicken
or turkey in this manner.

1 pound lean ground meat

Makes 1 pound

1 Break up 1 pound of ground beef into chunks and place in a microwave-safe plastic collander. Place a microwave-safe plate under the collander to catch any drippings.

2 Microwave beef on high power for 6 minutes, stirring the beef after 3 minutes of cooking time have elapsed. Discard drippings.

3 The meat is now ready for use in any recipe for browned ground beef.

Standing Rib Roast

H ere is the microwave
version of my oven-
roasted standing rib roast
recipe. It comes out perfect
every time.

1 4- to 5-pound rib roast
Lemon pepper to taste
Lulu's Special Seasoning

Serves 6 to 8

1 Sprinkle the roast to taste with the lemon pepper and special seasoning.

2 Place fat side down on the roasting rack set in a 2-quart glass dish.

3 Microwave on 70% power as follows:

3 minutes per pound for rare (120° internal temperature)
4 minutes per pound for medium (135° internal temperature)
5 minutes per pound for well-done (155° internal temperature)

4 Let beef stand 10 to 15 minutes. Check for desired degree of doneness before carving.

Peppered Pork Roast

A nice change from roast beef, this pork roast cooks to perfection in the microwave.

Serves 2 to 3

3/4 pound boneless pork loin
1 tablespoon dry sherry
4 small new potatoes, halved
1 medium onion, quartered
1 medium carrot, cut into 1-inch juliennes
1 teaspoon chopped fresh garlic
1/2 teaspoon dried rosemary
1/2 teaspoon dried thyme
1/2 teaspoon cracked black pepper
1/2 teaspoon garlic pepper
1/4 teaspoon Parsley Plus
1/8 teaspoon light salt
1/8 teaspoon ground nutmeg

1 In a skillet over medium-high heat, brown the pork on all sides. Transfer pork to a 2-quart microwave-safe pan. Add sherry to skillet. Scrape up drippings and pour them over the roast. Add water so liquid comes halfway up the sides of the pork.

2 Arrange vegetables around pork. Sprinkle with seasonings and cover with plastic wrap, venting one corner. Microwave on medium power for 15 minutes. Let stand 10 minutes before serving. The temperature of the pork should be 170°.

Per serving: *427 calories; 34 gm protein; 27 gm carbohydrates; 18 gm fat; 120 mg cholesterol; .97 gm fiber; 38% of calories from fat*

Chicken Breast

I f you do not have time to stew a whole hen or fryer, just microwave the chicken breast (skin on and covered with a piece of wax paper). The rule of thumb is 6 minutes per pound at high power. (You may have to make a minor adjustment for your microwave, but I cook a 6-ounce chicken breast on high power for 3 minutes.) Remove and discard skin, and use meat as needed. Leaving the skin on during microwaving helps keep the chicken moist. Microwaving no more than 4 breasts at one time prevents overcooking.

Tenderloin of Beef

T his marinade is great for any red meat —hamburgers, roasts, or steaks. Refrigerated, it stays fresh for several weeks.

Marinade

1 cup dry red wine
1/4 cup olive oil
1/4 cup light soy sauce
1/4 cup chopped fresh parsley
2 teaspoons coarse ground black pepper
1 teaspoon Lulu's Special Seasoning
1 teaspoon granulated sugar
1 teaspoon chopped fresh garlic

1 2-pound beef tenderloin
Lulu's Special Seasoning
Lemon pepper to taste
Garlic pepper to taste
Szechuan seasoning to taste

Serves 8

1 In a microwave-safe rectangular dish, blend all marinade ingredients.

2 Lightly sprinkle beef with special seasoning, peppers, and Szechuan seasoning. Marinate beef at room temperature for 1 hour, turning as desired. Pour off and store marinade.

3 Place a microwave-safe roasting rack in a 12 × 8 × 2-inch microwave-safe dish. Wrap ends and 1 inch down the side of the tenderloin with aluminum foil. Place beef on rack.

4 Microwave on high power for 3 minutes. Reduce power to medium (50% power) and microwave 5 minutes. Turn roast over. Rotate the dish, remove the foil, and microwave on 50% power 8 to 12 minutes or until the beef's internal temperature is 120°. Tent the beef with foil and let it stand for 10 minutes before carving. The beef's temperature will rise 15 to 20 degrees. Baste with pan drippings.

5 For medium beef, the internal temperature is 135°. I do not recommend cooking a tenderloin beyond medium.

Per serving: *280 calories; 32 gm protein; 1.31 gm carbohydrates; 14 gm fat; 95 mg cholesterol; .01 gm fiber; 46% of calories from fat*

Mango Sauce

S*erve this sauce over vanilla or fruit-flavored frozen yogurt, or pour over uniced cake.*

Makes 1 1/4 cups

1/2 cup water
1/4 cup granulated sugar
2 teaspoons cornstarch
1 1/2 tablespoons reduced-calorie butter
1 teaspoon fresh lemon juice
3 to 4 fresh, ripe mangos, puréed (about 1 cup mango purée)

1 Microwave water in a 1-quart glass measure for 1 minute on high power or until water boils. Stir in sugar and cornstarch. Microwave 1 minute longer on high power.

2 Stir in butter, lemon juice, and mango purée until blended. Serve warm or at room temperature.

Per tablespoon: *35 calories; .15 gm protein; 8.03 gm carbohydrates; .52 gm fat; 0 mg cholesterol; .26 gm fiber; 13% of calories from fat*

Melting Chocolate

Chocolate Morsels

C over dish containing 1 cup chocolate morsels with plastic wrap. Microwave on medium power for 3 minutes. Microwave 2 cups on medium power for 6 minutes.

Chocolate Squares

C hop coarsely 1 ounce chocolate squares and cover dish. Microwave on medium power allowing about 1 minute per square. Always stir melted chocolate until smooth.

Carrot Cake with Cream Cheese Glaze

T his cake is made in a microwave-safe bundt pan. To check for doneness, lightly press the moist top area of the cake with a paper towel. If the moisture lifts off and the batter is pulling away from the sides of the pan, it is done.

1 1/2 cups granulated sugar
1 cup safflower or corn oil
1 teaspoon vanilla
3 eggs or the equivalent egg substitute
1 1/2 cups unsifted all-purpose flour
1/2 teaspoon light salt
1 1/4 teaspoon baking soda
2 teaspoons ground cinnamon
2 cups grated carrots (about 6 medium raw carrots)
1/2 cup chopped walnuts or pecans
Non-stick cooking spray

1 In a mixing bowl, blend the sugar, oil, and vanilla. Add the eggs or egg substitute; beat well.

2 In another bowl whisk the flour, salt, soda, and cinnamon. Stir oil mixture into the flour mixture, mixing well.

263

3 Fold in the carrots and nuts.

4 Spray a 9-inch microwave-safe bundt pan with non-stick cooking spray.

5 Pour batter into pan. Microwave on medium power for 12 minutes. Increase to high power and microwave 3 to 5 minutes longer or until a cake tester inserted into the center of the cake comes out clean. Turn out onto cake rack to complete cooling.

Cream Cheese Glaze

3 ounces light cream cheese
$1/2$ cup granulated sugar
3 tablespoons reduced-calorie butter
$1 1/2$ tablespoons 2% milk
1 teaspoon vanilla

In a small microwave-safe bowl, microwave the cream cheese on high power 15 to 30 seconds. Add remaining ingredients and beat until smooth. Spread over cooled cake.

Per slice: *442 calories; 5.5 gm protein; 49 gm carbohydrates; 26 gm fat; 75 mg cholesterol; .91 gm fiber; 53% of calories from fat*

Softening Ice Cream

On low power, microwave 1 pint of ice cream for 30 seconds, or $1/2$ gallon of ice cream on low power for $1 1/2$ to 2 minutes.

SWEET
REWARDS

Peach Iced Tea

A great beverage for year 'round entertaining.

Makes 1 1/2 quarts

1 quart boiling water
1 quart-size tea bag
1 12-ounce can peach nectar
6 packets sugar substitute
Lemon wedges (optional)
Lime wedges (optional)

Steep tea bag in boiling water for 5 minutes in a 2-quart heatproof pitcher. Discard the tea bag. Stir in peach nectar and the sugar substitute. Serve over ice with a wedge of lemon and/or lime.

Per cup: 35 calories; .33 gm protein; 1.33 gm carbohydrates; 0 gm fat; 0 mg cholesterol; 0 gm fiber; 0% of calories from fat

Light and Luscious Waffles

Make these waffles on a regular or Belgian waffle iron. Serve with fresh fruit, reduced-calorie margarine, and light syrup.

Serves 2

1/3 cup plus 2 teaspoons all-purpose flour
1 teaspoon baking powder
1 teaspoon granulated sugar
1/2 teaspoon baking soda
1/2 cup low-fat buttermilk
1 egg yolk
2 teaspoons vegetable oil
1 teaspoon vanilla
2 egg whites
Non-stick cooking spray

1 Preheat waffle iron.

2 Whisk the flour, baking powder, sugar, and baking soda in a medium bowl.

3 In a small mixing bowl, blend buttermilk, egg yolk, oil, and vanilla. Add buttermilk mixture to dry ingredients, mixing until smooth.

4 In a separate small bowl, using clean beaters, beat the egg whites until stiff but not dry; fold into batter.

5 Spray waffle iron with non-stick coating. Pour batter into hot waffle iron and cook until golden brown, about 4 minutes.

Per waffle: *211 calories; 8.97 gm protein; 23 gm carbohydrates; 8.31 gm fat; 136 mg cholesterol; .28 gm fiber; 35% of calories from fat*

Oatmeal Buttermilk Waffles

T*he oatmeal and cornmeal in these light, crisp waffles give them an interesting texture. I serve them with light pancake syrup and reduced-calorie margarine. Freeze leftover waffles in plastic bags and reheat in a toaster.*

Makes 4 waffles

1 cup unbleached, all-purpose flour
¹/₄ cup white, yellow, or blue cornmeal (I prefer blue cornmeal)
1 cup uncooked rolled oats
2 tablespoons baking powder
¹/₂ teaspoon baking soda
¹/₂ teaspoon light salt
2 eggs (or egg substitute equivalent)
2 cups low-fat buttermilk
¹/₂ cup melted reduced-calorie margarine (microwave for 1 minute on high)
Non-stick cooking spray

1 Preheat a waffle iron.

2 In a large mixing bowl blend the flour, cornmeal, rolled oats, baking powder, baking soda, and salt.

3 In a 1-quart glass measure blend eggs, buttermilk, and melted margarine.

4   Pour the egg mixture into the dry ingredients, blending until barely combined. Do not over mix.

5   Spray waffle iron with non-stick cooking spray and fill waffle iron about two-thirds full with batter. Bake until golden brown and crisp, about 4 minutes.

Per waffle: *351 calories; 12 gm protein; 38 gm carbohydrates; 15 gm fat; 137 mg cholesterol; .66 gm fiber; 38% of calories from fat*

Honey Bran Muffins

These pretty, nutritious muffins are high in fiber; low in sodium and fat.

2 cups raisin nut-bran cereal
1 cup 2% milk
3 tablespoons honey
3 tablespoons safflower or corn oil
3 tablespoons egg substitute, or 1 egg
1 1/4 cups unbleached all-purpose flour
1 tablespoon baking powder
1/2 teaspoon ground cinnamon
1/4 teaspoon ground allspice
1/4 teaspoon lemon zest
1/4 teaspoon light salt
Non-stick cooking spray

Makes 10 to 12 muffins

1   Preheat oven to 400°. Insert paper liners in 10 muffin cups.

2   In a bowl or a glass measure, blend cereal and milk. Let stand about 5 minutes or until the cereal softens, then beat in the honey, oil, and egg substitute or egg.

3   In another bowl, whisk the flour, baking powder, cinnamon, allspice, lemon zest, and salt.

4   Stir the dry ingredients into the liquids, mixing until the dry ingredients are just moistened. Do not overmix.

5   Fill muffin cups about two-thirds full. Bake in the preheated 400° oven for 15 minutes or until a wooden toothpick inserted into the center of a muffin comes out clean.

Per muffin: *132 calories; 3.33 gm protein; 22 gm carbohydrates; 4.44 gm fat; 1.5 mg cholesterol; .46 gm fiber; 30% of calories from fat*

Dutch Apple Yogurt Bread

T his outstanding loaf contains low-fat yogurt and no added salt. It can be frozen, but at my house there is never any leftover to freeze! It's great toasted and spread with reduced-calorie margarine, low-calorie jam, or light cream cheese.

Makes 1 loaf

1 cup whole wheat flour
3/4 cup all-purpose flour
2 teaspoons baking powder
1 teaspoon baking soda
1/2 teaspoon ground cinnamon
1/4 teaspoon ground nutmeg
1 8-ounce container low-fat Dutch apple yogurt
2 beaten eggs
2 tablespoons 2% milk
1/3 cup packed brown sugar
1/4 cup vegetable oil
Non-stick cooking spray

1   Preheat oven to 350°. Spray a 9 × 5 × 3-inch loaf pan with non-stick cooking spray.

2   In a large bowl stir the first 6 ingredients together and set aside.

3   In a second large bowl, blend the yogurt, eggs, milk, sugar, and oil.

4   Stir liquids into the dry ingredients until the dry ingredients are barely moistened.

5 Pour batter into the prepared pan. Bake in the preheated 350° oven for 20 to 25 minutes or until a wooden toothpick inserted into the center of the bread comes out clean. Cool in pan for 5 minutes and turn out on a wire rack to finish cooling.

Per slice: *188 calories; 4.8 gm protein; 27 gm carbohydrates; 7.19 gm fat; 56 mg cholesterol; .87 gm fiber; 34% of calories from fat*

Spiced Pumpkin Bread

S*erve this delicate but easy-to-prepare bread as a snack or on a buffet table. It is delicious topped with light cream cheese and it freezes well.*

1 3/4 cups unbleached all-purpose flour
1/8 teaspoon baking powder
1 teaspoon baking soda
1/2 teaspoon light salt
1/2 teaspoon ground cinnamon
1/2 teaspoon ground cloves
1/2 teaspoon nutmeg
3/4 cup granulated sugar
3/4 firmly packed brown sugar
1/2 cup corn oil
1 cup cooked fresh or canned pumpkin
2 eggs
Non-stick cooking spray

Makes 1 loaf

1 Preheat oven to 350°.

2 In a mixing bowl, whisk the flour, baking powder, soda, salt, spices, and both sugars until well-blended.

3 Add oil and pumpkin, stirring until well-blended. Add eggs, one at a time, mixing well after each addition.

4 Spray a 9 1/2 × 5 1/2 × 2 1/2-inch loaf pan with non-stick cooking spray and pour batter into pan.

5 Bake in the preheated 350° oven for about 45 minutes or until a cake tester inserted into the middle of the cake comes out clean. Do not overbake.

Per slice: 310 calories; 3.5 gm protein; 48 gm carbohydrates; 12 gm fat; 55 mg cholesterol; .47 gm fiber; 35% of calories from fat

Cassis-Poached Pears

Present the pears on a glass dessert plate garnished with a cluster of fresh raspberries and a sprig of fresh mint. Otherwise, serve the poached pears à la mode —with a small portion of ice cream or low-fat frozen yogurt. Crème de cassis is a liqueur made from black currants.

1 fresh ripe pear (your favorite variety)
1 5¼-ounce can pear nectar
2 teaspoons reduced-calorie margarine
2 teaspoons honey
2 teaspoons crème de cassis
Cinnamon sugar

Serves 2

1 Preheat oven to 350°.

2 Wash, dry, and slice pear in half lengthwise and core with a melon baller. (Use a small, sharp knife to remove the stem and any fibrous material branching from the stem to the core.)

3 Place pear halves in a baking dish, sliced side up, and spread the cut surfaces with the margarine, honey, and cassis.

4 Pour in the pear nectar. Sprinkle lightly with cinnamon sugar, and bake in the preheated 350° oven for 20 to 25 minutes.

Per serving: 88 calories; 0 gm protein; 17 gm carbohydrates; 1.65 gm fat; 0 mg cholesterol; .37 gm fiber; 17% of calories from fat

Fresh Pear Cake

S ince this cake is not iced (saving calories), I sprinkle the top with sifted confectioners' sugar and garnish with sliced strawberries and kiwi fruit. I use a fluted flan or quiche pan with a decorative design for this simple yet elegant cake.

Makes 1 cake

3 fresh, ripe Bartlett pears, peeled, cored, and cut into large chunks
$1/2$ cup reduced-calorie margarine
1 cup granulated sugar
2 eggs
1 teaspoon grated lemon zest
2 cups unbleached all-purpose flour
1 tablespoon baking powder
1 teaspoon ground ginger
$1/2$ teaspoon ground nutmeg
$1/4$ teaspoon light salt
$1/4$ teaspoon ground cinnamon
$1/3$ cup chopped walnuts
Confectioners' sugar (optional)
Non-stick cooking spray

1 Preheat oven to 350°.

2 Purée pears in a food processor or blender. You should have 1 cup pear purée.

3 In a large mixing bowl, cream the margarine, sugar, eggs, and lemon zest until light and fluffy.

4 In a bowl, whisk together the flour, baking powder, ginger, nutmeg, salt, and cinnamon.

5 Add pear purée, flour mixture, and nuts to the creamed mixture, stirring until blended. Spray a $9 \times 1 1/2$-inch flan or quiche pan with non-stick cooking spray. Turn batter into pan.

6 Bake in the preheated 350° oven for 30 to 35 minutes or until a toothpick inserted into the center of the cake comes out clean. Let cake rest in the pan for 5 minutes. Turn cake out onto a serving plate.

Per slice: *343 calories; 6.21 gm protein; 58 gm carbohydrates; 11 gm fat; 69 mg cholesterol; 1.62 gm fiber; 29% of calories from fat*

Buttermilk Cake with Orange Glaze

S erve this light, moist cake as part of a buffet table for brunch.

Makes 1 cake

3/4 cup reduced-calorie margarine
1 cup granulated sugar
2 eggs
2 1/2 cups unsifted all-purpose flour
1 teaspoon baking powder
1 teaspoon baking soda
1 cup low-fat buttermilk
3/4 cup chopped dates
3/4 cup chopped walnuts
Non-stick cooking spray
Fresh mint leaves (optional)

Glaze

1 cup orange juice
1 cup granulated sugar

1 Preheat oven to 350°.

2 In a large bowl cream the margarine, sugar, and eggs with an electric mixer at medium speed until light and fluffy.

3 In a small bowl stir the flour, baking powder, and baking soda.

4 To the creamed mixture alternately add 1/3 flour mixture and 1/2 cup of buttermilk. Repeat, ending with the flour mixture and blending well after each addition. Fold in dates and nuts.

5 Spray a 9- or 10-inch tube or Bundt pan with non-stick cooking spray. Pour batter into pan. Bake 50 to 55 minutes or until a cake tester inserted into the center of the cake comes out clean. Remove from oven and let cool slightly.

6 Meanwhile, bring orange juice and remaining 1 cup sugar to a boil. Unmold cake and drench with the hot syrup. Serve while hot. Garnish with fresh mint leaves and an orange twist.

Per slice: 363 calories; 6.67 gm protein; 66 gm carbohydrates; 9.04 gm fat; 47 mg cholesterol; 1.02 gm fiber; 22% of calories from fat

Butterscotch Bars

T*hese tasty cookies have a delightful, nutty, cream cheese topping. They can be frosted if you don't mind the extra calories, but they are grand just plain.*

1 1/2 cups unbleached all-purpose flour
1 teaspoon baking powder
1/4 teaspoon light salt
1/2 cup reduced-calorie butter or margarine
8 ounces light cream cheese
2 cups packed brown sugar
3 eggs
2 teaspoons vanilla extract
Non-stick cooking spray
1/2 cup chopped walnuts

Confectioners' Sugar Frosting

1 cup sifted confectioners' sugar
2 to 3 tablespoons 2% milk
1/2 teaspoon almond extract (optional)

Makes 24 cookies

1 Preheat oven to 350°.

2 In a small bowl, whisk together the flour, baking powder, and salt. Set aside.

3 In a large bowl, cream butter, cream cheese, and brown sugar until light and fluffy. Remove and reserve half the cream cheese mixture.

4 To remaining cream cheese mixture add eggs, one at a time, beating until well-blended after each addition. Blend in vanilla and flour mixture.

5 Spray a 13 × 9 × 2-inch baking pan with non-stick cooking spray. Spread batter evenly into pan and sprinkle on chopped nuts.

6 Spread reserved cream cheese mixture evenly over nuts. Bake 25 to 30 minutes in the preheated 350° oven. Top should be golden brown. Do not overbake. Cool slightly.

7 In a small measuring cup, blend confectioners' sugar, milk, and almond extract. Drizzle frosting over the slightly cooled butterscotch bars.

Per cookie: 164 calories; 3.15 gm protein; 24 gm carbohydrates; 6.46 gm fat; 43 mg cholesterol; .26 gm fiber; 35% of calories from fat

Per tablespoon frosting: 33 calories; .08 gm protein; 8.46 gm carbohydrates; .05 gm fat; .19 mg cholesterol; 0 gm fiber; 1% of calories from fat

Walnut Meringue Bars

2 cups all-purpose flour
1/2 cup packed light brown sugar
1 cup reduced-calorie margarine
1 teaspoon vanilla
1 cup cherry preserves
1 cup peach preserves
5 egg whites, at room temperature
3/4 cup granulated sugar
2 cups walnut meats, finely ground in a food processor

Makes 35 cookies   Confectioners' sugar (optional)

1 Preheat oven to 350°.

2 In a mixing bowl, combine the flour, sugar, margarine, and vanilla, blending with a fork until the dough leaves the sides of the bowl. Press dough into a 13 × 9 × 2-inch pan.

3 In a small bowl blend both preserves. Spread the preserves evenly over the dough.

4 In a large clean glass or metal bowl, using clean beaters, beat egg whites until foamy. Gradually, 1 tablespoon at a time, beat in sugar, beating until meringue stands in stiff peaks. Fold in nuts and spread over preserves.

5 Bake in the preheated 350° oven for 30 minutes. Sprinkle lightly with powdered sugar. Cool and cut into bars.

Per cookie: *171 calories; 2.86 gm protein; 26 gm carbohydrates; 6.63 gm fat; 0 mg cholesterol; .64 gm fiber; 35% of calories from fat*

Sweet Apple Cake

T his delicious cake makes a wonderful dinner party dessert. To save calories, serve uniced squares, but I prefer iced squares.

3 eggs
1 cup granulated sugar
1 cup corn oil
1 cup unsifted all-purpose flour
2 teaspoons ground cinnamon
1 teaspoon baking soda
1 teaspoon vanilla extract
2/3 cup chopped walnuts
4 cups peeled, cored, thinly sliced apples
Cream Cheese Icing
Non-stick cooking spray

Cream Cheese Icing

8 ounces light cream cheese
1 1/4 cups sifted confectioners' sugar
1 teaspoon vanilla extract
1/2 teaspoon grated lemon zest

Makes 1 cake

1 Preheat oven to 350°.

2 Combine the eggs, sugar, and oil in a large bowl and beat until smooth and creamy.

3 In a separate bowl whisk the flour, cinnamon, and baking soda and add to the creamed mixture. Add the vanilla and stir in the walnuts.

4 Spray a 13 × 9 × 2-inch baking pan with non-stick cooking spray. Spread the apples over the bottom. Pour batter over the apples, spreading to cover.

5 Bake in the preheated 350° oven for 35 to 40 minutes or until cake is done. Remove from oven. Cool completely.

6 Meanwhile, beat the cream cheese until fluffy in a small bowl. Stir in the confectioners' sugar, vanilla, and lemon zest, mixing until smooth. Spread evenly over cooled cake.

Per cake slice: *346 calories; 4.23 gm protein; 31 gm carbohydrates; 24 gm fat; 69 mg cholesterol; .77 gm fiber; 62% of calories from fat*

Per tablespoon icing: *31 calories; .67 gm protein; 3.69 gm carbohydrates; 1.56 gm fat; 5.56 gm cholesterol; 0 gm fiber; 45% of calories from fat*

Fresh Fruit Crudités

P repare a heaping platter of your favorite fresh seasonal fruit and serve this sauce on the side. Or, serve the fruit in a glass compote with the cream piled on top. Thirty minutes before I whip the cream, I put bowl and beaters in the freezer and remove them moments before I whip.

Makes 2 cups

Fresh fruit prepared for dipping
1 cup whipping cream
3 tablespoons Bailey's Irish Cream
1 teaspoon brandy
3 tablespoons sifted confectioners' sugar
Sprinkle of ground cinnamon
Sprinkle of ground nutmeg

In a chilled bowl, using chilled beaters, whip the cream until stiff. Fold in all remaining ingredients.

Per tablespoon sauce: *31 calories; .16 gm protein; 1.75 gm carbohydrates; 2.31 gm fat; 8.28 mg cholesterol; 0 gm fiber; 67% of calories from fat*

Strawberry Napoleons

I f—in a moment of insanity—you have ever tried to make puff pastry from scratch, you'll appreciate the ready-made, frozen puff pastry sheets available in grocery stores. This impressive dessert pairs puff pastry squares with strawberry amaretto cream.

Makes 8 pastries

Pastry and Filling

1 sheet ready-made puff pastry
1.1-ounce box sugar-free instant vanilla pudding and pie filling
1 1/3 cup 2% milk
1 teaspoon unflavored gelatin
1 tablespoon water
1/2 cup whipping cream, whipped
2 tablespoons amaretto liqueur
1 pint fresh strawberries
Fresh mint leaves (optional)

Icing

1 cup sifted confectioners' sugar
1 tablespoon water
1 teaspoon almond extract

1 Preheat oven to 350°.

2 Thaw folded pastry sheet about 20 minutes on a lightly floured surface. Carefully unfold and cut sheet into 16 equal-size squares. Place on an ungreased baking sheet and bake in the preheated 350° oven for 15 minutes or until top is light golden brown. Remove from oven and cool.

3 Prepare pudding according to directions on box, using 1 1/3 cups milk. In a small bowl, dissolve the gelatin in 1 tablespoon of very hot water, then stir gelatin into pudding. Cover and chill.

4 Fold in the whipped cream and amaretto. Cover and chill until you are ready to assemble the Napoleons.

5 To prepare the icing, blend all icing ingredients together. Set aside.

6 To assemble, spread 8 baked pastry squares with pudding. Top with second 8 pastry squares. Drizzle icing over tops of the Napoleons. Garnish each Napoleon with a sliced fresh strawberry and a fresh mint leaf. (I slice the strawberry then fan it out.)

Per pastry: 254 calories; 3.41 gm protein; 30 gm carbohydrates; 13 gm fat; 20 mg cholesterol; .7 gm fiber; 46% of calories from fat

Candied Lemon Peel

T*his pretty garnish complements entrees, desserts, and steamed green or yellow vegetables where the bright yellow peel contrasts with the color of the vegetables. You can also use orange peel.*

2 blemish-free lemons
1 cup water
3 tablespoons sauterne or dry white wine
1 to 2 tablespoons sugar

Makes about 1/3 cup

1 Peel lemons (lengthwise) using a sharp vegetable peeler. Cut peel into very thin strips (almost strands).

2 Place peel and water in a small saucepan. Bring to a boil. Boil 1 minute, drain immediately.

3 Return strips to saucepan. Add wine and sugar and cook over low heat, swirling the pan occasionally, until the sugar dissolves. Simmer over medium heat until syrup coats the strips. Transfer to a plate. Separate the strips with a fork or your fingers, and let dry.

4 Store in a lidded container until ready to use.

Per tablespoon: 55 calories; .46 gm protein; 7 gm carbohydrates; 0 gm fat; 0 mg cholesterol; .08 gm fiber; 0% of calories from fat

Cranberry Glaze

T his *sugar-free glaze is made with low-calorie cranberry juice cocktail. Serve over frozen yogurt, Delicate Sponge Cake, or meringue nests.*

Makes 3/4 cup

3/4 cup low-calorie cranberry juice cocktail
2 teaspoons cornstarch
2 teaspoons fresh lemon juice
2 packets sugar substitute
1/4 teaspoon almond extract

In a small saucepan mix the cranberry juice, cornstarch, lemon juice, and sugar substitute. Over medium heat whisk the glaze constantly until it thickens. Remove from heat. Stir in the almond extract. Let cool.

Per tablespoon: *5.79 calories; .02 gm protein; 1.38 gm carbohydrates; 0 gm fat; 0 mg cholesterol; 0 gm fiber; 0% of calories from fat*

Delicate Sponge Cake

T his *light, moist sponge cake has no added salt and can be used as a base for many luscious desserts. Top with your favorite berries. This is my grandmother's basic recipe which I have modified to contain fewer calories and less salt and fat.*

1 cup all-purpose flour
1 teaspoon baking powder
1 cup granulated sugar
2 eggs
1 tablespoon reduced-calorie butter
1/2 cup evaporated skimmed milk
1 teaspoon vanilla
Non-stick cooking spray

Makes 1 cake

1 Preheat oven to 350°.

2 Place flour and baking powder in a food processor with the metal blade and process for 2 seconds. Transfer to a square of wax paper and set aside.

3 Place sugar and eggs in the processor and process for 1 minute. Stop once and scrape down the bowl.

4 Add butter and process for 1 minute. While the machine is running, pour the milk and vanilla in through the feed tube and process 20 seconds longer. Add the flour mixture. Pulse 5 or 6 times or until the flour just disappears. Do not over-process.

5 Spray an 8-inch-square baking pan with non-stick cooking spray. Pour batter in. Bake in preheated 350° oven for 20 to 25 minutes or until top is golden brown and the cake is moist, but set.

Per slice: 161 calories; 3.11 gm protein; 33 gm carbohydrates; 2 gm fat; 61 mg cholesterol; .17 gm fiber; 11% of calories from fat

Fresh Fruit Frappe

T*his beverage is a treat at any time. Good for a snack or for entertaining. For best flavor, be sure all the fruits are ripe.*

Makes 3 cups

1 cup sliced fresh or thawed frozen peaches
6 medium sliced strawberries
1/2 cup cubed fresh pineapple
1/2 banana
2 tablespoons fresh orange juice
2 tablespoons low-calorie cran-raspberry juice (or other blended low-calorie juice blend)
1 cup small ice cubes
1 packet sugar substitute
Strawberries (optional)
Fresh mint (optional)

Place all ingredients in a blender and purée on high speed. Serve at once in a chilled, stemmed glass. Garnish with a strawberry and a sprig of mint.

Per cup: 70 calories; .93 gm protein; 17 gm carbohydrates; .51 gm fat; 0 mg cholesterol; .77 gm fiber; 6.5% of calories from fat

Graceland Bananas

T hese are just
wonderful as is, but
try them à la mode.
Remember a small scoop
of ice cream or frozen
yogurt will do.

Serves 2

1 tablespoon reduced-calorie butter
1 banana, sliced lengthwise in half
2 tablespoons peach nectar
1 tablespoon crème de banana
1 tablespoon half and half
Cinnamon sugar to taste

Melt the butter in a skillet over medium heat. Sauté the banana slices for several minutes, turning as needed. Add the nectar, banana liqueur, and half and half and sprinkle lightly with cinnamon sugar. Cook several minutes longer until light golden brown. Serve immediately plain or à la mode.

Per serving: *124 calories; .5 gm protein; 20 gm carbohydrates; 4 gm fat; 3 mg cholesterol; .33 fiber; 29% of calories from fat*

Fresh Cantaloupe Sherbet

T his delightfully light
and refreshing
sherbet can double as a
reduced-calorie dessert for
formal entertaining. For
this recipe you will need
an ice cream maker.

Makes 2 quarts

1 2 1/4-pound cantaloupe, seeds
removed, cut into 1-inch chunks
2 tablespoons fresh lemon juice
1 cup granulated sugar
2 cups low-fat buttermilk
1/2 cup whipping cream

1 Purée cantaloupe in a food processor or a blender. You should have 1 1/2 to 2 cups purée. Stir in the lemon juice. Set aside or refrigerate. This can be done ahead of time.

2 Blend the sugar and buttermilk in a large bowl. Stir in the cantaloupe purée and the whipping cream.

3   Pour mixture into a 2-quart ice cream freezer. Freeze according to manufacturer's instructions.

4   Serve garnished with seasonal fresh fruit. To make ahead, cover and store in your freezer until ready to serve. Sherbet hardens when frozen.

Per cup serving: *192 calories; 3.08 gm protein; 34 gm carbohydrates; 5.38 gm fat; 17 mg cholesterol; .27 gm fiber; 25% of calories from fat*

Plum Sherbet

T *art, tangy, and somewhat sweet. Great for a dinner party dessert or as a nutritious after-school snack. You will need about 1 pound (7 to 8) ripe plums. If ripe plums are unavailable, purchase plums 4 to 5 days in advance and let ripen at room temperature.*

1 pound ripe fresh plums, washed and cut into chunks
2 tablespoons fresh lemon juice
1 cup granulated sugar
2 cups low-fat buttermilk
1/2 cup whipping cream

Makes 2 quarts

1   Purée plums in a food processor or blender. Stir in lemon juice. Refrigerate if preparing ahead of time.

2   In a large mixing bowl blend the sugar and buttermilk. Stir in plum purée and whipping cream.

3   Pour into a 2-quart ice cream freezer. Freeze according to the manufacturer's instructions.

4   Serve immediately garnished with seasonal fresh fruit, or cover and store in your freezer until ready to serve. Sherbet hardens when frozen.

Per cup serving: *197 calories; 3.39 gm protein; 36 gm carbohydrates; 5.13 gm fat; 17 mg cholesterol; .34 gm fiber; 23% of calories from fat*

Raspberry-Kiwi Frozen Yogurt

Y ou will need an ice
cream maker for this
refreshing dessert.

**Makes 6 1-cup
servings**

1 cup fresh or frozen raspberries
1 ripe kiwi, peeled and diced
1 cup granulated sugar
1 quart unflavored non-fat yogurt

Place the raspberries, kiwi, and sugar in your food processor or blender and purée on high speed. Pour this purée into the canister of an electric ice cream maker and stir in the yogurt until well blended. Freeze according to the manufacturer's instructions.

Per cup serving: *229 calories; 9 gm protein; 49 gm carbohydrates; .17 gm fat; 2.67 mg cholesterol; .75 gm fiber; 1% of calories from fat*

Very Berry Frozen Yogurt

I combine raspberries
and blueberries and
add a hint of raspberry
liqueur. You will need a
freezer for this recipe.

**Makes 6 1-cup
servings**

1 cup fresh or frozen raspberries
1 cup fresh or frozen blueberries
1 cup granulated sugar
3 tablespoons raspberry liqueur
1 quart unflavored non-fat yogurt

Place the raspberries, blueberries, sugar, and liqueur in a food processor or blender and purée on high speed. Pour purée into the canister of an ice cream freezer. Blend in the yogurt. Freeze according to the manufacturer's instructions.

Per cup serving: *264 calories; 9 gm protein; 54 gm carbohydrates; .33 gm fat; 2.67 mg cholesterol; .93 gm fiber; 1% of calories from fat*

Mount Fuji

T his is a wonderful, light ending to any meal. Select good quality pineapple sherbet.

Serves 4
Makes 1 cup sauce

1 10-ounce box frozen raspberries, thawed
2 ounces Cointreau (or any orange-flavored liqueur such as Grand Marnier or Arum)
Fresh mint leaves (optional)
1 pint pineapple sherbet

1 Purée raspberries and orange liqueur in a blender.

2 Place one scoop of sherbet in an individual glass compote. Top with the raspberry sauce and garnish with a fresh mint sprig. Serve at once.

Per serving: *267 calories; 1.5 gm protein; 56 gm carbohydrates; 2 gm fat; 7 mg cholesterol; 1.57 gm fiber; 7% of calories from fat*

Kiwi Ice

A refreshing blend of crushed kiwi fruit and orange extract. Serve to cleanse the palate between courses, or serve as a dessert or snack. Doubled, this recipe can still be made in an ice cream freezer.

Makes 2 cups

5 kiwi, peeled and coarsely mashed
3/4 cup granulated sugar
1/2 cup water
1 teaspoon orange extract
2 tablespoons fresh lemon juice
Fresh strawberries (optional)
Orange slices (optional)

1 Stir the crushed kiwi and sugar together. Let stand about 15 minutes or until sugar dissolves.

2 Stir in water, extract, and lemon juice.

3 Pour mixture into canister of an ice cream freezer and freeze according to the manufacturer's instructions.

Per cup: 406 calories; 2.5 gm protein; 103 gm carbohydrates; 0 gm fat; 0 mg cholesterol; 2.1 gm fiber; 0% of calories from fat

Light Strawberry Peach Freezer Jam

S ince you can freeze it, waxing the top is not necessary and less trouble. I am using the light fruit pectin.

Makes 6 cups

2 cups ripe cleaned, crushed strawberries
2 cups peeled, chopped, and slightly crushed ripe peaches
1 1 3/4-ounce box "light" fruit pectin
3 cups granulated sugar

1 In a large bowl mix the strawberries and peaches. In a small bowl blend the pectin with 1/4 cup sugar. Add sugar mixture to the mixed fruit. Let stand 30 minutes, stirring about every 10 minutes.

2 Gradually add the remaining 2 3/4 cups sugar to the jam, stirring until the sugar is dissolved.

3 Fill 6 1-cup freezer containers, leaving 1/2-inch headroom. Seal with lid, and let stand at room temperature for 24 hours.

4 Store in freezer. After using store in refrigerator. Keeps about 3 weeks.

Per tablespoon: 27 calories; .04 gm protein; 6.82 gm carbohydrates; .02 gm fat; 0 mg cholesterol; .04 gm fiber; .66% of calories from fat

GOURMET
VINEGARS
&
RELISHES

Herb and Fruit Vinegars

C reating your own vinegars is fun and easy. Gourmet vinegars add a tantalizing flavor to your sauces, salad dressings, and entrees. And they make excellent gifts. Here are some of my favorites, but don't let these recipes limit your imagination. I use 8-ounce cork-topped glass jars. These vinegars need about 2 weeks to mature.

Use any of the following vinegars:

Distilled white vinegar (40% acetic acid)
Cider or malt-based vinegars (50% to 60% acetic acid)
Red or white wine vinegars (50% acetic acid)

Tarragon Vinegar

1 cup vinegar
1 tablespoon fresh tarragon leaves, or 1/2 teaspoon dried tarragon
1 peeled and halved garlic clove (optional)

1   In a glass jar, crush tarragon leaves slightly to release aroma. Add vinegar and garlic. Cover with cork lid and set aside for 24 hours. Remove garlic and reseal.

2   Let steep for 2 weeks.

3   Two weeks later, strain and re-bottle vinegar in a labeled sterile jar. Vinegar is now ready to use.

Dill Vinegar

1 cup vinegar
1 sprig fresh dill or 1/2 teaspoon dried dill weed

Follow same procedure as for tarragon vinegar.

Mixed Herb Vinegar

1 cup vinegar
1 tablespoon of your favorite mixed fresh herb blend such as oregano, thyme, tarragon, or basil
8 black peppercorns

Follow same procedure as for tarragon vinegar.

Orange, Lemon, or Lime Vinegar

1 cup vinegar
1 tablespoon julienne orange, lemon, or lime zest

Scrub fruit well. Follow same procedure as for tarragon vinegar.

Beet and Peach Chutney

B esides tasting delicious, this chutney makes a lovely gift for friends. Serve it as a condiment with poultry, game, or sandwiches. Sometimes I make four times the recipe and store it in Mason-style jars for future use.

Makes 2 1/2 cups

1 1/2 pound fresh beets (about 3 large beets)
3/4 cup cider vinegar
1/2 cup granulated sugar
1/2 cup brown sugar
1 large, fresh, ripe, coarsely chopped peach
1/2 cup finely chopped onion
1 tablespoon horseradish
1/2 teaspoon ground cumin
1/2 teaspoon hot curry powder

1 Wash and trim the beets, leaving 2 inches of beet stalk and the root attached to prevent the color from bleeding out. Bring a large pan of water to a boil. Add beets and cook for about 30 minutes or until beets are fork tender. Drain and cool. This can

be done several days in advance. When you are ready to continue with the recipe, peel and grate the beets (I use the largest opening on an upright hand grater).

2 In a saucepan, combine the vinegar and sugars and cook until the sugars dissolve. Stir in the beets, peach, onion, horseradish, cumin, and curry.

3 Cover and simmer about 30 minutes or until almost all the liquid is evaporated and the chutney is very thick. Take care not to scorch. Cover and chill until ready to serve. Store leftover chutney in a jar with a tight-fitting lid. Refrigerate.

Per tablespoon: *23 calories; .11 gm protein; 6.27 gm carbohydrates; .01 gm fat; 0 mg cholesterol; .06 gm fiber; 0% of calories from fat*

Pico de Gallo

A Mexican staple, pico de gallo ("rooster's beak") is a tangy, versatile relish served with fajitas, grilled fish, omelettes, or as a low-calorie dip for corn and tortilla chips. I could eat my weight in it! Chop the ingredients chunky, not too fine or too coarse.

Makes 4 cups

1 pound cleaned, chopped tomatoes
1 cup chopped onion
1 cup chopped cilantro leaves
1/2 cup chopped green onions
1 Anaheim pepper, chopped
3 tablespoons lime juice
2 tablespoons olive oil
1 teaspoon chopped garlic
1 teaspoon light salt
1/2 teaspoon cracked black pepper (optional)
2 jalapeños, chopped (if you want it hot)

Blend all ingredients in a bowl. Serve immediately, or cover and chill.

Per tablespoon: *8.14 calories; .16 gm protein; .91 gm carbohydrates; .44 gm fat; 0 mg cholesterol; .13 gm fiber; 49% of calories from fat*

Seabury Pickled Peppers

My friends Suzette and Sam Seabury (fondly called "the family of hot lips") are famous for these pickled peppers. After eating one of these delicious peppers, hot lips are exactly what you have. If you don't like jalapeño peppers, you can substitute green, red, or yellow bell peppers. A combination of colors is quite pretty. To protect my hands from possible irritation, I always wear disposable surgical plastic gloves when seeding hot peppers.

15 to 20 jalapeño peppers, halved, seeded, diced, or enough similarly prepared bell peppers to fill a sterile 1-quart jar
1 medium onion, coarsely chopped
1 medium carrot, scraped and julienned
2 peeled garlic cloves
1/2 cup corn oil
1/4 teaspoon light salt
1 cup water
1/2 cup white vinegar

Makes 1 quart

1 Prepare the peppers.

2 In a small saucepan bring 3 cups of water to a boil. Add the onion, carrot, and garlic and cook for 5 minutes. Drain immediately.

3 In a bowl toss the diced peppers with the blanched vegetables. Fill a 1-quart jar with this mixture. Add the oil and salt.

4 In a small saucepan bring the water and vinegar to a boil and pour the mixture over the peppers and seal. Discard any excess water/vinegar mixture. Don't process. Let peppers cure at room temperature for 3 weeks.

Per tablespoon: *11 calories; .22 gm protein; 1.19 gm carbohydrates; .68 gm fat; 0 mg cholesterol; .19 gm fiber; 57% of calories from fat*

Spicy Tomato Relish

L ow in calories and tasty, this relish complements any meat dish or cooked beans. It can also be eaten as a salsa.

Makes 4 cups

8 medium tomatoes, peeled and coarsely chopped
1 medium green bell pepper, coarsely chopped (about 1 cup)
1 cup coarsely chopped onion
2 jalapeño peppers, seeded and coarsely chopped
1 cayenne pepper, seeded and coarsely chopped (optional)
1 cup cider vinegar
1/2 cup sugar
1 teaspoon ground cinnamon
1 teaspoon ground allspice
1 teaspoon light salt

1 In a large pot of boiling water, blanch the tomatoes for 3 to 5 minutes. Remove and let cool. Peel off skin and chop the tomatoes. Put the coarsely chopped tomatoes, green pepper, onion, and hot peppers in the food processor and process until this mixture is finely chopped, but not puréed. Depending upon the size of your work bowl, you may have to process half of the mixture, then the second half. Discard the water in the pot, and add this mixture back to the pot.

2 Add all the remaining ingredients and cook down for about 45 minutes. If you double this recipe, you will probably have to lengthen the cooking time. Pour relish into clean sterile jars, let cool, and seal.

Per tablespoon: *11 calories; .19 gm protein; 2.8 gm carbohydrates; 0 gm fat; 0 mg cholesterol; .14 gm fiber; 0% of calories from fat*

Fresh Corn Relish

This recipe goes with everything. It complements entrees and baked beans, and you can even sprinkle it over salads.

Makes 1 1/2 cups

1 10-ounce package cut corn, microwaved on high power for 5 minutes or cooked in a pan until tender, drained and cooled
1/3 cup diced red or green bell pepper
1/4 cup chopped Roma tomatoes
1/4 cup chopped green onion (use the whole thing)
1 heaping tablespoon chopped fresh cilantro
1 jalapeño pepper, finely chopped
1/4 cup seasoned rice wine vinegar
2 tablespoons sugar or 2 packets sugar substitute

Blend all ingredients in a bowl. Chill and serve.

Per tablespoon: *9.25 calories; .32 gm protein; 2.19 gm carbohydrates; .01 gm fat; 0 mg cholesterol; .08 gm fiber; 1% of calories from fat*

Jalapeño Jelly

There are other jalapeño jelly recipes around, but once you try this one, you'll forget the others! I enjoy serving this jelly with lamb or pork, but it also makes a great appetizer with light cream cheese.

Makes 7 cups

3/4 pound jalapeño peppers, seeded and ground in a processor or blender (makes about 1 1/4 cups ground jalapeño peppers)
1/2 cup green bell peppers, seeded and ground in a processor or blender
7 cups granulated sugar
1 3/4 cups cider vinegar
6 ounces liquid pectin (I use Certo)

1 Bring the jalapeños, bell peppers, sugar, and vinegar to rolling boil and boil for 10 minutes.

2 Remove from heat and add the pectin.

3 Pour into sterile jars and seal. It will keep longer if you seal the jelly with wax, but this is optional.

Per tablespoon: *49 calories; .04 gm protein; 13 gm carbohydrates; .01 gm fat; 0 mg cholesterol; .06 gm fiber; 0% of calories from fat*

Mint Basil Jelly

A wonderful complement to lamb or pork.

Makes 7 cups

2 cups water
3/4 cup cider vinegar
1/4 cup fresh lemon juice
1 packed cup fresh basil leaves
1/2 cup fresh mint leaves
6 cups granulated sugar
3 ounces liquid pectin

1 Bring the water, vinegar, and lemon juice to a boil in a 2-quart saucepan.

2 Bruise the basil and mint leaves with a potato masher and add to boiled liquids. Remove from heat and let steep 10 minutes. Remove herb leaves with a slotted spoon.

3 Add the sugar and bring to a boil. Boil until sugar is dissolved. When the syrup is at a rolling boil, add the pectin and boil 30 seconds longer.

4 Pour jelly into sterile jars and cool to room temperature, then seal. It will keep longer if the jars are sealed with wax, but this is optional.

Per tablespoon: *43 calories; .09 gm protein; 11 gm carbohydrates; .04 gm fat; 0 mg cholesterol; .13 gm fiber; 1% of calories from fat*

Apple Pear Mincemeat

Y ou can make a pie,
fill a peach half,
serve with toast, or add to
your favorite recipe for
spice cake or applesauce
cake with this mincemeat.
Most mincemeats call for
beef fat or suet, but I have
omitted the suet to lower
the fat content.

2 1/2 pounds fresh, firm, but ripe pears
(about 6), peeled, core removed,
and coarsely diced
1 1/2 pounds tart, red apples (about 3),
peeled, core removed, and
coarsely diced
2 large oranges, peeled, deseeded,
and chopped
1 cup dark or light raisins
1/2 cup sugar
2 packages sugar substitute
1 tablespoon fresh lemon juice
1 teaspoon ground cinnamon
1 teaspoon ground nutmeg
1/2 teaspoon ground ginger

Makes 5 cups

1/2 teaspoon light salt

1 Using your food processor, process the pears, then apples, then
oranges until lumpy but not puréed. Put the processed pears,
apples, and oranges into a large pot, add all the remaining
ingredients, mix well, and let stand for 30 minutes.

2 Turn heat to medium low and cook the mixture until the fruit is
tender, 30 to 40 minutes, stirring frequently.

3 Fill sterile jelly jars with the mincemeat, seal, and place the jars in
a boiling water bath for 5 minutes. The water should come to the
bottom of the lip of the jar, but do not submerge the jar in water.

Per tablespoon: *24 calories; .21 gm protein; 6.17 gm carbohydrates; .09 gm fat; 0 mg
cholesterol; .39 gm fiber; 3% of calories from fat*

Artichoke Relish

T here are many ways you can serve this low-calorie relish. If you wish to be fancy, fill a French endive leaf, garnish with julienned carrots, and arrange on a silver serving platter. It also makes an interesting sandwich filling. You can also serve it with sautéed mushrooms and/or cherry tomatoes.

Makes 1 cup

1 14-ounce can drained finely chopped artichoke hearts
1 2-ounce jar drained diced pimientoes
1/4 cup thinly sliced green onions
1/4 cup grated Parmesan cheese
2 tablespoons fresh lemon juice
2 tablespoons light mayonnaise
2 tablespoons chopped fresh parsley
1 teaspoon chopped fresh garlic
1/2 teaspoon dried oregano
1/2 teaspoon chopped fresh basil
1/8 or 1/4 teaspoon cracked black pepper

In a bowl, blend all listed ingredients. Cover, then chill several hours or overnight. Serve with crackers or crudités.

Per serving: 21 calories; 1.32 gm protein; 2.81 gm carbohydrates; .74 gm fat; 1.48 mg cholesterol; .28 gm fiber; 32% of calories from fat

INDEX

INDEX

INDEX